# GEORGE ELIOT AND THE BRITISH EMPIRE

In this innovative study Nancy Henry introduces a new set of facts that place George Eliot's life and work within the contexts of mid-nineteenth-century British colonialism and imperialism. Henry examines Eliot's roles as an investor in colonial stocks, a parent to emigrant sons, and a reader of colonial literature. She highlights the importance of these contexts to our understanding of both Eliot's fiction and her situation within Victorian culture. Henry argues that Eliot's decision to represent the empire only as it infiltrated the imaginations and domestic lives of her characters illuminates the nature of her realism. The book also reexamines the assumptions of post-colonial criticism about Victorian fiction and its relation to empire.

NANCY HENRY is Associate Professor in the Department of English at the State University of New York at Binghamton. She is the editor of George Eliot's *Impressions of Theophrastus Such* (1994), Elizabeth Gaskell's *Sylvia's Lovers* (1997), and Gaskell's *Ruth* (2001). She has published widely on George Eliot, including essays in *The Cambridge Companion to George Eliot*, *The Oxford Reader's Companion to George Eliot*, and *Victorian Literature and Culture*.

CAMBRIDGE STUDIES IN NINETEENTH-CENTURY
LITERATURE AND CULTURE

General editor
Gillian Beer, *University of Cambridge*

Nineteenth-century British literature and culture have been rich fields for interdisciplinary studies. Since the turn of the twentieth century, scholars and critics
have tracked the intersections and tensions between Victorian literature and the
visual arts, politics, social organization, economic life, technical innovations, scientific thought – in short, culture in its broadest sense. In recent years, theoretical
challenges and historiographical shifts have unsettled the assumptions of previous scholarly synthesis and called into question the terms of older debates.
Whereas the tendency in much past literary critical interpretation was to use
the metaphor of culture as "background," feminist, Foucauldian, and other
analyses have employed more dynamic models that raise questions of power
and of circulation. Such developments have reanimated the field.

This series aims to accommodate and promote the most interesting work being undertaken on the frontiers of the field of nineteenth-century literary studies:
work which intersects fruitfully with other fields of study such as history, or literary theory, or the history of science. Comparative as well as interdisciplinary
approaches are welcomed.

A complete list of titles published will be found at the end of the book.

# GEORGE ELIOT AND THE BRITISH EMPIRE

NANCY HENRY

*The State University of New York at Binghamton*

CAMBRIDGE
UNIVERSITY PRESS

PUBLISHED BY THE PRESS SYNDICATE OF THE UNIVERSITY OF CAMBRIDGE
The Pitt Building, Trumpington Street, Cambridge, United Kingdom

CAMBRIDGE UNIVERSITY PRESS
The Edinburgh Building, Cambridge CB2 2RU, UK
40 West 20th Street, New York, NY 10011-4211, USA
477 Williamstown Road, Port Melbourne, VIC 3207, Australia
Ruiz de Alarcón 13, 28014 Madrid, Spain
Dock House, The Waterfront, Cape Town 8001, South Africa

http://www.cambridge.org

First published 2002
Reprinted 2003

Printed in the United Kingdom at the University Press, Cambridge

*Typeface* Baskerville Monotype 11 / 12.5 pt.     *System* LaTeX 2$_\varepsilon$   [TB]

*A catalogue record for this book is available from the British Library.*

*Library of Congress Cataloguing in Publication data*
Henry, Nancy, 1965–
George Eliot and the British Empire / Nancy Henry.
p.     cm. – (Cambridge studies in nineteenth-century literature and culture; 34)
Includes bibliographical references and index.
ISBN 0 521 80845 6
1. Eliot, George, 1819–1880 – Views on imperialism.   2. Literature and society – Great Britain –
History – 19th century.   3. Great Britain – Colonies – History – 19th century.   4. Imperialism
in literature.   5. Colonies in literature.   I. Title.   II. Series.
PR4692.I46 H46   2002
823′.8 – dc21         2001037576

ISBN 0 521 80845 6 hardback

# Contents

# *Illustrations*

# Acknowledgments

I would like to thank the Dean of Harpur College at Binghamton University for a Dean's Semester Leave, the Union of University Professors and SUNY for a Dr. Nuala McGann Drescher Affirmative Action Leave, and the Beinecke Rare Book and Manuscript Library (especially Vincent Giroud) for a research fellowship. I would like to acknowledge the other libraries in which research for this book was undertaken: the British Library, the London Library, the National Library of Scotland, the Nuneaton Public Library, the Huntington Library, the New York Public Library and the Bartle Library (Binghamton University).

I am grateful to Mr. Jonathan Ouvry for permission to print previously unpublished George Eliot and G. H. Lewes manuscripts and to Mrs. Ursula Cash for lending me her photograph of Thornie Lewes. I also thank Dr. John Lyons for sharing with me his knowledge of the Lewes family history.

An early version of some of the ideas in this book appeared in the journal *Victorian Literature and Culture* (2001). I am grateful to Adrienne Munich and John Maynard for their comments on that essay.

I am indebted to Joel Snyder for reading and responding to the parts of this book as they gradually fell into place. If I have failed to push certain arguments far enough, it is not for want of his urging.

I would like to thank my colleagues, students, and friends in Binghamton, particularly Martin Bidney, Sarah Elbert, Paul Mattheisen, Brendan McConville, Philip Rogers, Gayle Whittier, and the members of the Victorian Studies Workshop. Jean Levenson, David Levenson, and Virginia Shirley took excellent care of Bitsy during my long summers in London. Those long summers apart, Bitsy has been my constant companion. The Sentry Sirens brought distractions from work that I now realize I needed. My friends in London provided support without which I could never have completed this book. I wish to thank Nick Shah, Ritula Shah, Tonny and Judy van den Broek, Katherine Bright-Holmes, and Barbara Handley. It would be impossible to thank Graham Handley adequately for the contributions he has made to the book and for his belief in me.

For help of various kinds, I am grateful to Bill Baker, Tina Ball, Rosemarie Bodenheimer, Neil Hertz, Claudia Johnson, George Levine, Chris Looby, Ellen Nerenberg, Stephanie Oxendale, Cannon Schmitt, Stuart Tave, and most of all to John Freccero.

Finally, at Cambridge University Press, Laura Davey was a life-saving copy editor, Linda Bree was a model editor, and Andrew Brown provided encouragement, criticism, and good conversation on George Eliot.

# *Abbreviations*

The following abbreviations are used for frequently occurring references:

| | |
|---|---|
| *Deronda* | *Daniel Deronda* |
| GE | George Eliot |
| *GEL* | *The George Eliot Letters*, ed. Gordon S. Haight, 9 vols. (New Haven: Yale University Press, 1954–5 and 1978) |
| GHL | George Henry Lewes |
| *Impressions* | *Impressions of Theophrastus Such* |
| *Journals* | *The Journals of George Eliot*, eds. Margaret Harris and Judith Johnston (Cambridge University Press, 1998) |
| Pinney | Thomas Pinney, ed., *Essays of George Eliot* (New York: Columbia University Press, 1963) |
| Yale | Beinecke Rare Book and Manuscript Library, Yale University |
| *WR* | *Westminster Review* |

## *Texts*

Page references to George Eliot's novels will be made internally and will refer to the Oxford World's Classics editions. References to *Silas Marner* and "Brother Jacob" will be to the Everyman edition, ed. Peter Mudford (1996), and references to *Impressions of Theophrastus Such* will be to the University of Iowa Press edition, ed. Nancy Henry (1994).

Page references to the *Westminster Review* and *Blackwood's Edinburgh Magazine* will be to the American editions. Page references for the *Leader* will be to G. H. Lewes's bound personal copy in the Beinecke Rare Book and Manuscript Library, Yale University.

# Introduction

> For learning to love any one is like an increase in property: it increases care, & brings many new fears lest precious things should come to harm.
>
> George Eliot to the Hon. Mrs. Robert Lytton (*GEL*, 5:106)

Upon his arrival in Cape Town on October 14, 1866, George Henry Lewes's youngest son wrote to his parents in London that he had visited the local library: "I saw the *Fortnightly Review* and all Mutters Books. They had also Felix Holt."[1] Herbert (Bertie) Lewes was waiting in Cape Town for a steamer that would transport him to Durban, where he would join his older brother Thornton (Thornie) and begin a new life. Bertie would never return to England and would die in 1875 – six years after the death of his brother – at the age of twenty-nine.

During their time in South Africa, the Lewes boys wrote dozens of letters to their father and George Eliot. Though Marian Evans had been living with Lewes since 1854, Lewes did not tell his sons about her or about his estrangement from their mother Agnes Lewes until 1859. They began to write to Miss Evans – who now called herself Mrs. Lewes – as "Mother" and to Agnes – who was still married to their father – as "Mamma." Rosemarie Bodenheimer has written in detail about Marian Lewes's "struggle to answer to the demands of her stepmotherhood," arguing that "to love Lewes perfectly was both to nurture his sons and to ensure at least Thornie's and Bertie's absence from the life of 'dual egoism.'"[2] This crucial familial context for Eliot's fiction is part of a larger social pattern of English life in which the decision was made to expatriate these young men. In her stepsons' letters from South Africa, Eliot read descriptions of landscapes and peoples she would never see. She followed their failures with the care of one who had invested emotionally and financially in their success. She knew a great deal about life in South Africa, and she had possessions there as well: she was a shareholder in the Cape Town Railroad, which gave her further cause to care about the South African colonies.

It is significant that one of Bertie's first sights in South Africa was the complete works of George Eliot, including the newly published *Felix Holt* (1866). These novels provided South African colonists with a nostalgic vision of England as well as a connection with the latest contemporary fiction. The *Fortnightly Review*, which Lewes edited from January 1865 through December 1866, brought them up to date on political and cultural issues at home. As a new and permanent emigrant, Bertie described the South African landscape and architecture to his parents. He also imagined sending someone home, as if in his place: "I should like to send you home a little niggar boy for a flunkey. They are such pretty little things."[3] The presence of new English writing and of new English colonists in South Africa is emblematic of the exchanges between England and its colonies in the 1860s – of books, people, and capital.

In 1870, when Eliot wrote to Mrs. Robert Lytton (Edith Villiers) – wife of the future Viceroy of India – that "learning to love anyone is like an increase in property," she confessed to a "proprietor's anxiety" for her friend's well-being. This metaphor in a letter that describes her sorrow over Thornie's death the year before highlights her association of ownership and affection at a time when her identity as a wealthy shareholder and stepmother was thoroughly established. The English had a proprietor's anxiety about their colonies – an emotional as well as material investment in life overseas – which matched in intensity, if not in character, the investment of English colonists at home.

There is no apparent warrant for associating Eliot's shares in Cape Town Rail with her stepsons' emigration or the sale of her novels to the colonies. Yet all are linked both to her domestic finances and to the consolidation of the South African colonies. The export of English literature, money, and sons to the colonies formed a pervasive and diverse culture of empire in mid-nineteenth-century England. But the systemic totality of that culture was not perceived or articulated by those who were implicated in it. *George Eliot and the British Empire* assumes the existence and coherence of nineteenth-century British imperialism, but only as a retrospective construction. In the years covered by this study (1850–1880), the Victorian experience of the empire was local and fragmented. The benign pursuit of caring for family by providing financial security through investments and finding colonial careers for young men helped to consolidate notions both of imperialism and of Englishness. The social conditions that permitted the Lewes boys to end their lives in South

Africa, and Eliot to amass a portfolio of colonial stocks, were the same social conditions in which she wrote her fiction – itself a valuable export to the colonies. Although there was no imperialist agenda behind either her actions or her writing, the empire and the domestic culture that sustained it are crucial to understanding both.

*George Eliot and the British Empire* reexamines some of the assumptions of post-colonial criticism about Victorian fiction. Among them is the notion that the author's experiences are irrelevant to understanding her writing. Another is that we can explain the presence of the empire in British fiction through the retrospective imposition of terms such as "imperialist ideology" or even the concept of imperialism itself. As Richard Koebner argued in his classic study of the word "imperialism," between 1852 and 1870 the British public "was not conscious of the idea that the problems of British rule could be surveyed or made the subject of criticism on the basis of so comprehensive a notion as the term *imperialism* implied."[4] Eliot's comments about various aspects of British colonial rule around the world in her letters, as well as her essays and fiction, support this claim. Imperialism was associated with others – the Turks, the Russians, the French. Even as they began to formulate the broad objectives of English rule, the English did not yet see their rule as imperialism. As C. K. Dilke wrote in his *Greater Britain* (1869), "not only is our government in India a despotism, but its tendency is to become an imperialism, or despotism exercised over a democratic people, such as we see in France, and are commencing to see in Russia."[5]

Eliot was aware of colonial reform movements, and of anti-colonialist views, such as those of the radical politicians Richard Cobden and John Bright.[6] Yet while she was critical of what she read about the empire, she could not formulate a critique of British "imperialism" as it would later be defined. Just as she reacted against fiction that seemed to depart fancifully from the observed details of daily life, her conscious response to the pervasive writing about the colonies confirmed her belief in realistic representation. The fact that she turned to the colonies to establish careers for her stepsons and to maximize her income from writing does not mean that she was subject to a monolithic "imperialist ideology." With the advantage of hindsight, *George Eliot and the British Empire* brings the various aspects of her experience together, and also elucidates the fragmentary nature of the empire as perceived by Victorians at home during her lifetime.

Eliot wrote her fiction between 1857 and 1878, during the phase of British colonialism that preceded the New Imperialism and "scramble for Africa" that began in the decade after her death in 1880. She began "The Sad Fortunes of the Reverend Amos Barton" in 1856 – a year in which she wearied of reading about "Indian mutinies" (*GEL*, 2:383). She published her last novel, *Daniel Deronda* in 1876, when Queen Victoria was crowned Empress of India. Colonial events such as the Indian Mutiny, the crowning of Victoria as Empress, and the Governor Eyre controversy (contemporary with the action of *Deronda*) receive just enough attention in her letters and fiction to assure us of her familiarity with them. While some critics have noted correspondences between British colonial activity and Eliot's fiction, the more immediate aspects of her colonial knowledge and experience have gone unrecognized.[7]

In 1860, she purchased her first shares in The Great Indian Peninsular Railway. In the same year, she helped Thornie Lewes to prepare for his Indian civil service examination, the failure of which would lead him to the colony of Natal. These domestic decisions influenced Eliot's perspective on English society and her portrayal of characters facing similar familial and financial pressures. Whereas her earliest use of the colonies as a narrative solution is the transportation of Hetty Sorrel to the penal colony of Botany Bay, Australia in *Adam Bede* (1859), characters such as David Faux in "Brother Jacob" (1864), Will Ladislaw in *Middlemarch* (1871–2), and *Daniel Deronda*'s Rex and Warham Gascoigne look to the empire – in all but the last case fancifully – as a career.

*George Eliot and the British Empire* argues for the importance of the colonial context to our understanding of Eliot's fiction and to a fuller and more accurate picture of her situation within Victorian culture. To this end, it combines cultural studies, literary criticism, and biographical analysis. All lives are unique; they are also typical. I read the particulars of Eliot's life as instances of patterns and habits among the upper-middle-class London society to which she gained access by virtue of her success as a novelist. Such a perspective on Eliot's quotidian relationship to the empire may demystify her status as an artistic genius, but it need not neglect or oversimplify the exquisite complexity that sustains our ongoing attempt to interpret her fiction. With a fuller understanding of her typicality, we can see more clearly her popularity among Victorian readers, who appreciated the realism of her representations in ways that are frequently lost to us.

It is my contention that biographical analysis is essential to any form of literary studies that seeks to place literature in historical context, and that evading facts and issues that are central to the author's life can lead to misinterpretations of both texts and contexts. Biographical analysis as I use it makes no attempt to link an author to the interpretation of a text via psychological speculation, or to limit interpretations of her fiction to what we know about her "intentions." Though the "intentional fallacy" does not create the anxiety it once did, it is nonetheless a legacy, the effects of which literary scholars and critics continue to feel. The methodological developments of New Historicism and Cultural Studies, while breaking away from New Criticism and rediscovering history by acknowledging all forms of discourse as legitimate material for illuminating literary texts, have nonetheless incorporated a belief in the "death of the author," which persists even in literary criticism for which establishing historical context is the stated aim.

In questioning the assumption that the author is irrelevant to her writing, I want to make clear that the biographical facts that interest me are not the subjective marks of authorial personality. What can and should be gained from biography is an appreciation of the framework in which lives were led, issues debated, and decisions made. In the nineteenth century, colonialism is part of that framework. The known facts about Eliot's active role in her society's promotion of colonialism can provide insights into the knowledge and expectations shared by readers, writers, and even fictional characters.

We are fortunate to have a great deal of historical documentation of Marian Evans Lewes's life. Her daily activities and impressions are recorded in her surviving letters and journals. Bodenheimer argues that letters as well as novels are "acts of self-representation in writing" and both may be taken as fictions.[8] While letters and even private journals are acts of self-representation, they are also cultural artifacts – texts that provide clues to the broader cultural contexts in which authors wrote. Together with the letters and journals of Lewes, with whom she lived for twenty-four years, these documents show the continuity of private and professional lives – of Marian Evans Lewes and George Eliot. They reveal her concerns about family, friends, and finances, as well as her engagement with the intellectual and political issues of her time. The development of her art is central in this material, which has been mined for its relationship to her fiction since the publication of John Walter Cross's *George Eliot's Life as Related in her Letters and Journals* (1885). Certain events in her life have become canonical in the study of her work. "Originals" have been discovered for characters in *Scenes of Clerical Life* and *Adam Bede* since their publication. Her break with her brother Isaac Evans over her relationship with the married Lewes is accepted as the impetus for her perspective on their childhood together as recalled in

*The Mill on the Floss*. The evangelical phase of her young adult life is thought to be a model for Dorothea Brooke's religious ardor. These sometimes reductive equations, which focus on her early life and assume that her memory of the past was more important than her experience of the present, draw on a standard biographical narrative that has become as familiar to contemporary students of her writing as any of her novels.[9] I am presenting a new George Eliot, whose imagination and aesthetic principles were shaped by her experiences as a reader and reviewer of colonial literature, a colonial shareholder, a stepmother to colonial emigrants, and, ultimately, a critic of colonial war. This new focus clarifies her metaphoric and her explicit references to the empire, as well as her realism, moral perspective, and sense of English identity.

Eliot's novels preserved a distinctive Englishness and provided a touchstone of national identity for colonial emigrants and readers throughout Great Britain. In her late works, she perceived this Englishness to be in a state of transformation under the pressures of colonial dispersion and cosmopolitanism at home. Her last book, *Impressions of Theophrastus Such* (1879), self-consciously reconciles the fragmenting intrusions of colonial knowledge and the need to consolidate Englishness. Theophrastus, in making an analogy between Englishmen and Jews, observes that "our own countrymen who take to living abroad without purpose or function to keep up their sense of fellowship in the affairs of their own land are rarely good specimens of moral healthiness," yet the consciousness of having a motherland preserves these "migratory Englishmen from the worst consequences of their voluntary dispersion" (156). As Eliot's only contemporary fiction, *Impressions* defines character types as products of late nineteenth-century culture, assessing the future of England and Englishness in an era of "cosmopolitan indifference" and an English diaspora to the colonies of which she had direct experience.

Critics have noted the role Eliot's fiction played in consolidating English identity. Some have touched on the empire as a disruption to visions of rural England. Elizabeth Helsinger argues that Eliot's novels "contradict their own project of creating a cohesive national identity because they register painful memories of exclusion, and still more dangerously, of complicity in excluding others, at the center of images meant to bridge difference and construct new national communities."[10] In fact, Eliot's fiction is conscious of the distinctions between self and other. Theophrastus writes: "It is my way when I observe any instance of folly, any queer habit, any absurd illusion, straightway to look for something of the same type in myself, feeling sure that amid all differences there will be a certain correspondence" (104). And he extends the individual case to the general, the geographic and geological differences by which England defined itself – "just as there is more or less correspondence in the natural history even of continents widely apart, and of islands in opposite zones" (104).

Eliot's fiction was trained from the start on representing life in England, and the moral imperative of her realism had its nationalist component: to expand limited notions of Englishness by including "otherness." "The Natural History of German Life" (1856) is one of her most important aesthetic statements preceding the realist fiction she would begin writing in 1856. In it she describes the "picture-writing of the mind," the psychological process by which we associate images with abstract words or concepts. She is interested in *how* we imagine in relation to what we know, speculating that "the fixity or variety of these associated images would furnish a tolerably fair test of the amount of concrete knowledge and experience which a given word represents" (Pinney, p. 267). Although we are all in the habit of visualizing what we have not seen, such mental pictures depart from reality and are not to be trusted. To illustrate her point, she chooses a word familiar to all her contemporaries:

The word *railways*, for example, will probably call up, in the mind of a man who is not highly locomotive, the image either of a "Bradshaw," or of the station with which he is most familiar, or of an indefinite length of tram-road; he will alternate between these three images, which represent his stock of concrete acquaintance with railways. But suppose a man to have had successively the experience of a "navvy," an engineer, a traveller, a railway director and shareholder, and a landed proprietor in treaty with a railway company, and it is probable that the range of images which would by turns present themselves to his mind at the mention of the *word* "railways," would include all the essential facts in the existence and relations of the *thing*. Now it is possible for the first-mentioned personage to entertain very expanded views as to the multiplication of railways in the abstract, and their ultimate function in civilization. He may talk of a vast network of railways stretching over the globe, of future "lines" in Madagascar, and elegant refreshment-rooms in the Sandwich Islands, with none the less glibness because his distinct conceptions on the subject do not extend beyond his one station and his indefinite length of tram-road. But it is evident that if we want a railway to be made, or its affairs to be managed, this man of wide views and narrow observation will not serve our purpose. (Pinney, pp. 267–8)

The tendency to entertain expanded views exists in inverse proportion to experience – that is, the less one has observed of a thing, the easier it is to generalize. In 1856 railways signified not only progress within Great Britain but the spread of "civilization" around the globe, particularly in those parts where the British were laying the "lines." The familiarity of railways made them a conceptual link between the concrete and the abstract – the local tram-road and the vaguely imagined tracks emerging from jungles and passing through deserts.

The invocation of railways in an essay that argues for social realism in fiction reveals a connection between the geographical and imaginative expansion of England to the empire and Eliot's narrowing of the field of fictional representation to what has been observed by the author. The unlikely advent in 1856 of lines in Madagascar and the absence of railways in the Sandwich Islands (i.e. Hawaii) make her hypothetical first man's wide views an apt illustration of the inaccurate associations against which her theory and practice of fiction developed, as she goes on to suggest by comparing "railways" to "the masses" and elaborating on misconceptions about the peasant classes as presented in art.

With railway investment such a prominent part of English life, it is worth asking whether and how Eliot and others visualized the colonial railroads they were helping to build. Anthony Trollope, who owned colonial stocks and was a frequent traveler on colonial railways, described the South Central Pacific and Mexican Railway scam in *The Way We Live Now* (1875). Eliot's fellow realist took the consequences of misrepresentation to their logical extreme. His imaginary railway was invented to defraud English investors, who were only too willing to speculate on what did not exist. Eliot, too, was anxious about the English habit of imagining foreign places on the basis not of observation but of fanciful associations to which they were all the more susceptible for being ignorant.

Eliot's notion that images invoked in speech and writing are a test of "concrete knowledge and experience" raises the question of what counted for her as concrete knowledge. Her aesthetic position and its relationship to her own representations challenge us to understand the world she knew. The narrator of *The Mill on the Floss* remarks that, "our instructed vagrancy . . . is nourished on books of travel and stretches the theatre of its imagination to the Zambesi" (263). In her fiction, Eliot redirected the "theatre of the English imagination" to commonplace reality within England. The empire was an inherent if abstract part of that reality and thus was present even in Eliot's domestic fiction. The imaginative vagrancy of her contemporaries was extended through books of travel that Eliot read and reviewed. She could not hope to curtail that instruction, but sought rather to concentrate her readers' attention on the English landscape and on knowable ways of life overlooked in the vagrant passion for exploration and travel.

In Victorian culture and society, representations of the British colonies filled the imaginations of those at home with images that constituted a shared basis of knowledge. Beliefs about the indigenous inhabitants of colonies emerged into what Eliot, describing the traditions of representing the English peasantry, called "prejudices difficult to dislodge from the artistic mind" (Pinney, p. 269). The name that has been given to one form of nineteenth-century colonial discourse is "Orientalism." Edward Said's *Orientalism* (1978) argues that nineteenth-century British and French writers, in attempting to represent the East, unconsciously reproduced a self-referential set of images which became intransigent prejudices in Western thought and art, and, as Said writes, created "not only knowledge but also the very reality they appear to describe."[11]

The representations of colonized people that post-colonial critics have shown to be instrumental in legitimizing imperialism were precisely the kind of romanticized misrepresentations that Eliot saw as distorting middle-class perceptions of the English peasantry. In *Adam Bede*, she wrote that the need to represent the "common, coarse people" as they really were was political and social: "It is so needful we should remember their existence, else we may happen to leave them quite out of our religion and philosophy, and frame lofty theories which only fit a world of extremes" (Pinney, p. 178). Eliot applied the same analytic standards to representations of the empire, which she recognized as treacherous for readers who could not verify published accounts by their own observation. While she could not formulate her critique in the terms used by late twentieth-century post-colonial theorists, she saw the danger of looking to "literature instead of life" (Pinney, p. 269). She argued against English pastoralism as a "tradition" – the kind of cultural formation that Said, following Foucault, calls a "discourse."[12]

This book explores a disjunction between the expressed politics of a realist aesthetic that did not permit Eliot to represent what she had not seen, and life in a society that encouraged practical decisions based on abstractions – "the colonies." That is, contemporary sources of knowledge about the colonies were not reliable enough to form the basis of artistic representations but were sufficient to support the emigration of sons and the investment of capital. Eliot's knowledge of what she was investing in was abstract. The exile of her sons to an unrepresentable world abstracted them too, rendering them unknowable except through letters that were themselves a patchwork of colonialist discourses mediating their lived experience.

Written in 1860 when she had just begun to invest the profits from
*The Mill on the Floss* in Indian railways and was considering colonial careers for her stepsons, Eliot's story "Brother Jacob" displays a striking
self-consciousness about the forms of representation we now call Orientalism. "Brother Jacob" addresses the consequences of false conceptions
about the colonies. Under the assumed identity of Edward Freely, David
Faux is able to dupe the Grimworth people on the basis of his experience
in Jamaica. What they know of the West Indies comes from books, and
Eliot registers the tendency of provincial villagers to conflate explicitly
Orientalist images in ways that prepared them to believe canny travelers.
For example, Freely's customer, Mrs. Steene, "knew by heart many passages in 'Lalla Rookh,' the 'Corsair,' and the 'Siege of Corinth,'" and
regrets that her husband was "not in the least like a nobleman turned
Corsair out of pure scorn for his race, or like a renegade with a turban and crescent" (245–6). In "Brother Jacob," Eliot not only refuses to
represent what she does not know (Jamaica), but makes ignorant and
false representations the subject of her fiction. Rather than encouraging
stereotypes, she mocks them and suggests the immorality of exploiting
them. David Faux is not only a thief and an imposter: this would-be
colonizer and fortune-seeker is an absolute failure whose preposterous
assumptions about Jamaican culture clash with colonial reality. Yet his
fabrications are validated by his equally ill-educated listeners at home.

As examples of realism, Eliot's novels have come under criticism for
generic properties which allegedly evince complicity in imperialism. In
the late twentieth-century critique of realism, the realist novel is thought
to have given form to the ideologies of bourgeois individualism, capitalism, and imperialism. The narrator who views the world as from
a panopticon is thought to concentrate control in a single omniscient
English individual in a manner that reflected and subsequently encouraged the control that England exerted over its empire. Firdous Azim
summarizes the post-structuralist premise of this argument by explaining that the novel is "an imperial genre, not in theme merely, not only by
virtue of the historical moment of its birth, but in its formal structure –
in the construction of that narrative voice which holds the narrative
structure together."[13] In addition to such formalist claims, there is an
argument about representation: middle-class novelists unwittingly represented the world in a way that validated the politics and practices
of British colonialists, even when their novels are not explicitly imperialist. Said argues: "It is striking that never, in the novel, is that world
beyond seen except as subordinate and dominated, the English presence

viewed as regulative and normative."[14] But seen by whom? By "seen" Said means the references to or glances at colonial spaces in domestic novels. In Eliot's case, such spaces are not seen at all, though they are alluded to in revealing ways. Both the formalist and the representational arguments fail to consider what the author might have known about the multifaceted ways in which the British interacted with the cultures and peoples in the world beyond their novels.

While "The Natural History of German Life" and "Silly Novels by Lady Novelists" are acknowledged to be important statements about her realism, her reviews of colonial literature by authors such as C. J. Andersen and Richard Burton have gone unexamined as evidence of the development of her aesthetic. In chapter 1, I explore a variety of colonial discourses that were evaluated by Eliot in the years before she began writing her fiction. In one review, for example, she measured the impact of myths and erroneous information on both British society generally and her own imagination in particular. African explorers, she believed, were slowly correcting the images of Africa drawn from the Arabian Nights and familiar from "our childhood."[15] She recognized the commingling of science and fiction, fact and fancy, that filled in the blanks of the English imagination with intriguing images of Africa. She looked forward to the clarifications of scientific discovery, but remained vigilantly skeptical of all the popular accounts she read and reviewed.

Lewes's thinking and writing about colonial exploration and emigration provide an immediate context for Eliot's fiction. His sons, whose colonial ventures Eliot supported, were an important though dubious source of her information about colonial life in South Africa – dubious because their failure to turn supposed colonial opportunities to their advantage called into question their reliability as accurate narrators of their experiences in Africa. Thornie and Bertie wrote intermittent but substantial letters to Lewes and Eliot throughout the 1860s, Bertie's continuing into the early 1870s, and the texts of these letters are the basis for chapter 2. In considering the South African letters, we must imagine Eliot as a reader of unsettling accounts of colonial warfare, poverty, and failure. Thornie and Bertie were "bad colonists."[16] They failed to become bureaucratic functionaries, and they succeeded neither as explorers/hunters nor even as self-supporting emigrants. Thornie in particular evinced enthusiasm for a genre – the colonial adventure novel – that Eliot's fiction directly challenged and sought to displace. His unrealistic expectations and inability to see beyond the romance of his situation as a settler colonist epitomize the dangers she recognized

as resulting from a diet of unrealistic fiction. I examine the relationship
between boys' adventure fiction and Thornie's colonial experiences as
narrated in his letters home, to argue that Eliot's domestic experience of
colonialism reaffirmed her commitment to realism.

The value of children is related for Eliot to predictions about the
future. In Charles Dickens's *Dombey and Son* (1846–8), offspring are assessed in monetary terms. Girls, in Mr. Dombey's view, are debased
currency: "In the capital of the House's name and dignity, such a child
was merely a piece of base coin that couldn't be invested – a bad Boy –
nothing more."[17] Eliot's ambivalence about assessing individual worth
in this manner is seen in parent–child relationships in her fiction. As
Mr. Tulliver says of Maggie, "an over-'cute woman's no better nor a long-
tailed sheep – she'll fetch none the bigger price for that" (12). Gwendolen
is viewed similarly by her uncle Gascoigne – worth an investment only
because she promises to pay off in a successful marriage. In "Debasing
the Moral Currency," Eliot's Theophrastus uses a financial metaphor
to decry contemporary English attitudes toward literary traditions that
convey the moral values of society. Failing to respect the inherited texts
transmitted over the ages amounts to a desecration of the moral sentiments that bind a people and a culture – a debasing of the moral currency
that lowers "the value of every inspiring fact and tradition" and impov-
erishes "our social existence" (84). In his concern for English children
and posterity, Theophrastus wonders where parents "have deposited that
stock of morally educating stimuli which is to be independent of poetic
tradition" (84). Teaching our children is an investment that will pay
dividends far into the future, and failing to invest wisely, Theophrastus
argues, could have disastrous consequences for the nation.

The dire projections of Theophrastus (who is notably childless) for the
moral future of the nation synthesize anxieties about English identity
during a period in which colonial markets were expanding and foreign cultural influences multiplying. Chapter 3 investigates the forms of
empire-building with which Eliot's investments made her complicit. With
her first purchase of shares, she began to accumulate a portfolio of domestic, foreign, and colonial stocks that gave her an investment in British
colonialism and distanced her material interest in the progress of imperial
expansion from the moral problems that expansion entailed. I argue that
the conflict of personal and, more broadly, social interests was significant
in shaping the moral outlook of her fiction. The choice between material comfort and moral rectitude is one faced repeatedly by women in
Eliot's novels, including Esther Lyon, Dorothea Brooke, and Gwendolen

Harleth. In these fictional situations Eliot idealized behavior that she herself could not emulate: renouncing money that was in some way tainted.

In *Daniel Deronda*, Eliot went furthest to investigate the experiences of people who lived beyond the bounds of her personal lot. She studied Jewish history, culture, and religion to better know the "other" within England. She made herself an expert on Jewish subjects, but upheld her notion of realism to the extent that she demurred from representing places, specifically "the East," which she had not seen. In chapter 4, I examine how Eliot aligned her knowledge about contemporary Jews and their nascent nationalism with her realist aesthetic. The complexity of her artistic and political motivations in *Deronda* challenges readings of the novel that are limited to critiques of its alleged imperialist ideology. Said accuses Eliot of perpetuating in the novel a myth of empty land: "On one important issue there was complete agreement between the Gentile and Jewish versions of Zionism: their view of the Holy Land as essentially empty of inhabitants."[18] His condemnation, which transforms Eliot into a Zionist and an imperialist, has played a key part in subsequent criticism of *Deronda*, and its impact exceeds his own limited yet repeated claims.

Because of Said's influence, I evaluate his position and those of his followers, not as a defense of Eliot, but rather to clarify an understanding of the colonial and aesthetic contexts in which she wrote. When we look at her statements about fiction as well as at her work as a whole, we can see that her treatment of "the East" at the end of *Deronda* is analogous to that of "the Indies" in "Brother Jacob." Said argues that Eliot writes about the East as if the Arabs do not exist, that she represents the land as available for the taking. This criticism would have more validity had Eliot actually represented any part of "the East" and had she been less aware of the fallacies of representations that merely reproduced other representations. Mordecai's conception of the Holy Land is dependent upon discursive constructions and traditions – a combination of religious texts and accounts by contemporary travelers. When he speaks of Israel, his "voice might have come from a Rabbi transmitting the sentences of an elder time" (636). His visions are hallucinatory combinations of textual fragments bearing virtually no relationship to contemporary reality, and Daniel's plans are contingent upon what he will find in a future beyond the text.

Understanding these and similar aspects of Eliot's fiction depends upon an awareness of the language and knowledge available to her. In my conclusion I bring together the issues discussed in the book as a whole by focusing on the synthesis of economic, colonial, and literary discourses represented by Eliot's relationship with her banker John Walter Cross. Cross was an intimate friend throughout the 1870s, during which time he also wrote a number of essays on finance, emigration, and literature. He wrote about railroads from his direct experience in the United States and Australia and it was on his advice that Eliot invested heavily in New World railways. His influence was both directly personal and discursive.

With Cross to guide her, Eliot knew more about her investments than most ordinary shareholders. This raises the question of how her decisions about participation in the affairs of empire, specifically emigration and investment, differed from decisions about representing colonial spaces in fiction: could the economy and the society of England be extended overseas without the sympathy that realist fiction generated? In *Impressions*, Theophrastus contrasts the effects of railroads on the English landscape to "those grander and vaster regions of the earth" (24). Offering an image of foreign "lines," he asks: "What does it signify that a lilliputian train passes over a viaduct amidst the abysses of the Apennines, or that a caravan laden with a nation's offerings creeps across the unresting sameness of the desert?" (24–5). What does it signify? Having "learned to care for foreign countries" (26), Theophrastus projects the railroad – symbol of British technology and progress – into romantic landscapes familiar to his readers through literature. His phrase "learned to care" echoes Eliot's letter to Lady Lytton, in which "learning to love is like an increase in property." The foreign scenes had become part of the English theatre of imagination, just as railroads had become part of the English landscape. The incorporation of the foreign into English culture was an occasion for the reassessment of that culture. Following the examination of an inextricable relationship between English and Jewish cultures in *Deronda*, *Impressions* tightens that association and points forward to a new, less insular Englishness that Eliot might have represented, had she lived to see it.

In *Impressions*, Theophrastus's denunciation of false outward vision recalls the statements about realism in Eliot's early essays, which worried about the neglect of the marginal English classes and the English preference for images of foreign places. In the years between "The Natural History of German Life" and *Impressions*, Eliot's life and art changed in many ways that were reflective of its colonial and imperial contexts. Her reading about the spaces of empire in travel writing and newspapers, her direct involvement in the emigration of her stepsons, and her extensive colonial investments amounted to a multifaceted engagement with the material reality of imperial expansion and contributed to transformations in her political, moral, and aesthetic perspectives.

# CHAPTER I

# *Imperial knowledge: George Eliot, G. H. Lewes, and the literature of empire*

... and yet, how little do we still know of Africa.

George Eliot[1]

Like many of her contemporaries, George Eliot looked to the empire for solutions to poverty and unemployment in England. In January 1851, she moved from Coventry to London, and between 1851 and 1854 she edited the *Westminster Review* for its publisher, John Chapman. On December 20, 1851, her brother-in-law Edward Clarke died, leaving her sister Chrissey with six children and a considerable debt. Although Eliot had emigrated to London rather than to a colony to escape the "moral asphyxia" of the Midlands, she thought Australia was just the place for her widowed sister and six orphaned children. Chapman had traveled to Australia before becoming a publisher and he was at the time engaged in preparing Sophia Tilley, the sister of his mistress, Elisabeth Tilley, to emigrate to Australia (*GEL*, 2:93). Writing to her friends Charles and Cara Bray in Coventry, Eliot asked: "What do you think of my going to Australia with Chrissey and all her family?" According to this plan, Chrissey was to relocate permanently because she seemed to have so few alternatives in England; it may have been the one way to keep the family together. Eliot did not intend to stay, merely "to settle them and then come back" (*GEL*, 2:97). Chrissey's emigration would give her a chance to travel, see the world, and return home, perhaps to write for an English audience about what she had seen in Australia.

Eliot's vision of Australia as a salvation from the physical hardships and the social disgrace of poverty into which Chrissey had fallen derived from the reading and reviewing that made her life so radically different from that of her sister. Her position as editor of the *Westminster* was transforming her into a member of the London literary elite, the type of person who would never emigrate, but who would express opinions about the emigration of others. Several books about Australia had been reviewed recently in the *Westminster*, including "the book of books for the emigrant," Samuel Sidney's *The Three Colonies of Australia*.[2] Samuel Sidney and his brother published many books on Australia, as well as articles in Charles Dickens's *Household Words*. In 1850, Dickens wrote to his friend Miss Burdett-Coutts that he had gained from guidebooks some little knowledge of the state of society in New South Wales "of which one could have no previous understanding, and which would seem to be quite misunderstood, or very little known, even in the cities of New South Wales itself."[3] Dickens felt that this and other sources of second-hand information provided a sufficient basis for understanding and knowing Australia. His "little knowledge" was enough for him to support the emigration of others – of "fallen women" as part of the Urania House project beginning in 1847 and of his own sons in the 1860s.

Similarly, in 1850 Eliot looked to the popular guidebook for justification in urging the emigration of her sister, who had "fallen" in a different sense. Her plight was more like that of the Micawber family in Dickens's *David Copperfield*. The initial plan had been to send Chrissey's son Edward to Australia, where an acquaintance had "offered to place him under suitable protection at Adelaide" (*GEL*, 2:88). Eliot "strongly recommended" that Chrissey accept the offer and, perhaps under Chapman's influence, continued to push the idea of the whole family's emigration. She bought Sidney's book and sent it to Chrissey "to enlighten her about matters there and accustom her mind to the subject" (*GEL*, 2:88). Sidney advocated "an influx of well-disposed, educated, intelligent families, prepared to carry on colonization by cultivation," and clearly this was the image Eliot had of orderly settlement and a new life in the colonies.[4] But Chrissey refused to go. She died in 1859, and her sons Edward and Charles eventually emigrated to Australia and New Zealand.

This moment of enthusiasm in 1853 was the closest Eliot ever came to visiting a colony. In 1854 she began living with G. H. Lewes and embarked on a shared intellectual life in which the two often read the same books. Their reading formed a common basis of knowledge, including knowledge about the empire, on which they drew to make joint decisions about issues such as emigration and investment. This reading included theories of, as well as practical advice about, the colonies. The case that colonization was regenerative for some Germans was made in W. H. Riehl's *Die Naturgeschichte des deutschen Volkes* (1854). In her review essay "The Natural History of German Life" (1856), Eliot notes that Riehl "points to colonization" for the peasant class as the remedy for the degenerative effects of civilization. She seems to concur that on "the other side of the ocean, a man will have the courage to begin life again as a peasant, while at home, perhaps, opportunity as well as courage will fail him" (Pinney, p. 281). Just as Riehl believed that the peasants were the most successful of German agricultural colonists, so Sidney remarks that British attempts to "fill ships with the higher and middle classes" have failed because "they are not the class who, in a body, can succeed" under colonial conditions in Australia.[5]

In the early 1850s, Eliot believed that emigration would enhance the development of the English race. She was thrilled at the thought of the "great Western Continent, with its infant cities, its huge uncleared forests, and its unamalgamated races" (*GEL*, 2:85). She recalled these early impressions of North America in an 1872 letter to Harriet Beecher Stowe, in which she confessed that she "always had delight in descriptions of American forests since the early days when I read 'Atala.'" She enjoyed the primeval setting of Chateaubriand's 1801 romance about French colonizers and the American Indians they encountered in the Louisiana territory at the end of the eighteenth century, even though it was "half-unveracious" (*GEL*, 5:279–80). In the same letter, Eliot recalled admiring Stowe's descriptions of the American South in *Dred, a Tale of the Great Dismal Swamp*, which she had reviewed when it appeared in 1856. The freshness of her early reading had faded by 1872, when she knew that she would never see the New World except, as she wrote to Stowe, "in the mirror of your loving words" (*GEL*, 5:279).

## REVIEWING COLONIAL LITERATURE

Throughout the nineteenth century, the expanses of Australia, Canada, Africa, India, or "the East" were colored for those at home by the accounts of explorers, missionaries, emigrants, colonial officials, and novelists. Among the many categories of books Eliot read, travel and exploration narratives comprised a significant portion. Because she reviewed extensively in the 1850s, she read many classics of travel writing, such as Captain James Cook's *Voyages around the World* and Alexander von Humboldt's *Travels and Discoveries in South America*, as well as the most recent accounts of David Livingstone, Richard Burton, John Hanning Speke, and others. This reading established the groundwork of her knowledge about the empire, and textual information was infused later with personal experience of the imperial bureaucracy at home and correspondence with friends and relatives in the colonies.

In the 1850s, Eliot's writing negotiates the uneven ground of her knowledge about the empire in ways that contributed to her developing realist aesthetic. Like any other genre, colonial literature demanded critical evaluation. Her standard for the judgment of such books was not personal experience: she could not assess the descriptions of geography, natural life, and indigenous peoples based on her own travel. She could ask only, as she would of any book, whether it was well-written, informative, and consistent with similar accounts. In her 1856 review of Ruskin's *Modern Painters* (vol. III), she defined "realism" as "the doctrine that all truth and beauty are to be attained by a humble and faithful study of nature." While the objectives of travel and exploration literature were to inform and entertain rather than to achieve "truth and beauty," we find her suspicious that travel writing, like painting and fiction, could fail by "substituting vague forms, bred by imagination on the mists of feeling, in place of definite, substantial reality."[6]

The social need for realistic representation was especially great in the descriptions of unfamiliar, foreign places. With the expansion of the empire through exploration and colonization, the observations of travelers had considerable cultural significance.[7] In 1854, Eliot reviewed the Rev. N. Davis's *Evenings in My Tent; or, Wanderings in Balad Ejjareed.* "In comparison with other quarters of the globe," she wrote, "Africa may be considered almost as a *terra incognita.*"[8] Ever precise in her expression, Eliot summarizes the received wisdom about Arabs, neither crediting nor doubting it on her own authority: "Modern travellers concur in representing the Arab as singularly cunning, rapacious, and cowardly, apparently incapable of truth, and sunk in abject superstition; in fact, as exhibiting all the vices of an oppressed race."[9] The depressed state of the Arabs is made known to her by Davis's account of their moral failings. As she would do later in her fiction, Eliot looks immediately to the conditions that created the alleged demoralization. She speaks against the negative effects of Christian missionaries, referring to the "evil that has been done by an *ill*-organized missionary system in some of our colonies, the irreparable injury to progress and to real civilisation."[10] Real civilization resists the "narrow bigotry and intolerance" of missionaries and depends on "progress" of a more scientific nature.

Two years later, she made a similar case about representations of moral degeneration in her review of Stowe's *Dred*. According to Eliot, Stowe's social criticism is weakened (she commits "argumentative suicide") because her Negro characters are too good and fail to capture "the Nemesis lurking in the vices of the oppressed." Stowe "alludes to demoralization among the slaves, but she does not depict it; and yet why should she shrink from this?"[11] A strict commitment to what Eliot sees as the realistic condition of demoralization among American slaves would show readers the consequences of slavery. Unflinching realism would lead readers to condemn slavery all the louder, just as Davis's account of the Arabs led Eliot to criticize the missionary system.

From her reviews in the 1850s through her last book, *Impressions of Theophrastus Such*, Eliot expressed the conviction that oppression leads to a collective degeneration, whether in slaves, in the English working classes, or in colonized peoples. In *The Mill on the Floss*, her narrator observes of Philip Wakem: "Ugly and deformed people have great need of unusual virtues," but "the theory that unusual virtues spring by a direct consequence out of personal disadvantages, as animals get thicker wool in severe climates, is perhaps a little overstrained" (331). Similarly, in "The Modern Hep! Hep! Hep!" Theophrastus observes: "An oppressive government and a persecuting religion, while breeding vices in those who hold power, are well known to breed answering vices in those who are powerless and suffering" (152). Together with realistic descriptions of landscape, architecture, or physiognomy, Eliot believed that the artist was obliged to represent such hard truths.

Eliot's reviews suggest that it was partially by balancing the claims of veracity and artistic merit in fiction and travel writing that she came to formulate her theory of fiction. The themes of her reviews, whether of fiction or non-fiction, are consistent. In an 1855 review of Charles Kingsley's historical romance *Westward Ho!*, she showed her willingness to appreciate his story while judging its realism cautiously. "We dare not pronounce on the merit of his naval descriptions," she wrote, "but to us, landlubbers as we are, they seem wonderfully real" (Pinney, p. 128). The next year she reviewed Richard Burton's *First Footsteps in East Africa* (1856). For her, accuracy of description in the literature of exploration was not sufficient. The author must also hold the reader's attention. Here Burton failed, and Eliot complained that his book "labours under the sin (unpardonable in the production of so extremely clever a man) of being dull." She objects that "we are hungry, and are not fed, we are thirsty, and find no drink."[12]

In other reviews, she speculated about the veracity of travelers' accounts with an implied concern that any inaccuracies or distortions would be perpetuated by less cautious readers. In a review of C. J. Andersen's *Lake Ngami*, she applauds the author's contribution to British geographical knowledge of southern Africa. Correcting the reports of missionaries (received "second hand from Arab travellers") about an enormous inland lake, Andersen shows that the lake "turns out to be a mirage – a mythus with the smallest conceivable nucleus of fact." "So perishes a phantom," she writes, "which has excited London geographers for a whole season."[13] Andersen, she remarks, is more hunter than scientist, but it is on these testimonies that scientists must depend. It took explorers like Andersen and Burton, she believed, to separate the facts from the myths. Eliot acknowledges that information about Africa was inconsistent and fragmented, and that unconfirmed reports could leave even men of science chasing phantoms.[14]

Eliot wrote in "The Natural History of German Life" that art is "the nearest thing to life; it is a mode of amplifying experience and extending our contact with our fellow-men beyond the bounds of our personal lot" (Pinney, p. 271). Her historical romance *Romola* (1863) illustrates her interest in reconstructing a non-English past based on her readings about it. *Daniel Deronda* shows her entering into the lives of European and English Jews, about whom her research made her expert. Yet her writing shows a decided avoidance of the realities of British colonialism. Considering her belief in emigration as a solution to domestic problems, she might have striven to extend the contact of her readers to the experiences of English colonists. Or, with her critical attitude toward missionaries, she might have shown the vices and answering vices of the oppressors and oppressed in any number of places about which she had read. But with the British empire, Eliot seems to have run up against the limits of her realism, or at least the limits of what she was willing to represent.

Mid-century fiction that does more than allude to parts of the empire is noteworthy in that action and violence in the colonies, whether in sport or in warfare, was consigned primarily to boys' literature until the late nineteenth-century emergence of a new generation, most notably Kipling and Conrad.[15] In the early part of the century, novels set in India would have been familiar to the British reading public. Scott's *The Surgeon's Daughter* (1827), for example, extended a Scottish romance plot to India. Novels were also written by Englishmen who had served in India, such as Colonel Meadows Taylor, author of *Confessions of a Thug* (1839) and four other Indian romances. W. D. Arnold's *Oakfield; or, Fellowship in the East* (1853) was based on his experiences in India, as Henry Kingsley's *Geoffrey Hamlyn* (1859) was based on his five years in Australia.

But authors such as Eliot, Trollope, Dickens, and Thackeray had a more oblique relationship to the empire. They resisted extending to the colonies their representations of English life, yet the colonies are present in their fiction. Thackeray was born in India. Eliot, Trollope, and Dickens all sent sons to the colonies. Trollope represented the Australian colonies he had visited, but in the work of Dickens and Eliot colonial spaces constitute the margins of their fictional worlds, simultaneously lands of opportunity and dumping grounds: the "Indies" to which David Faux emigrates in "Brother Jacob"; the Botany Bay to which Hetty is transported in *Adam Bede*; the Australia to which Dickens's Magwitch is transported in *Great Expectations* and to which Martha the reformed prostitute and Micawber the reformed debtor emigrate in *David Copperfield*. Eliot did not represent the colonies, which could seem alternately ominous and prosperous, but the tension between their image as "new worlds" for starting life over and as desolate, perilous margins of an empire to which the unwanted could be conveniently removed is evident in her life and fiction.

Although she never set a novel in the colonies, Eliot described those aspects of British imperialism that were part of her daily life as a resident in the metropolis of London. We can see her own experiences breaking in on her aesthetic argument. Correcting false images of English peasants in "The Natural History of German Life," she applies a metaphor drawn from her own decontextualized observation. Speaking of the English ploughman, she writes that "the slow utterance, and the heavy slouching walk" remind one of "that melancholy animal the camel" (Pinney, p. 269). Such an exotic analogy is part of Eliot's stated aesthetic project of representing the common English folk to English readers. It is possible that a greater number of urban middle-class readers had seen live camels than had seen live peasants. Where, we might ask, did Eliot encounter a camel? In a painting? A novel? Most likely it was at the London Zoological Gardens.

Once she moved to the Priory in Regent's Park in 1863, the Royal Zoological Gardens were within walking distance. Through Lewes's scientific observations, she became aware of the differences between animals in captivity, which she was able to view, and animals in the wild, about which she read, and this distinction is registered in her fiction. The imperialist nature of nineteenth-century zoos has received much critical attention. Harriet Ritvo argues that "[t]he maintenance and study of captive wild animals, simultaneous emblems of human mastery over the natural world and of English dominion over remote territories, offered an especially vivid rhetorical means of reenacting and extending the work of empire."[16] Robert W. Jones argues that in zoos "it was possible to suggest, indeed to insist, that the animals were to be viewed as metonyms for imperial triumph, civic pride, the beneficence of God or scientific discovery."[17] Eliot assumes that even those who had never traveled to the natural habitat of camels – to northern Africa or northern India – would have been familiar with the vivid theatrical reenactment of the empire to be found in zoos and menageries.

In *Adam Bede*, she distinguished between the observed and the merely imagined in art: "Falsehood is so easy, truth so difficult." Her example of falsity is a drawing of a griffin – easy enough to do when there is no reality against which to test it, but "that marvelous facility which we mistook for genius, is apt to forsake us when we want to draw a real unexaggerated lion" (177). While no one can doubt that the drawing of a lion in a zoo represents a "real" lion, both Eliot and Lewes made a point of differentiating lions in zoos and menageries, which they had seen, and lions in Africa, about which they had only read. As Ritvo notes, the display of animals in zoos was a reenactment, a representation, of natural life in colonial places inaccessible to average zoo goers. Animals in captivity became symbols of British exploration and power. As we shall see, such animals, particularly lions, function as metonymic illustrations of Eliot's knowledge of British conquest throughout the empire. Her dependence on zoos, like books about hunting, travel, and emigration, accentuated the limitations of her authority to represent the real. In her fiction, she highlights the differences between the real and the represented colonial experience, rather than attempting to represent realistically what she had not seen.

MANLINESS AND COLONIALISM

Lewes's readings and reviews are relevant to Eliot's experience in that they respond to colonial writing published in popular periodicals of the time. In 1850, Lewes and his friend Thornton Hunt established the *Leader* (1850–57), a weekly newspaper with a radical political agenda and commitment to literature and the arts. In his role as editor and primary contributor to the literature and arts section, Lewes reviewed some noteworthy publications and listed others. The lists, and frequently the review section, included books relating to the empire. Lewes's writing shows that he was concerned with the moral effects of travel writing, as well as of literature and drama. Through his reviews, he scrutinized fundamental issues of English national character, including the stereotypes and conventions of manliness.

One of his harshest reviews was of R. Gordon Cumming's *Five Years of a Hunter's Life in the Far Interior of South Africa*. Cumming, who abandoned a colonial military career to devote himself to field sport, was the premier big-game hunter of the period and one of the first to capitalize on his success.[18] Lewes objected to the brutality and bravado that character-ize this account of lion-hunting in the same country to which his son Thornie would be sent thirteen years later with, as Eliot wrote, "a very sanguine expectation of shooting lions" (*GEL*, 4:117). Lewes confesses that in encounters between man and beast, "we heartily wished the lion success." He mocks Cumming's bluster, asking: "If a lion, obeying the impulses of his own nature, seeks for food and finds it in the flesh of a man whom he subdues, deserves to be tortured alive, what does the man deserve who, in mere wanton sport, slaughters animals with every circumstance of cruelty, and glories in the deed as if it proved his manliness?"[19] The infliction of pain without limits and without sympathy signifies a descent into savagery that undermines any claims to manliness by which colonial activities might be justified. Further chiding Cumming, he writes: "Our sense of courage, hardihood, adventure, is lost in that of butchery . . . The page reeks with blood; and the writer smears himself all over with it as if blood in itself were ornamental!"[20] In Lewes's metaphor, the writer becomes the stereotype of a "savage," besmeared with the blood of his victim. The ultimate civilized act – writing – becomes a barbarous ritual, the very ink figured as blood.

Hunting narratives described performances that took place on a colo-nial stage and epitomized the relationship between conventional man-liness and the empire. With his experience as an actor, playwright, and theatre critic, Lewes was insightful about performances on and off the stage. "Vivian," Lewes's persona in his theatre reviews for the *Leader*, was a bachelor dandy, who, in reviews with titles such as "Vivian in Tears," fusses about his clothing, teases and flirts with his readers, and self-consciously inquires into his manliness. Vivian's challenge to mas-culinist stereotypes carries over into Lewes's comments on books such as Cumming's. He is not afraid to berate inferior authors, nor to tweak fel-low reviewers who "have touched but gently on its brutal and demoraliz-ing tone, probably from some secret fear of being thought effeminate!"[21] In undermining what passes for manly behavior in popular hunting narratives, Lewes accuses other literary men of insecurity about their manliness and neglect of their duties as reviewers. Such an offensive book should have been condemned by critics, but male reviewers shrink from speaking out against the hyperbolic manliness in the lion hunter's story. Neither true manliness nor good literature, he implies, is to be found in the bloodthirsty pursuit of big game.[22]

The distinction between adventure and butchery has implications for the behavior of the English in the colonies generally, and, by extension, for the treatment of native peoples. John MacKenzie argues that the "emergence of natural history specialisms, the division and ordering of the scientific effort, reflected the accelerating urge to order the world of nature, which was itself both an impulse towards and a symptom of the developing yearning to order and classify human affairs through imperialism."[23] MacKenzie shows that scientific collecting meant "killing on a large scale." Classifying and destroying, he argues, "epitomised Western man's command of a global natural world."[24] Yet as Lewes's interest in hunting as mere sport was supplanted in the 1850s by a conception of hunting in relation to science, he continued to value the kind of manliness that avoided cruelty. He wrote, for example, that John Petherick "shows how a man may be strong and terrible without being brutal."[25]

"Lions and Lion Hunting," written six years after his review of Cumming, discusses *Le tuer de lions* (1855) and *Chasse au lion et les autres chasses de l'Algérie* (1854), both by the Frenchman Jules Gérard.[26] More than the previous review, this article is concerned with natural history and what it has to tell us about lions. Lewes begins with the characteristically direct statement: "We know very little about lions," and suggests that if scientists could only observe the lion in his natural environment as carefully as Gérard has done, "we should have another conception of the lion from that to be derived by a study of books or an inspection of menageries."[27] Of course Lewes's information is derived from Gérard's book, but his point is that the hunter's first-hand knowledge is valuable and his techniques instructive to the naturalist, who, with similar methods of observation, might produce a truer picture of natural life, rather than another lion-skin rug or trophy head.

The moral tone of the earlier article is missing from his reading of Gérard (whom he compares to Cumming), perhaps because he had begun to embrace the association between hunting and science and wanted to stress the contribution to knowledge that might be made by those who knew lions in the wild, even if they were hunters. Lewes implicitly criticizes menageries as productive of incomplete knowledge about animals, in part because the animals themselves are inferior specimens, 'taken from the mother's breast, bred like rabbits, deprived of the fresh mountain-air and ample nourishment."[28] The pathos of captivity is confirmed by an anecdote from Gérard's book that describes the slow wasting of a lion, Hubert, caught by Gérard and brought to the Jardin des Plantes in Paris. When Gérard, who had raised Hubert from a cub, visits him in the zoo, "He stood up, pressed against the bars, striving to break through the obstacle which separated us."[29] Much affected, the hunter resolves to "kill as many lions as he could, but to capture no more."[30] Gérard thus affirms killing manfully but despises the humiliations of captivity – a code of honor for lion-hunters.

As if to challenge the stereotypical manliness of the lion-hunter, Lewes's article takes a whimsical turn, and describes his own encounters with two lions in the London Zoological Gardens. "We were once embraced by an affectionate young lioness," he boasts, "who put her paws lovingly round our neck, and would have kissed our cheek, had not that symptom of a boldness more than maidenly been at once by us virtuously repressed."[31] Gone are the bars that separated Hubert and Gérard, whose manly love affair ended in tragedy. Turning tragedy to farce, Lewes presents a man's love for lions, troping the conventions of courtship. In a tone more like that of "Vivian," who rebuffed the advances of marriage-minded women, Lewes invokes an endearing if ludicrous image of the author standing face to face with a female lion, an experience surely missed by hunters in the wild. The lioness is not only personified, but cast as a leading lady to Lewes's anti-hero, the man who loves rather than kills lions. Lewes experiences the lion as he would a pet; he takes great delight in the animals in this instance and in numerous other trips to the zoo described in his and Eliot's diaries.

In the description of his second encounter with a lion, Lewes diminishes himself further by his willingness to appear ridiculous. He tells of his fascination with the angry roars of the "noble lion who occupies the last den" at the Zoological Gardens, and how "we one day got over the railing opposite his den, and began dancing and *hishing* before him, in a wild and, as we imagined, formidable manner." Starting with this improbable image, Lewes continues:

Instead of flashing out in wrath and thunder, the lion turned his eye upon us, and in utter contempt continued licking his leg of beef, perfectly untroubled by our *hishing*, probably asking himself the meaning of those incomprehensible gesticulations. We felt small. He evidently did not think us worth even a growl; and we were forced to get back over the railing, utterly discomfitted by the quiet dignity of his majesty.[32]

Following an account of the many episodes in which Gérard is rushed by angry, roaring lions in the wild, Lewes's failure to make this less threatening lion so much as growl, leads him not only to feel, but to appear, small. For the sake of comic relief and his readers' entertainment, Lewes displays his domestication and humiliation. Crossing the boundary that separates the passive spectator from the captive and recalcitrant leonine performer, Lewes undercuts the notion that manliness is to be found in combat with wild animals, and makes such combat absurd through his parody of it. Here Lewes is the performer; the lion is the unimpressed audience.

However lightly done, this juxtaposition in the same article of the hunter's dramatic triumphs in Africa and the spectator turned spectacle in the London Zoo, is an important indication of Lewes's skepticism about displays of bravado and his self-consciousness about the relationship between gender and performance. Writing itself is a performance, and just as Cumming had smeared his pages in blood, so the critic exposes through mimicry the façade of manliness in the lion-hunter's text.[33]

Eliot made a similar criticism of Charles Kingsley's *Westward Ho!*. In her generally favorable 1855 review of this immensely popular novel by the foremost proponent of "Muscular Christianity," she found fault with the violence that seemed to conflict with the sensibilities of the author. She wrote that the "ruddy and, now and then, rather ferocious barbarism, which is singularly compounded in Mr Kingsley with the susceptibility of the poet and the warm sympathy of the philanthropist, while it gives his writings one of their principal charms, is also the source of their gravest fault" (Pinney, p. 126). Her rebuke of the novel's representations of the Elizabethan age takes on a contemporary colonial significance when we consider that the novel is dedicated to "Rajah" Brooke, who had recently been censured in Parliament for his excesses against natives in Sarawak, and that Kingsley's depiction of the eviction of the Spaniards from Ireland was intended as a justification for such violence. Then and later, the figure of Rajah Brooke epitomized masculine imperial conquest, as in, for example, Kipling's "The Man Who Would Be King," in which Daniel Dravot fantasizes, "we shall be Emperors – Emperors of the Earth! Raja Brooke will be a suckling to us."[34] Eliot complained of Kingsley that the "battle and the chase seem necessary to his existence" (Pinney, p. 126). This violence with which she found fault as art was a component of colonial manliness. In their reviews, both Eliot and Lewes condemned such glorified violence as unmanly.[35]

## THE MILL ON THE FLOSS

Much has been written about women and gender in Eliot's life and art, but there have been few considerations of how she experienced masculinity in her personal relationships or how she examined the category in her fiction.[36] *The Mill on the Floss* (1860) traces the painful process of socialization by which conventional masculinity is constructed. Rosemarie Bodenheimer notes that *The Mill on the Floss* "has always been understood as the last of the fictions to be generated directly from her provincial childhood," but that it also "marked a farewell to little sister-hood and a reorientation in Marian's experience of family life."[37] The young Maggie and Tom were created in part from the memory of her childhood relationship to her brother Isaac, yet while writing the novel she received letters from the Lewes boys, who were away at school in Switzerland. Thornie Lewes in particular wrote to her about hunting and about his schoolboy fights and war games. Tom Tulliver emerged from a combination of intense recollection of the past and present reflections on the struggle of teenage boys to establish themselves as men by the standards of their society, often in counter-distinction to their fathers' perceived failures by those same standards.

Issues of manliness in *The Mill on the Floss* circulate around images of hunting wild animals and of military combat and are linked by the larger themes of reading and imagination. Engaged in conversation with the mill-hand Luke, who is opposed to books on the grounds that "they're mostly lies," Maggie argues that through books we learn about other people, and "we ought to know about our fellow-creatures" (30). She offers the example of Goldsmith's *Animated Nature* with its "elephants, and kangaroos, and the civet cat, and the sun-fish" (30). "There are countries full of those creatures," she explains, "instead of horses and cows, you know."[38] Maggie is distinguished by her sympathetic imagination, which allows her to feel for "fellow creatures" of the animal and human kind. Her imagination takes flight with her knowledge of wild and exotic animals while Tom's remains grounded by ignorance.

It is typical of Maggie that she takes Tom's pedestrian account of schoolboy combat – giving Spouncer a black eye – and elevates her expectations of his bravery to mythic levels:

"O how brave you are, Tom! I think you're like Samson. If there came a lion roaring at me, I think you'd fight him – wouldn't you, Tom?"

"How can a lion come roaring at you, you silly thing? There's no lions, only in the shows."

"No; but if we were in the lion countries – I mean in Africa, where it's very hot – the lions eat people there. I can show it you in the book where I read it."

"Well, I should get a gun and shoot him."

"But if you hadn't got a gun – we might have gone out, you know, not thinking – just as we go fishing; and then a great lion might run towards us roaring, and we couldn't get away from him. What should you do, Tom?"

Tom paused, and at last turned away contemptuously, saying, "but the lion *isn't* coming. What's the use of talking?"

"But I like to fancy how it would be," said Maggie, following him. "Just think what you would do, Tom." (34–5)

Tom's desire for mastery, linked implicitly to his intellectual insecurity, requires him to deny the reality of animals of whose existence in the wild he is ignorant: "There's no lions, only in the shows." Maggie combines what she has read in the bible (the story of Samson) and what she has read in *Animated Nature*. She conflates the story of Samson slaying the lion with contemporary images of African lion-hunting. She inserts Tom into narratives unfamiliar to him, and he responds reflexively with simple solutions, first of shooting the lion, and then of silencing his sister. He ends the discussion with an assertion of literalism: "But the lion *isn't* coming. What's the use of talking?" Maggie's intellectual emasculation of Tom (as if, like Delilah, she had shorn her Samson of his strength) is met with an outleap of metaphoric talons. Lacking both knowledge and imagination, Tom extinguishes Maggie's fantasy about his bravery as completely as he smashed the earwig about which she had been making up stories "as a superfluous yet easy means of proving the entire unreality of such a story" (99).

*The Mill on the Floss* is structured by the gradual divergence of Tom and Maggie in response to specifically gendered social expectations. As her world expands through reading and becomes diffuse through her apparent superfluousness to her family, Tom's views narrow and focus through an almost monomaniacal sense of purpose. He transforms his limitations into strength, working to save the mill and losing his already limited capacity for sympathy in his vow to avenge his father's name. Their emotional differences are made explicit by the narrator when Mr. Tulliver emerges from his illness and faces the reality of his financial losses. The children wait in terror for their father's response. Maggie "yet felt as if the sorrow made larger room for her love to flow in, and gave breathing-space to her passionate nature" (259). "No true boy feels that," asserts the narrator: "he would rather go and slay the Nemean lion, or perform any round of heroic labours, than endure perpetual appeals to his pity, for evils over which he can make no conquest" (259–60). Here the narrator echoes Maggie's casting of Tom as Samson, who killed a lion with his bare hands, by invoking Hercules, whose first great feat was to throttle the Nemean lion. And Tom is a "true boy," representing "the generic character of boyhood" (33) with a want of sympathy that leads even his loving sister to condemn him: "You have no pity: you have no sense of your own imperfection and your own sins" (347).

Tom Tulliver's sole imaginative moment in the novel is his hyper-masculine performance with the sword. He prepares to frighten his sister with small gestures toward making his "round pink cheeks" look formidable – blackening his eyebrows and winding a red handkerchief around his head to give it "the air of a turban" (179). Maggie misconstrues the costume, thinking Tom has made himself "like Bluebeard at the show" – an image threatening specifically to women. Tom corrects her by proclaiming "I'm the Duke of Wellington! March!" and frightens her onto the bed "as the only means of widening the space between them" in the small theatre of Tom's bedroom (180). Tom, "happy in this spectator of his military performances," marches on until the sword becomes too heavy and he drops it on his foot, fainting in pain.

This scene of masculine performance to a female audience occurs during that period in Tom's life when he has been explicitly feminized. Poor Tom, as the narrator reflects, has his male supremacy dislodged by his "education" at Mr. Stelling's. He "began even to have a certain scepticism about guns, and a general sense that his theory of life was undermined" (134). Ironically, by forcing Tom to learn Latin and refusing to "enfeeble and emasculate his pupil's mind by simplifying and explaining," Mr. Stelling makes Tom "more like a girl than he had ever been in his life before" (141). His self-image is further compromised by the "pretty employment" designed for him by Mrs. Stelling, of watching her baby girl. The narrator remarks that Tom might have come to hate "the little cherub Laura," but "there was too much in him of the fibre that turns to true manliness, and to protecting pity for the weak" (142–3). Yet that fibre is overcome by Tom's need to perform a masculine role that combines martial and sexual domination but that only emasculates him further, turning him temporarily into an invalid and forcing him to accept the sympathy of both Maggie and his natural enemy Philip Wakem, whom he had previously accused of being "no better than a girl" (173).

In her analysis of gender roles in *The Mill on the Floss*, Eliot focuses on Tom's performance, not his imagination. Ironically, Tom's literalness and lack of imagination do not secure his masculine identity, which, when under assault, is held together by force of will and by forceful acts. While Maggie's imagination takes her out of herself, in her daily life she nonetheless refuses to perform the role of the good girl that would make her family happy. Tom, who never imagines, is always acting as is expected, as a man should. Eventually he learns what it means to be manly through the hard work of redeeming the mill, but the sword scene and other performative moments in the first two books of the novel expose the gap between what Eliot considered real manliness and the displays of violence that passed for manliness.

Here, as elsewhere, Eliot is engaged in scrutinizing the process by which the English learned about other places and peoples through representations and thus came to understand the meaning of home. Characters in the novel, like the Dodsons, know who they are by knowing who they are not; they are not, for example, Tullivers. While critical of provincialism, the narrator is sympathetic to the domestic attachments that make a secure sense of identity possible. The description of Mr. Tulliver's feelings about the mill and the land on which he was raised calls attention to contemporary (*circa* 1860) reading about foreign travel and the very accounts of African exploration that Eliot reviewed in the 1850s. The narrator muses:

Our instructed vagrancy, which has hardly time to linger by the hedgerows, but runs away early to the tropics, and is at home with the palms and banyans, – which is nourished on books of travel, and stretches the theatre of its imagination to the Zambesi, – can hardly get a dim notion of what an old-fashioned man like Tulliver felt for this spot, where all his memories centred, and where life seemed like a familiar smooth-handled tool that the fingers clutch with loving ease. (263)

Through instruction, or reading, "our" imaginations "run away" and we are "at home" in foreign lands, rather than in England. Mr. Tulliver's vision of past and future is limited to this spot of ground. His love is the stronger for its narrowness. Modern sensibilities are wider and more inclusive, but, like Maggie's, more fractured and conflicted as a result. This is a difference between the English past and present as established by Eliot: her readers face the modern dilemma, as she did herself, of understanding where home was when "books of travel" made the foreign seem familiar. Surveying the British empire from the South Pacific palms to the Indian banyans and the African river Zambesi, *The Mill on the Floss* is both nostalgic for the hedgerows and old-fashioned ways of thinking and critical of the restricted imaginations that constrain Maggie and Tom.[39]

Although set in an earlier period, *The Mill on the Floss* is an indictment of the "moral asphyxia" that generations of sameness prepared for Mary Ann Evans and from which she saved herself by moving to London. She would have saved her sister Chrissey Clarke, the missing sibling from the autobiographical portrait of herself and Isaac, through emigration to Australia. Yet for Maggie, whose imagination extended to Africa and into worlds of sympathy and romance where Tom's could not follow, there can be no solution apart from home. Both Maggie and Eliot's earlier heroine Milly Barton, whose experiences of childbearing and poverty resemble those of Chrissey, are released only through death from predicaments that migration (to the city or to the colonies) appeared capable of solving in the Evans family.

## COLONIAL EMIGRATION AND TRAVEL LITERATURE

Lewes, in his review of Livingstone's *Missionary Travels and Researches in South Africa*, described the Zambesi as a "magnificent stream, which permits navigation all the year round" and "as fine a path into the interior as commerce could desire."[40] Lewes also shared Livingstone's optimism about the opening up of African commerce, noting that "for civilization, there must be commerce." Colonial exploration and the expansion of commercial routes were among the modern changes that contrasted with the simpler life of the setting of *The Mill on the Floss*. Eliot's vagrant imaginings were instructed by books of exploration and emigration, and the map of her imagination charted the *terra incognita* of Africa, even as her books focused intensely on the hedgerows and on the "familiar smooth-handled tool" of life in the rural Midlands.

By invoking travel literature as a common experience in *The Mill on the Floss*, Eliot recalled her own reliance on similar guidebooks in considering the future of her family members. Sidney's book on Australia and other emigrants' guidebooks advised on matters such as the best emigration agent to use and clothes to pack, what weather to expect and crops to plant. They also described the behavior of a desirable new colonist. Long before Lewes thought of sending his sons to Africa, he reviewed Charles Barter's *The Dorp and the Veld; or, Six Months in Natal*. He called the book "very acceptable to emigrants," observing of the author with some ironic distance: "He has 'strong views,' and expresses them without equivocation. He 'goes in' for the extirpation of the Kafir."[41]

Here his skepticism and implied disapproval is expressed through quotation marks, but the review evades the common if not majority view that the native South Africans should and would be exterminated as a result of British settlement. Some Englishmen approved of "extirpation" because they feared that continued exposure to "savages" might lead to their own moral degeneration, a backward sliding from moral progress of which the Boers were their prime example.

Emigration literature frequently addressed the potential for moral degeneration among English colonists. One guidebook, *The Settler's New Home* (1849), is quoted in Dr. Robert James Mann's *The Colony of Natal.*[42] It advised against emigration to the newly acquired colony of Natal because of the "unsettled and unsafe state of the Kafir population." The settlers themselves risk falling into a state of "barbarism" when the "antagonism of races degenerates into a loss of respect for humanity and life." "Where there is no power of enforcing respect for the law," this guide warns, "each man must depend on his bowie knife and revolving pistols."[43] In the main, *The Settler's New Home* is alarmist and racist. Yet, rather than assume a stable moral superiority in the English, it worries about the moral consequences for the English of racial conflict in the colonies.

By the early 1860s, when Natal was more settled with Englishmen, official government propaganda was adept at promoting the virtues of frontier life and downplaying the brutality of some English settlers as well as the twin threats of physical danger and moral degeneration through contact with native populations. Mann wrote from his knowledgeable position as Superintendent of Education in Natal and could evaluate competing claims to correct rumor and misinformation: "Land is so cheap, that for the mere sum which would be paid in England for a single year's rental, a man may purchase hundreds of acres of his own fields, fell his own trees, and gather his own fruits."[44] He stresses that life in Natal is "rude, rather than hard" and free from "the artificial restraints imposed by society at home."[45] He concludes that reports of native hostility and warfare are greatly exaggerated, and that since 1849, when such warnings were issued, Natal has become "a flourishing colony of more than eight thousand prosperous European inhabitants, and with prospects brightening day by day."[46]

For anyone living in mid-nineteenth-century London who was attempting to assess the situation in Natal based on information available at home, the messages were mixed at best. Hunting was abundant and unrestricted; the Zulus were threatening warriors; Kaffirs were to be extirpated like so much wild game; land was cheap and life was hard but good; English society had been replicated; opportunities for advancement exceeded those in the climate of restricted employment at home. It is easy to understand from a survey of emigration propaganda how a family in England, relying on its information, would be optimistic about the opportunities for their children in the developing British dependency, especially if they downplayed or failed to imagine race relations. The lure of opportunity was too strong to resist in the practical matter of finding careers for English sons. Eliot and Lewes's belief that the weather was fine and the land cheap, combined with a willful disregard for what they had read about the dangers and difficulty of life in South Africa, affected their deliberations about the emigration of Lewes's sons in the 1860s.

In reviewing travel literature, both Eliot and Lewes searched for the appropriate models for evaluation. What was scientifically proven and therefore credible and what subjective and dubious? To what extent were these representations, which claimed to contribute to knowledge, to be viewed as literature? In a favorable review of the *Narrative of a Mission to Central Africa* by James Richardson, Lewes reports simply: "No extract can convey anything like the picture here given of African character, especially in its barbarian aspects of sensuality, lying, and fanaticism, because the picture is painted by a series of minute touches, jotted down as experience furnished them."[47] The metaphor of the painted picture suggests that the narrative's contribution is artistic, but that its supposed realism also adds to English knowledge of "African character." Perhaps he chose the painting metaphor because he was aware that words such as "sensuality," "lying," and "fanaticism" inevitably represented subjective moral judgments rather than scientific information.

Five years later, when he reviewed Livingstone's *Missionary Travels*, he struck an optimistic tone about Africa: "Missionary zeal, trading enterprise, and love of sport, together with the native restlessness and spirit of adventure animating the Anglo-Saxon race, will soon bring us acquainted with the whole habitable surface of our globe."[48] Enterprise, sport, and adventure animated Lewes's emigrant sons, while scientific and technological advancements animated their father, who adds with enthusiasm that the English are "gradually mapping the whole earth; and our children may live to see railroads across the desert."[49]

It was scientific knowledge that most interested Lewes and many of his contemporaries, and explorer-authors like Livingstone forced readers to revise previous beliefs by furnishing "a mass of precise information which materially modifies our previous conceptions of the African races."[50] The emphasis that Lewes was coming to place on the scientific rather than aesthetic value of colonial books is reflected in his change of terms from "African character" in 1853 to "African races" in 1858. Livingstone's book makes Richardson's painted picture look less reliable. Lewes writes that with Livingstone, "we feel perfect confidence that what he narrates really did present itself to his mind in the way he mentions," concluding that "his evidence is trustworthy, as far as it goes."[51] A reliable narrator like Livingstone encourages him to see similarities between Africans and Europeans and, revising his previous conclusions, he asserts that "all [Africans] are unequivocally endowed with the same faculties and tendencies, and in the same degree, as Europeans" and that their intelligence equals that of "any race known to us."[52] These conclusions, perhaps echoing Livingstone's more altruistic motives for exploration, are a notable contrast to the previous picture of African "lying" and "fanaticism." Lewes's racial views were evolving based on the available, contradictory accounts of travelers; with more reading, he encountered more opinions.

*Blackwood's Edinburgh Magazine* was a primary source of African exploration narratives as well as reviews of travel literature. John Blackwood provided a personal connection to great explorers of the age. In 1859, he wrote to Eliot describing John Hanning Speke, Richard Burton's companion (and ultimately his rival), as "a fine manly unaffected specimen of an Englishman," who is "very innocent of literature having since he went to India at 17 been devoted to wild sports and geographical discovery" (*GEL*, 3:131). Blackwood explains that despite "dangers and suffering" in Africa, Speke is "determined to go back and carry out his discovery." Eliot replied that she envied Blackwood's acquaintance with a "genuine non-bookish man," adding that she wondered "when men of that sort will take their place as heroes in our literature, instead of the inevitable 'genius'" (*GEL*, 3:133). Eliot turns the implied deficiency of not being literary into a strength appropriate for admirable characters in literature.

Her preference here for the non-bookish over the bookish man as a hero in literature is enigmatic but suggestive. She seems to imply an admiration for the kind of manly, if unliterary, figure represented by Speke. Her own heroes, Adam Bede and later Felix Holt, were intent on education, though not bookish. Tom Tulliver is explicitly not bookish but likes to be told "a good many fighting stories" by bookish Philip Wakem (165). Later male characters such as Will Ladislaw and Daniel Deronda are more literary, but not bookish in the sense that Casaubon is. Yet neither they nor any of her future heroes resemble an African explorer.[53] Perhaps the men of action like Speke were seen to be doing what they could do best, and it is possible that this image of the man of empire fed into her self-deceiving hopes for the Lewes boys in the colonies.[54]

By 1859, after the publication of *Scenes of Clerical Life* in *Blackwood's*, Eliot and Lewes had become intimately associated with the magazine. It was in *Blackwood's* that both Burton and Speke published some of their most important contributions to the nineteenth-century literature of discovery.[55] Lewes participated in the ongoing dialogue about travel and exploration literature published in "Maga," as *Blackwood's* was called. His article, "Uncivilized Man," is an attempt to discredit Rousseau's notion of the "noble savage" by showing, in a humanistic view similar to that of Eliot, that all peoples share positive and negative moral qualities. In this piece, Lewes disapproved of Burton, whose observations of Africans in *The Lake Regions of Central Africa* were suspect because "in general we find him harsh and ungenerous in his judgments."[56]

As if anticipating such criticism, Burton wrote in his Preface to the *Lake Regions*: "We are told somewhat peremptorily that it is our duty to gather actualities, not inferences – to see and not to think; in fact, to confine ourselves to transmitting the rough material collected by us, that it may be worked into shape by the professionally learned at home." Here the resentment of the man of action against the emerging scientific establishment at home is evident. "But why may not the observer be allowed a voice concerning his own observations, if at least his mind be sane and his stock of collateral knowledge be respectable?"[57] Burton answers his critics, among whom may be counted Eliot and Lewes. Eliot wrote in her review of Burton's *First Footsteps in East Africa*: "While complaining of the book, we must express, at the same time, our admiration of the exploit which it relates. The writer only is to blame – the man is all which a man ought to be."[58] She and Lewes were part of the centralizing process by which information arrived from the margins of empire to be assessed and assimilated as colonial knowledge.

When considering the representation of the Ojibbeway Indians in Johann Georg Kohl's *Kitchi-Gami, Wanderings Round Lake Superior*, Lewes seems to contradict his earlier reflections about the equality of Africans and Europeans in order to accentuate the virtues of native North Americans, suggesting that "in most of the moral qualities, these Indians are not only immeasurably above the Africans – they are quite on par with Europeans."[59] Even considering some inconsistencies in his conclusions based on wide reading, Lewes warns against the application of "our European standards" to non-Europeans. He points out, for example, that the belief in witches and witch doctors is no less un-scientific than "the spirit-rapping *séances* of our own day."[60] Given the persistence of superstition in European culture, he asks, "[w]hy, then, can we wonder at savages . . .?"[61] Without abandoning a belief in progress, he, like Eliot, urges the English to understand others by comparison with themselves.

The confusion about our "fellow creatures" for those who read widely in the literature of travel and exploration in the mid-nineteenth cen-tury was produced by contradictory reports from authors of varying degrees of reliability. Authors like Eliot and Lewes, who were obliged to assess the accounts contained in colonial literature, were inconsistent when they attempted to be authoritative. There was some satisfaction for them, then, in the staged performances of exotic animals and humans that claimed entertainment and scientific value. Lewes was attracted to these exhibitions, and his responses to them provide some insight into the conflicting representations of "other" races for the benefit of those at home. Ritvo notes that the publication of Cumming's *Five Years of a Hunter's Life* coincided with a London exhibition, which included his trophies, a Bushman boy, and a Cape wagon, and was supplemented by nightly lectures accompanied by music.[62] Such performances drew large and diverse crowds and received notices in the major periodicals. Lewes encountered "natives," like lions, only in captivity.

In 1853, an advertisement in the *Leader* announced that a man named Caldecott, a merchant of Port Natal, South Africa, had brought to London "with the sanction of the colonial authorities" a "Troupe and Family of Native Zulu Kafirs."[63] Lewes went to see the Zulus perform at the St. George's Gallery and "Vivian" contributed a review to the arts section of the *Leader*:

Thirteen veritable Zulus – eleven men, a woman, and a child (the child engaging enough to make all mothers and fathers, putative and real, go off into small ecstasies of sympathy) – are made to represent, amid painted scenes, as on the stage, various aspects of their wild life, so that the spectator assists at a Kaffir drama at which the actors are no wretched "supers" at one shilling a night, but the free, graceful warriors themselves, *being* what they *represent*. We see them in their Kraals – we see them at their meals – at their dances, at their councils of war, at their hunting, at their quarrels and fights, at their marriage ceremonies, and "witch findings" – we hear them sing, we hear their poet laureate recite his savage ode, accompanied by dance and gestures not in the least resembling those I presume Mr. Wordsworth was wont to employ! We are at home among these wild animals. In a way no previous exhibition has ever attempted, we are made spectators of something more than a few specimens of a savage tribe – we begin to understand their life. If the philosopher can go there without learning much, I would not give much for his philosophy![64]

This exhibition, treated as a theatrical performance, is not only enjoyed, but taken seriously by "Vivian" as original and unique of its kind. Although it is a "Kaffir drama," this drama is "real." The Zulus are "*being* what they *represent*" – a surprising observation from Lewes/Vivian, the self-conscious philosopher and theatre critic. It seems almost paradoxical. To the London audience, they *represent* all Zulus, perhaps all Africans, even all savages. Yet they are being themselves. They really *are* Zulus, and they are anthropologically accurate, at least as far as Lewes can tell, based on the convincing quality of the drama and the "ecstasies of sympathy" they excited in him (he was after all a real father in 1853). These are no black-faced actors and in their authenticity they instruct and delight.[65] The Zulu Kaffirs provide all the elements of good theatre, adding to this the virtue that comes from being authentic. Lewes could not know that ten years later his son Thornie would encounter these "savages" in their "native habitat," and would display toward them all the disdain and superiority that a colonial context permitted and encouraged, taking less notice of what he could learn from them in Africa than had Lewes when the Zulus came to London.

What these examples of Lewes's overlapping interests in London's performing Zulus and captive lions suggest is a fluidity of the categories on which the consolidation of the later empire would depend: civilized and savage, human and animal, captive and free. Lewes's objection to Cumming's brutality as unmanly reflected an anxiety that in the colonies Englishmen could become barbaric. As a believer in the development of a "moral sense" among human beings, along with the evolution of physical characteristics, Lewes saw the cruelty of the lion-hunter as an anomaly in the nineteenth century. His role as a reviewer of books about such behavior was to check their consumption and glorification at home. His commingling of dramatic and scientific criteria for evaluating the spectacle of "real" Zulus on a London stage reflected a confusion about the value of importing human beings from Africa for popular entertainment.

The moral question for Eliot and Lewes, which was related to the problem of reliability in colonial literature, was not so much whether the English ought to be appropriating Zulus for display in England as one raised by the emigration literature: did colonization contribute to the progress or the degeneration of the colonizers? Theories relating to the "moral sense," which Spencer, Darwin, Lewes, Eliot, and their contemporaries attempted to formulate and negotiate, were developing in conjunction with the empire and had a complex relationship to its expansion. Nancy Paxton argues that in *Daniel Deronda*, Eliot responded to Spencer by exploring the notion of degeneration and "questioning the imperial mission that Great Britain assumed in the 1870s."[66] Eliot, Paxton argues, "saw the dissemination of sympathy and altruism as the best means to combat the 're-barbarization' that both she and Spencer perceived in Britain's more aggressive imperialist policies."[67] The moral inferiority of non-Europeans could be a justification for domination or paternalism, but the potential regression of Europeans in these foreign environments was also an argument against colonialism. Colonialism was a serious matter with racial and moral implications for the English. These theories are worth examining briefly so that we may see the significance of Eliot and Lewes's failure to apply them to the personal cases of their own emigrant sons.

For many Victorians, the distinction between nature and nurture, or heredity and social conditioning, was unstable, and particularly difficult to maintain for non-physical attributes. Lewes welcomed a theory by which moral advancement might be explained scientifically (i.e. biologically). In 1856, he defined the moral sense as an "aptitude to be affected by actions in their moral bearings."[68] He believed that this aptitude in individuals "varies not according to their intellect but according to their native tendencies" and is "transmitted from forefathers." In "Hereditary Influence, Animal and Human," Lewes observes: "Boys or pug dogs, all children resemble their parents." Except of course when they don't: "Nay, the children are sometimes not only unlike their parents, they are, in important characteristics, unlike their Species. We then call them Deformities or Monsters."[69] Just as the pup pointer has inherited an aptitude to point, "so also has the European boy inherited an aptitude for a certain moral life, which to the Papuan would be impossible."[70]

In Lewes's view, what is inherited is the *aptitude* to be affected. And aptitude suggests potential to respond, which must be cultivated, as the pup pointer is taught to point. The potential is *to be affected*. A highly developed moral sense will be affected by actions as the audience is affected by a play. In his theatre criticism, the performance is evaluated according to its ability to affect the audience. In his theory of moral development, he judges the viewer according to his or her aptitude for feeling. He suggests that individuals who are not affected by actions in their moral bearings have inherited this lack of sensitivity. A European with no apparent aptitude for a moral life is a moral "monster" because he is morally unlike his parents. But what is a European who lives under conditions in which the aptitude is not encouraged and may be thwarted, as, for example, when he lives in an "uncivilized" colony?

Eliot's views about moral development and degeneration are not synonymous with Lewes's, but it is always safe to assume that her ideas were worked out in conversation with him and his writing. While Eliot treats most of her villains with sympathy and shows the conditions that produced their behavior, a few among them might be considered moral monsters for whom no social or psychological explanation is offered. Dempster in "Janet's Repentance" and Raffles in *Middlemarch* are degraded characters whose behavior is blamed partly on alcohol, yet both seem to arrive on the scene with a depraved character. Tito in *Romola* is more insidious because more calculating; the dim promptings of consciousness are easily overcome as the performer comes to believe his own lies. David Faux in "Brother Jacob" and Henleigh Grandcourt in *Deronda* are perhaps her most morally reprehensible characters. Significantly, both have exercised their assumptions of supremacy in the colonies – David in his attempts to exploit the West Indians and Grandcourt in his tiger-shooting and pig-sticking in "the East." But the colonies provide an outlet rather than an excuse for their depravity.

In *The Mill on the Floss*, she emphasizes the combination of factors that determine Maggie's destiny. As the narrator explains to the reader "[you] need to be told, not her characteristics, but her history, which is a thing hardly to be predicted even from the completest knowledge of characteristics" (401). Character is not destiny, for circumstances shape character just as character creates circumstances. Maggie's destiny is "like the course of an unmapped river" (402) and the novel follows the course of her aptitude for sympathy as it follows the growth of Tom's "fibre" of manly feeling. Eliot's understanding of how certain innate capacities are acted upon by external conditions was typical of the view that was more anxious about English degeneration than confident of English superiority.

Three years after "Hereditary Influence," Lewes recorded in his journal some responses to Henry Thomas Buckle's *History of Civilization in England*, which he thought accounted inadequately for the developmental process by which human beings had become more civilized – not, in his view, through preaching but through changes in the constitution of the mind.[71] He writes:

When people are cruel, barbarous, unsympathetic, delighting in war as the activity of an instinct, and witnessing dog fights, gladiators, executions, & c. it is of little use for the moralist to preach; the intellect acquiesces, the man rebels. Precisely because our moral feelings have enlarged have duels & wars lost their prestige.[72]

Here Lewes minimizes the effect of teaching in favor of a biological explanation for the enlargement of "our moral feelings." His belief in 1859 that war had lost its prestige was formulated in the wake of the national demoralization over the Crimean War. In "Hereditary Influence," he identifies the Crimean War as the occasion for the manifestation of a particular, evolved sensibility, asking, "How could that new, unheard-of feeling for the wives, widows, and orphans of soldiers, which so honourably distinguished the war just closed, have ever arisen, had not the sympathetic feelings of the race been cultivated during centuries of slow evolution?"[73] His emphasis on the aftermath of the war, rather than the war itself, reflects his own optimism and distaste for violence.

In her 1855 review of Tennyson's "Maud," Eliot had criticized the poet for his support of the Crimean War: "These family sorrows and mortifications the hero regards as a direct result of the anti-social tendencies of Peace, which he proceeds to expose to us in all its hideousness; looking to the war as the immediate curative for unwholesome lodging of the poor, adulteration of provisions, child-murder, and wife-beating – an effect which is as yet by no means visible in our police reports" (Pinney, p. 193). She complains that the "ground-notes" of the poem include "hatred of peace and the Peace Society . . . and faith in War as the unique social regenerator" (Pinney, p. 197). This objection to violence, also expressed in her review of Kingsley's *Westward Ho!*, is upheld in her letters. In 1860, she offered a different reflection about the future of war. Commenting on Tom's enthusiasm for war stories, her narrator remarks: "It is doubtful whether our soldiers would be maintained if there were not pacific people at home who like to fancy themselves soldiers. War, like other dramatic spectacles, might possibly cease for want of a 'public'" (176). We must ask to what extent she associated colonialism with violence and how much violence she thought might be justified in the process of civilization, especially as her stepsons were settling in South Africa.[74]

For Lewes, the despair was the violence of the war; the pride came in the "new unheard-of feeling" that the war engendered. He was perhaps part of the "vertiginous ideological rift" which Mary Poovey argues was opened by the Crimean War "in which the very conditions that generated pride also provoked despair."[75] Poovey argues that the image of Florence Nightingale was divided between the self-sacrificing angel and the "iron will and indominable spirit," and that she "contributed to the construction of an image of the English national character, which deployed the domestic ideal to support both Britain's imperial designs in India and the expansion of state administrative control over the poor at home."[76]

To make this assertion about moral progress, Lewes had to ignore the glorification of violence against animals and humans in the literature of the period in which his children were growing up. Lewes's hopeful reading of his own time looked for "progress," a new sympathy at the very time brutality continued throughout the empire. In the mid-nineteenth century, Victorians looked enthusiastically toward the potential of a society in which the highly evolved cultivation of sympathetic feelings might take new forms: a society in which wives, widows, orphans, and animals would be protected, in which the barbarisms of dog-fights, gladiators, executions, dueling, and even war would lose their prestige.

After the publication of Darwin's *On the Origin of Species* (1859) and *The Descent of Man* (1871) with the latter's section on "The Moral Sense," Lewes would qualify and complicate his own argument, giving more emphasis to culture, or the "social medium." Eliot would contribute to refining his argument in her revisions of *The Study of Psychology* (1879). In 1856, the notion of an inherited moral sense in his writing reflects a strain of thinking in scientific discourse just prior to the emigration of his sons. Except for his colonial illustrations (Australians, Hindoos, etc.), Lewes does not mention the process of English colonization in this article. Yet in his articulation of theories about the transmission of familial and racial characteristics, we can see a confluence of issues that would soon impinge on his own and Eliot's parental feelings. They would decide, based on the aptitudes of his sons, that they were "fit" only for a colonial life. In time, Thornie ("our Caliban") and Bertie (the "backward" one) would supply him with examples of behavior that posed an implicit challenge to his theory of moral evolution.

Emigration to the colonies was not a solution to which Eliot turned in her fiction, as did contemporaries such as Dickens, Gaskell, and Trollope. It was rather a misguided fantasy that she satirized in "Brother Jacob" and later in *Daniel Deronda*. But as a solution to actual domestic problems, the lure of the empire was too great to resist. She tried unsuccessfully to persuade her impoverished sister to emigrate to Australia. With Lewes, she succeeded in effecting the emigration of her stepsons to South Africa. In the next chapter, I consider the cultural influences that convinced both the sons and the parents that the colonies offered opportunities for personal and financial advancement that could not be found at home.

CHAPTER 2

# *"Colleagues in failure": emigration and the Lewes boys*

> If we have young friends whom we wish to send forth into the world,
> we search the maps with them at our elbows.
>
> Anthony Trollope[1]

By the 1860s, the colonies had become a repository not only for crimi-
nals, fallen women, and the poor, but also for the sons of wealthy middle-
class parents such as Eliot, Dickens, and Trollope. India remained the
imperial outpost of choice, but Australia, Canada, and South Africa offered alternatives for young men who, despite educational and financial
advantages, were able to succeed neither at home nor in India. Lewes
and Eliot faced their own version of a larger social problem, what in
the 1880s came to be called the "younger son question." According to
Patrick A. Dunae, a growing number of middle-class sons and of public
schools to educate them meant that "the professions which were regarded
as being most suitable for gentlemen could not accommodate this greatly
enlarged pool of gentlemanly aspirants."[2] Many of these "supernumer-
ary gentlemen" turned to the colonies. For Lewes and Eliot, who sought
positions for Lewes's younger sons that were consistent with their middle-
class life yet geographically far from it, the empire offered a particularly
attractive solution.

The story of the Lewes boys' colonial careers is an early instance of
the "younger son question," remarkable but typical in its lack of structure and imperialist motive. No desire to civilize or conquer, no sense of
patriotism or the "white man's burden," is evident in the series of events
that led to the eventual emigration and deaths of the two younger Lewes
boys. Such values and missions would emerge later in the education of
the more established middle class. In 1863, failure, luck, illusion, misinformation, and personality played equal roles in the ultimate decision
that Thornie and Bertie should make their future and their fortune in
the South African colony of Natal.

This chapter will explore the typicality in the particularity of the Lewes boys' story by examining its historical and discursive contexts: social conditions such as the absence of jobs at home, representations of the colonies in boys' adventure fiction, and the lives of other middle-class sons. It will also look closely and specifically at their experiences as colonists in South Africa and at the way their representations of themselves in letters were inflected with the colonial discourses available to them. Between 1860 and 1880, Eliot was never without letters from or about the empire. The issues raised by these colonial communications – parenthood, children, and, as will be discussed in chapter 3, money – made the empire a part of her domestic life and consciousness. It is no wonder that the empire can be seen and heard as a presence or subtext in her fiction precisely when these issues are engaged. What follows will combine historical narrative and literary criticism to emphasize the inextricability and intertextuality of Eliot's life and writing and to show the typicality of her experiences as parent to emigrant sons, a role she shared with authors such as Dickens and Trollope, as well as with many of her readers.

INDIA AND THE CIVIL SERVICE

In the mid-nineteenth century, middle-class parents negotiated the complicated British systems of patronage and merit in order to assure their sons' financial independence, which could be at odds with their physical safety. As we saw in chapter 1, Eliot and Lewes read accounts of emigration and travel with characteristic scrutiny and skepticism. For them, as for many of their contemporaries, confidence in colonial prospects was based on fragmentary information; every hopeful anecdote was countered by an alarming one. In 1857, the year of the Indian Mutiny, the eldest Lewes son Charles wrote to his mother Agnes about a young man presumed killed at Lucknow: "A little time ago he was in the list of the dead." Later they received news that he was alive. "Since then," Charles wrote, "no news has been heard respecting him" (*GEL*, 8:191). This disturbing report did not deter Agnes Lewes from suggesting in 1859 that Charles try for a cadetship in the Indian army. Other young men known to Lewes and Eliot, such as Dickens's son and John Blackwood's nephew, had recently followed this route, but Charles chose a position in the Post Office.[3] His younger brother Thornie, however, was destined for India. In 1860 Thornie began a year of preparation in Edinburgh for the Indian civil service examination.

Despite Lewes's unconventional career as a radical journalist, actor, and author, he wanted his sons to rise in a conventional fashion.[4] When Thornie passed the first Indian examination in 1861, Lewes wrote to his friend Wathen Mark Wilks Call that Thornie "goes out next year with a salary of 450£ & by the time he is 25 will have 1200£." Providing an insight into the specific nature of his ambitions for his sons, he adds: "*That* isn't to be made by Aristotle or Reviewing!"[5] Thornie's examination ordeal introduced Lewes and Eliot to the ambiguities of the merit system. When Thornie failed the second part of the exam, they were thrown back on the practice of patronage for which they, as exemplars of what merit could accomplish, were not well placed.

Thornie's fall from potential Indian bureaucrat to African settler requires some contextualization if we are to understand its implications for him and for Eliot. In the mid-1850s, when the domestic and Indian civil service sectors were in transition from a system of entrance dependent on patronage to one based on examination, both received attention and criticism as a result of these changes. Trollope, who had served in the Post Office since 1834, aligned himself with the conservative position, lamenting the waning of patronage as a forecast of decline in the service. His novel *The Three Clerks* (1857) is a part-satirical, part-sympathetic representation of the lives of young civil servants that expresses the predicament confronted by fathers of sons, including Trollope himself. A man does what he can, explains Trollope's narrator, and hopes that "he may descend to his grave without that worst of wretchedness, that gnawing grief which comes from bad children."[6] Lord Gaberlunzie has the "terrible task" of providing for eleven sons: "There were three in the army, two in the navy, and one at a foreign embassy; one was at the diggings, another was chairman of a railway company."[7] That such a scenario is representative may be concluded from Dickens's account of his sons in a letter written in 1862:

My eldest boy . . . is in business as an Eastern Merchant in the City. My second boy, with the 42nd Highlanders in India, spends more than he gets and has cost me money and disappointed me. My third boy, a good steady fellow but not at all brilliant, is educating expensively for engineers or artillery. My fourth (this sounds like a charade), a born little sailor, is a Midshipman in H.M.S. Orlando now at Bermuda, and will make his way any where. Remaining two, at school.[8]

The bad son of *The Three Clerks*, Undy Scott, spends his time corrupting Alaric Tudor, the young civil servant rising in the Department of Weights and Measures through what Trollope saw as the bogus system of examination. In the novel, Trollope summarizes the stereotypical image of the civil service propagated by its critics: "The Civil Service is a kind of hospital, in which the parents of sickly sons seek for employment for their puny offspring."[9] In his defense of the civil service, he notes: "The Crown has greatly lamented that the aspiring, energetic, and ambitious among British youths do not flock into its Civil Service."[10] And why should they, he asks, seeing that there was so little incentive or advantage compared to trade, finance, law, or even politics? Trollope's stance on the issue of examinations is clear from the novel's plot, in that the admirable Harry Norman is defeated in a competitive examination (and in love) by the corrupt Alaric Tudor.

It is clear that a stigma of sorts attached to the civil service and that Victorians were divided during the period of civil service reform as to how a better-quality civil servant could be attracted. This debate applied to the Indian as well as the domestic service. The transition from patronage to competitive examination took place in 1853 as a tentative step toward the eventual dismantling of the East India Company and the double government system of ruling India. With such reform, and with a new emphasis on public works projects in India, the government hoped, as Timothy Alborn writes, to "silence charges of corruption, 'civilize' the natives, and turn India into the robust trading partner of the Manchester merchants' dreams."[11] Eliot was aware of these debates, which took place during the period of her editorship of the *Westminster Review*. Radicals such as Richard Cobden and John Bright were calling for more extreme measures against the East India Company. John Stuart Mill, editor of the *Westminster* in the period of its greatest influence, supported the examination system and defended the East India Company for which he worked.

After the demise of the company in 1858, the debates about competitive examination for positions at home and in India continued. No longer associated with the liberal *Westminster*, Eliot and Lewes were now writing for the conservative *Blackwood's*, which in 1861 published a two-part article opposed to democratic reforms, "The Indian Civil Service: Its Rise and Fall." This article argued that the "men who go in for the Indian Civil Service, under the competition system, are men who neither have nor think that they have any brilliant prospects at home." They are "content to earn a competence, isolated and forgotten, in a remote Eastern settlement, rather than to incur the risk of being utterly beaten in the great battle of life at home." They are satisfied with "being left, stranded and forlorn, without profit and without preferment, in some precarious profession, the prizes of which, if great, are few, and only to be won by men of greater ability and perseverance than themselves."[12] From this perspective, those who can win in the examination system are actually losers, deserters from the "great battle of life." In a patronage system, by contrast, those most prepared and committed by birth and training assume their natural roles as Indian administrators.

Lewes and Eliot certainly read this article as Thornie was preparing for his examination. Lewes published six articles in the same volume of *Blackwood's*, including "Uncivilized Man" and "Life in Central Africa." Despite the possibility of Thornie's being "isolated and forgotten," they agreed that he had no "brilliant prospects at home." They would have been aware of the view, as expressed in the *Blackwood's* article, that if the civil service of India "is to be thrown open to the general public, the interlopers to be looked for are the failures of the imperial country."[13] But disdain for exam-takers was a luxury of the well-connected elite. Thornie stood to benefit from the competitive system, since his father had no influential connections through which to get him a position. By the logic of the examination's critics, Thornie was already a failure when he sat for the examination.

In *Daniel Deronda*, Eliot wrote cynically of Warham Gascoigne's "cram" for the civil service examination, "which might disclose the welfare of our Indian Empire to be somehow connected with a quotable knowledge of Browne's Pastorals" (46). This perspective was based on her memory of Thornie, whose letters from Edinburgh gave her a glimpse of the aspiring "competition wallah," in the terms of G. O. Trevelyan's 1864 book of that title, which popularized the figure of the young civil servant in India. Thornie wrote to Eliot asking for books on the history of English and German literature and requesting that she "ask Pater to get *all* the *examination* papers of the Indian civil service" so that his tutor could see what sort of questions were to be expected.[14] The period was one of educational confusion, and Thornie wrote to Eliot announcing that "Misther Paternal Paternity" was mistaken because the examination questions "are not getting more difficult, but easier."[15] This willful self-confidence would bring Thornie into conflict with his parents over his future.

After Thornie's failure, there was more confusion about the procedure, calling into question the training he had received as well as the fairness of the test. Eliot wrote to her friend Sarah Hennell that Thornie's "colleagues in failure have agitated and got up a memorial to Sir Charles Wood [Secretary of State for the Colonies] against the injustice done them in making the examination final (contrary to precedent) after it was too late for them to take an additional year for study before passing the initiatory examination last year" (*GEL*, 4:105). There is a sharpness, perhaps sarcasm, in Eliot's phrase "colleagues in failure." Nothing came of the petition to Charles Wood, and Lewes wrote that Thornie "refused to go through the two years' ordeal again" (*GEL*, 4:102). After all his costly schooling, Thornie disappointed his parents and lost his prospects. Eliot's first emotional and financial investment in her stepson had not paid off, and this younger son's sudden lack of direction threatened to disrupt her hard-won career and domestic harmony, placing her in "a nightmare of uncertainty about our boys – awaiting one letter here and another there, and feeling in many ways the wide gap between theoretic longing and possible practice" (*GEL*, 4:106).

It is at this time that we begin to see in Eliot's fiction a theme of parental expectations at odds with the capacities and inclinations of sons. Tom Tulliver's trials at Mr. Stelling's were conceived in the period in which Thornie was writing regularly to Eliot from Hofwyl, his school in Switzerland. The delinquency of the Cass brothers in *Silas Marner*, the defection of Dino to the clergy against his father's wishes and Tito's treachery to his adopted father in *Romola*, and Fred Vincy's rejection of the clergy for which his father intended him in *Middlemarch* are variations on this theme. In *Felix Holt*, Mrs. Transome, whose son Harold disregards her wishes and expectations that he carry on the family's Tory tradition, suffers profound disappointment. Finally, the entire structure of *Daniel Deronda* depends on a mother's trying to determine the future of her son. Leonora Halm Eberstein gives Daniel up in an attempt to engineer his life as a wealthy English gentleman, only to find that he has embraced the Jewish identity she rejected.

After *The Mill on the Floss*, *Silas Marner*, *Romola*, and *Felix Holt*, and before *Middlemarch* and *Deronda*, Eliot lived through the disappointments of Thornie's colonial career. The Indian examination was the first of many failures. It redirected his life irrecoverably away from India and the social legitimacy of a civil service position – a narrow window of opportunity. The plans for his conventional career gave way to a desperate search for somewhere, anywhere, for him to go. The colonies provided a solution. Instead of an Indian bureaucrat earning £450 a year, he would become a pioneer in a white settler colony where land was cheap and success was achieved by muscle and diligence, rather than by examination or social connections. Instead of being bound by the rules, hierarchies, and wage scales of the civil service, an emigrant would be free to make or lose his own (or his parents') money. There were perhaps greater opportunities for success in a white settler colony, but there were equally great risks of failure. Eliot and Lewes, like other middle-class parents, engaged in tremendously wishful thinking when they rationalized that sons who were not "suited" to a disciplined professional life at home and who could not pass the Indian test, were suited to farming and trading in an unfamiliar, unstructured environment. Finally, Eliot's friend Barbara Bodichon, a half-year resident of French Algiers and advocate of British emigration, suggested the relatively under-developed colony of Natal and supplied the names and addresses of her emigrant friends.

Thornie knew about Natal only what he could learn from guidebooks of the sort both Eliot and Lewes read and reviewed in the 1850s. As discussed in chapter 1, books like *The Settler's Home* and Mann's *The Colony of Natal* were full of warnings about rough settlers and threatening natives, but on the whole emphasized the cheapness of the land and the freedom of the society. Letters that Lewes secured for him at home introduced Thornie to a small circle of emigrants, but he knew almost nothing about farming, trading, or the native peoples whom he would encounter. He was not a state-sponsored emigrant, nor was he part of the administrative bureaucracy. He was a nineteen-year-old Englishman who left, as Eliot wrote, with "a large packet of recommendatory letters ... and with what he cares much more for – a first-rate rifle and revolver – and already with a smattering of Dutch and Zulu" (*GEL*, 4:109). The intensive preparation for a career in the Indian civil service – a year in Edinburgh studying languages, literature, and mathematics – had given way to a "smattering" of local knowledge, a strained attempt at social connections, and guns. As Dunae points out, it was this casual middle-class attitude toward emigration – and the dire and wasteful consequences of which Thornie's life is an example – that led to the founding of institutions such as the Colonial College in 1885 to train middle-class boys.[16] But in 1863, by failing the examination, Thornie had taken a step down in the eyes of his society and parents. He had simply to make his way and to pass a different test of his merit – one of financial and physical survival without preparation.

### FICTION AND SELF-FASHIONING

We know from Thornie's letters that he was, like his father, a performer with his own "mask of flippancy" (*GEL*, 2:98). Rosemarie Bodenheimer observes that "it is sometimes difficult to tell whether he is actually representing his life as an adventure story or whether he is conscious of tongue-in-cheek self-parody."[17] The unreality of the self he projected into his colonial narratives epitomized Eliot's fears about self-deception and misrepresentation. For her, misrepresentation amounted to a kind of lie that eroded credibility, morality, and sanity. This belief formed the basis for her moral and aesthetic commitment to representing the world in an accurate and realistic fashion. In the "Natural History of German Life," she wrote of "our social novels" that "the unreality of their representations is a grave evil" (Pinney, p. 270). Inaccurate literary representation misleads readers and degrades all forms of writing, from colonial travel to romance. Her moral theory of what fiction should do blurs a line between fact and fiction: misrepresentation is evil in writing because it is evil in life. And misrepresenting oneself, consciously like Tito, or through self-deception, like Mr. Casaubon, can have devastating consequences for others, like Romola and Dorothea. Her artistic life was devoted to realistic representations of outer and inner landscapes, which would bring readers closer to some aspect of life that was remote to them as well as show them the dangers of deceit and falsity.

At the end of her career, she believed the stakes of accurate representation were even higher both for society and for the individual mind. In the chapter of *Impressions of Theophrastus Such* entitled "How We Come to Give Ourselves False Testimonials, and Believe in Them," her narrator Theophrastus defines "the sane mind in the sane body" as a "security of distinction between what we have professed and what we have done; what we have aimed at and what we have achieved; what we have invented and what we have witnessed or had evidenced to us; what we think and feel in the present and what we thought and felt in the past" (108). In his analysis of self-deception, or "traditions about ourselves," Theophrastus posits the notion that sanity depends upon a security of distinction between the real and the unreal, or a certainty of self. *Impressions* as a whole argues that we fashion ourselves – are both author and character in narratives of our own construction – and that, as far as we are able, we have an obligation to represent ourselves and the world around us with honesty.

Eliot remade herself repeatedly: by moving from Coventry to London, living with Lewes and taking his name, and adopting a masculine pseudonym. In her fiction she developed a theory about individual identity as the product of domestic ties. Later, she extended the notion of community bonds to the national and transnational connections which Deronda recognizes in the Jews. The idea of emigration is opposed to one of the central themes of Eliot's fiction, expressed in *The Mill on the Floss* by the question, "what grove of tropic palms, what strange ferns or splendid broad-petalled blossoms, could ever thrill such deep and delicate fibres within me as this home-scene?"(41).

The absence of touchstones such as parents and homeland threatens the integrity of individual and collective identity. In her portraits of "ordinary" characters, Eliot examines the extreme conditions of psychological and social disintegration. The psychological instabilities and physical deterioration that she witnessed in the Lewes boys after their separation from family and nation through emigration recall the concerns about the moral degeneration of English settlers in the colonies discussed in chapter 1. This was not merely a matter of contagion by "savages"; rather, it was a feared consequence of severing social ties and abdicating responsibility to society and to the land. The absence of social constraints resulting from relocation led to, for example, the decadence of Harold Transome in Smyrna in *Felix Holt*.[18] Knowing that she watched the decline of the young men she called sons helps to explain the evolving position in her fiction on the importance of familial and national ties to the "sane mind in the sane body."

Between 1860 and 1863, the years of anxiety about Thornie's career, Eliot wrote several works that explore the theme of dislocation and self-fashioning. The cryptic and comic "Brother Jacob" represents the colonies as a place of escape and fraudulent remaking for the selfish and deceitful David Faux. *Silas Marner* rewrites this story sympathetically, as Silas leaves his sad past behind to become a settler in Raveloe. Running through both these stories is a warning about the dangers of violating family bonds. *Romola* is also a work of psychological realism that explores more profoundly than any of her other novels the possibilities offered by relocation for transformations of identity. With Tito, the Greek orphan who remakes himself in Savonarola's Florence, she portrayed the hazards of deception and self-deception. Tito's betrayed stepfather Baldassarre, who struggles to retain his grasp on reality, is her most explicit portrait of insanity. The consequences of denying family and nation are fatal to Tito and destructive for those around him.

In contrast to deceitful sons such as David Faux, Dunstan Cass, and Tito, who forsake their ties to place and family, later novels introduce indecisive but likeable young men, who reaffirm their English roots. Bodenheimer writes that in *Middlemarch* Eliot created a "full-blown study of young men in search of elusive vocations," and that in the characters of Will Ladislaw and Fred Vincy she "rewrites Thornie's story of failure in two different ways."[19] *Middlemarch* looks intensely inward and trivializes the idea of a colonial life, which was a less realistic solution in 1830 than it was in 1860.

Will Ladislaw is one of Eliot's aimless young men whose search for a vocation is resolved over the course of the narrative. Upon meeting Will, Mr. Brooke asks Mr. Casaubon whether the young man might "turn out a [James] Bruce or a Mungo Park" (66), explorers of the generation before Livingstone and Burton. Casaubon replies:

"No, he has no bent towards exploration, or the enlargement of our geognosis: that would be a special purpose which I could recognize with some approbation, though without felicitating him on a career which so often ends in premature and violent death. But so far is he from having any desire for a more accurate knowledge of the earth's surface, that he said he should prefer not to know the sources of the Nile, and that there should be some unknown regions preserved as hunting-grounds for the poetic imagination."(66)

Here everyone is risible. Mr. Brooke for his romantic notions, Casaubon for his imperviousness to romance, and Will for his impetuous metaphors and preference "not to know." There is truth in the humor. Explorers were known for "premature and violent death," as Eliot wrote of Africa in 1855: "Within a very few years, – almost within the memory of the present generation, – the adventurous traveller who essayed to penetrate into its interior, was regarded less as a pioneer of civilisation, than as a forlorn hope, – whose escape from destruction was scarcely to be anticipated."[20] No man of action, Will is a stereotype of a poet, rejecting "accurate knowledge" of the elusive geographical facts for which explorers died. The metaphor "hunting-grounds" contrasts Will to Thornie, who imagined that in Africa he would have "big game" to hunt. It is significant that Will does not become a poet, but rather a journalist and political reformer – practical vocations that situate him firmly within English society and make him heir to ideals that emigrants necessarily forfeited.

Mrs. Cadwallader asks why Casaubon did not "use his interest to get Ladislaw made an *attaché* or sent to India" – what families do with "troublesome sprigs" (312). When the codicil to Casaubon's will threatens scandal about Will's relationship to Dorothea, Sir James Chettam exclaims, "let us get him a post; let us spend money on him" (397). In a parody of aristocratic patronage, he thinks that Will might "go in the suite of some Colonial Governor! Grampus might take him – and I could write to Fulke about it" (397). Mr. Brooke, whose laissez-faire attitude was arguably responsible for Dorothea's marriage, objects to the notion of packing off troublesome young men to the colonies: "But Ladislaw won't be shipped off like a head of cattle, my dear fellow; Ladislaw has his ideas" (397). Will himself feigns interest in an "intended settlement on a new plan in the Far West" (654), but drops the pretense upon his reunion with Dorothea. In *Middlemarch*, love gives Will and Fred reasons not to leave home and strengthens their connections to England. The idea of reform and the practice of working the land are the essence of Englishness, precisely the connections the Lewes boys lacked. Will and Fred are tied to place and family and both become saner for giving up their earlier, fanciful notions.

### MANLINESS AND NATIONALISM

Having looked at the cultural contexts that explain how Thornie ended up in Natal, we can now examine his experiences there and, most importantly, how he represented them to Eliot and Lewes. His letters bear the traces of an ideological conflict between his culture's promotion of organized emigration (families, farming, discipline) and adventure (single men, hunting, battle). Thornie knew he was "going out" to pursue a practical career, but his language was that of romance, much to the distress of Eliot and Lewes, who urged him to tell them the facts of his situation so that they could understand it. There are also conflicts between his anti-imperialist politics and the colonial temptations to mastery to which he was exposed. Finally, Thornie's emigration throws some interesting light on the pressure to perform conventional manliness and on Eliot's rejection of that model as reflected in her feminized heroes from *Silas Marner* to *Daniel Deronda*.

Thornie was at once the most like Lewes in his interests in natural science, poetry, and journalism, and the most unlike him in his pursuit of manly activities such as horseback riding, hunting, and fighting. Lewes, with his "Vivian" persona, intellectualism, and domesticity – his preference for kissing rather than shooting lions – displayed a self-consciously unconventional masculinity. He was small and slight. He suffered from constant ill health, too delicate even for horseback riding, which he tried and gave up: "The exercise seemed to stir up my liver into unpleasant activity."[21] In *The Mill on the Floss*, Eliot's narrator observes of boys like Tom Tulliver that it is "only when you have mastered a restive horse, or thrashed a drayman, or have got a gun in your hand, that these shy juniors feel you to be a truly admirable and enviable character" (91). Thornie identified with his father, but resisted him and defined himself against Lewes's less than manly image. He must have known eventually, despite the silences and fictions that characterize the family's letters, that his mother Agnes's relationship with Thornton Hunt (Thornie's namesake) placed Lewes in the socially humiliating position of cuckold.

In an episode highlighted by Gordon Haight in his biography of Eliot, Thornie found himself locked out of George Robertson's house, where he lodged in Edinburgh. Thornie sneaked in through a window. When Robertson confronted him about violating his curfew, an altercation ensued. Thornie wrote to his father: "You need not ask me what I did; I did what you would have done in my place – knocked him down" (*GEL*, 8:295). From what we know of Lewes, the notion that he would knock anyone down seems ridiculous, and naturally he reprimanded his son. Thornie's attempt to coax Lewes into colluding with his defiance suggests that he wished that his father would display a more conventional manliness.

This confrontation, which occurred on 22 December 1861, is an example of Thornie's scripting his own life after the literature he read. Just one year earlier, on 11 December 1860, he wrote home that he was reading Dickens's *Nicholas Nickleby*. In that novel, Nicholas, with a "long series of insults to avenge," and the part of "helpless infancy" to defend, beats the cruel schoolmaster Squeers.[22] While this act loses him his job, Nicholas feels he has right on his side and becomes a hero in the telling of his tale, as when John Browdie congratulates him, "Beatten the schoolmeasther! Dang it, I loove thee for 't."[23] It seems to be just such acknowledgment that Thornie sought when he included a drawing of Robertson's black eye in his letter.

In addition to this boyish sense of honor and self-defense and this defiance of specifically paternal authority, Thornie's letters before his emigration lack explicit English nationalism and show instead a general sympathy with the oppressed. In the late 1850s and early 1860s, he took an inevitable interest in events affecting the empire, particularly the Indian Mutiny. In 1857, he asked his father to tell him how the "Indian War" was getting on: "What are your opinions respecting it, that we shall win or lose?"[24] He did not, however, take the figures of the Indian war for his heroes.[25] From his school in Switzerland Thornie was captivated by anti-imperialist movements within Europe. In 1859, for example, a Sardinian–French alliance was at war with Austria – one stage in the long struggle to throw off the imperialist Hapsburg yoke. Reminiscent of Tom Tulliver's dress-up as a soldier, Thornie and his schoolmates made Austria their enemy, and he described the "Hofwyl Regiment" as the "bravest regiment in the world and quite ready to meet the Austrians."[26]

Like his parents, he followed the developments of the Italian nationalist movement with much interest. On 11 September 1860, just before leaving Hofwyl for Edinburgh, he learned that a son of Garibaldi would be a student at the high school. He fantasized that he might run away with him and "make the world ring with the glory of my name, so that when in future any one asks, who were the three liberators of Sicily? the answer will be Garibaldi, Türr and Thornton Lewes" (*GEL*, 8:271).[27] Thornie's heroes are anti-imperialist nationalists to whom he is connected by his belief, as an Englishman living outside England, in the ideals of freedom and national self-determination. To the extent that he showed any desire to direct his own future, he imagined himself participating in a national liberation movement, not a colonizing project.

Thornie also found heroes in poetry. He mentions to Eliot that he is reading a poem by Viscount Maidstone, adding that Abd el Kader is "one of my favourite heroes."[28] *Abd-el-Kader* (1851) is a book-length ballad about the Algerian nationalist who fought the French imperial army in 1848, was subsequently imprisoned, and became a celebrated cause among English radicals, or, as in the case of Maidstone (George-James Finch-Hatton, later Earl of Winchilsea), anti-Catholic Tories.[29] As part of the general anti-imperialist sentiment of the poem, Maidstone compares Abd el Kader to the Chechen leader Schamyl: "Clad in link'd mail, a noble man and free,/ The Tchekesse stoops like eagle on the flock:/ The lines are driven in – some fall – most flee./ Fierce is the dint of Schamyl's battle-shock!"[30]

Thornie showed the most enthusiasm for Schamyl. In 1859, he wrote to Eliot and Lewes: "You must know, that Schamyl is my favourite hero," enclosing a poem he had written, titled "Schamyl's Capture."[31] Schamyl had been a popular hero with the English since before the Crimean War. In 1854 Lewes had written of the "Lesgian chief": "Gifted with a vitality so mysterious, boundless in resources, eloquent, he has all the qualities to inspire enthusiasm."[32] His son was certainly one of those so inspired. Thornie delighted in the news that "the Russians had been signally defeated in the Caucasus by Scheikh Mehemet, Schamyl's noble successor," writing in his long poem:

> But Russia beware, though Schamyl lies low
> Thou hast not yet conquered his land,
> For his valiant Murides have another chief found
> To command in the battle his band.[33]

Thornie's verses fall into the tradition of Wordsworth's poems dedicated to national independence. They show English sympathy for national liberation movements and abstract the specific reference into a struggle for freedom. His poem displays even more affinity with those contained in W. M. Rossetti's "Democratic Sonnets," many of which were written in the 1850s and 1860s and include "Poland, 1863." Such pro-democratic poetry coexisted in English society with pro-empire verses – by Tennyson, for example – and with romantic fiction that championed the glory of colonial adventure.

Like Will Ladislaw, Thornie, too, had his "ideas." Emigration was a way of restraining him from pursuing his intention to become a volunteer soldier with the Polish insurgents against Russia in the "January Uprising" of 1863, which began before he left for Natal and ended in April 1864, shortly after his arrival. Eliot wrote to her friend François D'Albert-Durade that they "felt that it would be a sin to allow a boy of nineteen to incur the demoralisation of joining [the] coarse men engaged in a guerilla warfare, to say nothing of Thornie's utter unfitness for military subordination and other inevitable hardships" (*GEL*, 4:117).

Thornie's multinational education in Switzerland prepared him for his Pan-European identity in South Africa. Together with the journalistic accounts of struggles for independence and the popular poetry of nationalist movements, the multinational genre of boys' adventure fiction was also an important influence on his imagination. In adult genres, such as R. Gordon Cumming's hunting narrative, Lewes recognized a moral regression in Englishmen. The conditions in Africa were not conducive to the development of the European boy's aptitude for a moral life. Boys' adventure fiction reconciled the killing of animals and people with English Christian values. Since the atheist Lewes looked to science for an explanation of moral behavior and personally eschewed masculine performance, such propaganda should have been doubly distasteful to him. Yet his attitude to children's books foreshadows his acceptance of the colonies as a future destination for his boys.[34]

The first indication we have of books read by the Lewes boys, aged eleven, nine, and seven, is in the *Leader*. Among the books listed in the arts section, but only occasionally reviewed, were books for children. In 1853, Lewes wrote that "we have had much more pressing calls upon our time than the reading of a pile of children's books," and therefore his remarks will be "guided by juvenile critics who have read them, and pronounced very unbiased, if not very discriminating verdicts."[35] Willingly guided by his juvenile (boy) critics, Lewes reserves special praise for "the spirited volume by Captain Mayne Reid, *The Young Voyageurs; or, The Boy Hunters in the North*. Emphatically to be recommended."[36]

*The Young Voyageurs* (1853) by Mayne Reid is typical of adventure fiction of the period. It is addressed to boy readers and intends to be educational as well as exciting. It pays close attention to the fauna and flora of its setting in northwest Canada, and begins with the invitation: "Enough, brave boy! You shall go with me to the wild regions of the 'North-west,' to the far 'fur countries' of America," and entreats young readers to "Take down your Atlas."[37] *The Young Voyageurs* involves the quest of three French Creole brothers from Louisiana – Lucien, Francois, and Basil – for their uncle, a fur trader in a far outpost of French colonial Canada, whose son, Norman, acts as their guide. Characteristic of the genre, each brother falls into type. Basil is a robust hunter and Lucien a slight, fair naturalist, both likely to appeal to Thornie, whose personality combined the hunter with the naturalist son of his father. The book is divided according to the interests of the brothers, and Lucien the naturalist gives veritable lectures on the species he encounters, including Canadian swans – just before the boys shoot them. Yet his intellectual enthusiasm does not dampen their collective lust for blood. Reid is halfheartedly apologetic about the behavior of his boy characters and their gratuitous killing of swans, explaining that "the hunter is hard to satisfy with game, and but too often inclined to 'spill much more blood' than is necessary to his wants."[38]

Thornie kept Eliot informed about his reading, writing from Edinburgh that he had read R. M. Ballantyne's *The World of Ice; or, Adventures in the Polar Regions* (1861) and Gustave Aimard's *The Tiger-Slayer, a Tale of the Indian Desert* (trans. 1863). Ballantyne, one of several Scottish authors Thornie read in Edinburgh, wrote stories set in territories from Canada (*The Young Fur Traders*) to Africa (*The Gorilla Hunters*) that exemplify the genre of boys' adventure fiction.[39] *The World of Ice* tells the story of Fred Ellice, a "stout, fair-haired boy of fifteen,"[40] and his friend Tom Singleton (who studies medicine in Edinburgh), a "sturdy boy of about fifteen."[41] The usual division obtains between Fred the adventurer/hunter and Tom the naturalist/scholar. There is plenty of hunting. When Fred sees a bird, he "particularly want[s] that fellow because he's beautifully marked,"[42] whereas Tom "went into raptures" at the scenery and "stuffed his botanical box with mosses and rocks until it could hold no more."[43]

Fred sets out on a whaling expedition to the Arctic in search of his father, who has been lost on a similar voyage. Most striking about this adventure narrative are its parallels to Thornie's later experiences, as well as its pronouncements about masculine values when we imagine Thornie as a reader. For example, the narrator proclaims: "All honour, we say, to the boy who *dreams* impossibilities, and greater honour to him who, like Fred, *resolves to attempt them*."[44] The irony, at least in retrospect, is that Thornie dreamed much grander dreams than he was ever able to attempt, and failed at most of the adventures, quests, and projects on which he embarked. Yet, as we shall see, his representations of himself as a young man on shipboard during his voyage to South Africa echo this book in particular.

Thornie also mentions reading a book by Gustave Aimard, a French author who wrote about North America and was popular in England.[45] Much more romantic (full of duels, betrothals, violations of honor), *The Tiger-Slayer* begins ominously with "the discovery of the rich Californian plains" which "awakened suddenly the adventurous instincts of thousands of young and intelligent men, who, leaving country and family, rushed, full of enthusiasm, towards the new Eldorado, where the majority only met with misery and death, after sufferings and vexations innumerable."[46] The plot follows El Tigrero and his pursuit of Anita, the beautiful daughter of Don Sylva de Torres. Its various subplots portray racial wars between Comanches and Canadians, Comanches and Mexicans, and Comanches and Apaches. At one stage, Aimard speculates that war between Europeans and Indians resembles "war in Africa."[47] Ultimately, war is bloody and brutal: "The combat had degenerated into a horrible carnage, in which the fighters clutched each other, stabbing and mangling, without loosing hold."[48] While participating in a different tradition from that of English boys' literature, Aimard's text (which Thornie read in French) represents the multinational character of colonialism. Ranging from South America to Canada, the novel blames the Spaniards for colonial exploitation: "The grinding tyranny which for several centuries weighted Indians down, by rendering them the utter slaves of haughty and implacable masters, has given them the characteristics of slaves."[49] In this sense, a criticism of past colonialism is mixed with, and perhaps seeks to justify, its acceptance as a subject for romance.

Of these three books by an Irishman, a Scot, and a Frenchman, only Ballantyne's concerns the English. Thornie's South Africa was as multinational as Aimard's North America; he spent at least as much time with Boers and Germans in South Africa as he did with Englishmen, and he met, fought, and employed Basutos, Zulus, and members of other

1. Thornton (Thornie) Arnott Lewes (*circa* 1861).

African tribes. Boys' adventure fiction prepared Thornie less to be an Englishman than to expect and condone violence of all sorts.

## DANIEL DERONDA

Eliot's decision in the 1870s to set the action of her last novel, *Daniel Deronda*, in the mid-1860s indicates, among other things, her perceptions of the cultural influences on Thornie's generation, whose reading would be, for boys, the same as Thornie's, and, for girls, of the type she had satirized in her 1856 article "Silly Novels by Lady Novelists." Gwendolen Harleth, aged twenty in 1864, is an exact contemporary of Thornie (born in 1844). The setting of *Deronda* (1864–6) falls precisely during the years in which Thornie was in South Africa (1863–9), and Eliot's portrait of Gwendolen suggests a version of Thornie's experience from a woman's point of view, a simultaneously lived woman's drama. It is possible that the lament over Gwendolen's lack of some "spot of native land" may have been intensified by Eliot's observation of the rootless and ultimately exiled lives of Thornie and Bertie.

After his rejection by his cousin Gwendolen, Rex Gascoigne decides to "take another course" from the university education he has begun, explaining to his father that he "should like to go to the colonies and work on the land there" (72). Bodenheimer argues that "the story of Rex Gascoigne reverses the decision to send [Thornie and Bertie] abroad, contributing in this way to the novel's persistent critique of colonialism."[50] There is no doubt that Rex recalls Thornie. For example, Thornie had a habit during his school days at Hofwyl, where he was studying Latin, to sign his letters Thorntonius Arnottus Ludovicus, Ranarum Rex, and Rex Ranarum. Yet Rex's case is interestingly different from that of the Lewes boys. Rex's brother Warham is the Indian civil servant Thornie might have been, but Rex is the eldest son (like Charles Lewes), with the promise to repay the investment in his education. To put down his colonial plans, Rex's father makes the appropriate parental intervention, telling him, "you have no right whatever to expatriate yourself until you have honestly endeavoured to turn to account the education you have received here" (73). In other words, a boy with an Oxford degree need consider neither the second-rate option of the Indian civil service nor the third-rate option of emigration.

The kind of colonial life Rex imagines – "I should like to build a hut, and work hard at clearing, and have everything wild about me, and a great wide quiet" (71) – is consonant with a non-violent facet of the boys' literature of the 1850s. Anna Gascoigne's contribution to the fantasy emphasizes the point. In this conversation, the siblings Rex and Anna have defined their destination in no more precise terms than "Canada, or somewhere of that sort" (70), yet Anna is sure that she would "sooner go there than stay here in England . . . It would be nicer than anything – like playing at life over again, as we used to do when we made our tent with the drugget, and had our little plates and dishes" (71). Anna's comments accentuate Rex's intention to escape as well as the typical emigrant dream of "playing at life over again."

As Eliot captures the ill-informed romance surrounding the colonies, she embeds adventure fiction as a comic subtext in her novel. This is characteristic of *Deronda* and marks a development in her realism. She does not represent the colonies, nor does she need to argue against unrealistic genres as she had in earlier works, such as *Scenes of Clerical Life* and *Adam Bede*. Rather she turns her narrative into a web of allusion and representations of representations – the music, acting, and diverse forms of writing, such as girls' fiction (particularly *Little Women*), that are associated with the Meyrick household.

Like Thornie's nationalist dreams, Gwendolen's greater aspirations find no outlet, for "her horizon was that of the genteel romance where the heroine's soul poured out in her journals is full of vague power, originality, and general rebellion, while her life moves strictly in the sphere of fashion" (43). She teases Rex by saying that she would like to "go to the North Pole, or ride steeplechases, or go to be a queen in the East like Lady Hester Stanhope," but the narrator observes: "Her words were born on her lips, but she would have been at a loss to give an answer of deeper origin" (57). With Grandcourt she complains that "We women can't go in search of adventures – to find out the North-West Passage or the source of the Nile, or to hunt tigers in the East" (113). These images are, in Eliot's metaphor, on the surface, caught by Gwendolen's lips as familiar cultural markers of freedom and adventure. When faced with real financial hardship, Gwendolen thinks she would rather "emigrate than be a governess" (199), the narrator adding: "What it precisely was to emigrate, [she] was not called on to explain."

Rex is saved from emigrating to escape a failed romance when his father clarifies his prospects and responsibilities at home. He pursues the rising-middle-class profession of law and the emigration interlude becomes a part of his childish past. The image of Rex farming in Canada is absurd, while Deronda's decision to reject Sir Hugo's practical suggestions for his career in favor of leaving England and pursuing his Jewish interests is ennobled as a higher calling, despite its impracticality. These two men in their early twenties facing career decisions in the mid-1860s, the one rejecting emigration, the other embracing it, recall the situation of the Lewes boys in the mid-1860s, but Thornie and Bertie were less like any characters in Victorian novels than like the sons of other Victorian novelists.

### OTHER YOUNGER SONS

Many of Eliot and Lewes's contemporaries had comparable problems with unemployable sons and turned to similar colonial solutions. Among the friends and acquaintances in their London literary and social circle, Trollope and Dickens had sons who emigrated to various parts of the empire at approximately the same time as Thornie and Bertie. Like Eliot and Lewes, Trollope and Dickens had read a great deal about the colonies, but their sons were as ill-prepared for colonial careers as were the Lewes boys. The experiences of the Trollope and Dickens boys are worth examining for what they reveal about aspirations for children and assumptions about the future of the empire among this ambiguously situated segment of the middle class in the 1860s, before the need to prepare middle-class sons for emigration had been recognized as a national problem.

As a postal inspector, Trollope's job was to increase the efficiency of communication between England and its colonies and within individual colonies. The travel books that resulted from his business trips were an important source of income for him from 1859 to 1879. Their popularity is suggested by the fact that Lewes read them all. Trollope acquired an emotional investment in Australia when his son Fred emigrated to New South Wales in 1865 at the age of eighteen. Fred returned to England briefly in 1869, but settled permanently in Australia in the same year, purchasing a large sheep farm. After 1875 he could no longer maintain his farm, and his father visited (for the second time), helping out financially and also writing a series of letters home for publication in the *Liverpool Mercury*. After the loss of his farm, Fred took a position in the Lands Department. He worked as a public servant for the rest of his life in different locations around New South Wales. Fred's biographer writes that Fred's colonial life "left him at heart disappointed and unsatisfied."[51] He is yet another exception to the standard representation of English colonists as imperialist ideologues. Although he did not lose his life, his compromised ambitions made him a victim of the Victorian projection of the colonies as a land of opportunity.

Unlike Dickens and Eliot, Trollope traveled throughout the colonies and represented those places he had visited not only in travel writing, but in fiction. He wrote two Australian novels, *Harry Heathcote* (1874) and *John Caldigate* (1879), the latter dealing with the corruption of young English men in the colonies. His *Tales of All Countries* (first series, 1861) includes "Miss Sarah Jack of Spanish Town, Jamaica." Furthermore, as part of Trollope's realistic representation of English society, references to India and the colonies turn up throughout his fiction, especially in relation to sons. Just as Sir James Chettam wanted to get rid of Will by sending him to India, so Roger Carbury in *The Way We Live Now* (1875) suggests sending the troublesome Felix there: "The young man should make up his mind to do something for himself. A career might possibly be opened for him in India."[52] Trollope was a more explicit supporter of British colonial projects than Eliot, Lewes, or Dickens, yet was the only parent who did not want his son to leave England.

Fred Trollope ended up in Wilcannia, New South Wales, at the same time as Dickens's youngest son, Edward "Plorn" Dickens. Plorn's nickname, after Mr. Plornish in *Little Dorrit*, emphasizes the connections between Dickens's characters and his children. Plorn and his brother Alfred, like Fred Trollope and the Lewes boys, emigrated in the 1860s, by which time two of their brothers had already left for India. Dickens had seven sons to worry about placing, and he urged emigration for those he perceived to be less than competitive for jobs at home. In 1857, Walter, aged sixteen, obtained a cadetship in the East India Company. Dickens wrote that "he will probably be sent out soon after he has passed, and so will fall into that strange life 'up the country' before he well knows he is alive."[53] Walter was immediately involved in the Mutiny, and as a result of his service was promoted to lieutenant. His father's comment that Walter would "fall into that strange life . . . before he well knows he is alive" is both ironic and tragic in view of the fact that Walter died of a brain hemorrhage in Calcutta in 1863. Peter Ackroyd writes of Walter's death as "one of the many tragedies and disappointments that were to mark Dickens's children; as if his own great success had left some kind of stain upon his offspring." "As if," he continues, "in some form of natural compensation, they *had* to fail."[54] But as a look at the larger picture suggests, failures and even tragedies were common among middle-class sons who found colonial careers. Walter, however proud his father became of his military success, was sent off initially, like Bertie Lewes, because he was "a little slow" with no "uncommon abilities."[55]

In 1867, Dickens wrote of Plorn: "His want of application and continuity of purpose would be quite extraordinary to me if I had not observed the same defect in one of his brothers, and tried to trace it to its source."[56] The other son was Francis Jeffrey (Frank) and the implied "source" was Dickens's estranged wife Catherine. Frank had wanted to emigrate to a settler colony with "fifteen pounds, a horse, and a rifle," but his father was skeptical, writing: "I perceived that the first consequence of the fifteen pounds would be that he would be robbed of it – of the horse, that it would throw him – and of the rifle, that it would blow his head off."[57] So Dickens tried him in the *All the Year Round* office. Frank performed so poorly that his father next made efforts to get him a post in the registrar's office in Chancery Lane as well as in the Foreign Office (which he lost by examination).[58] Finally, Dickens thought India was the best option. He applied to the Lieutenant-Governor of Bengal and obtained for Frank the position of District Superintendent, Bengal Mounted Police. Frank arrived in India in 1864, shortly after Walter's death on December 31, 1863.

Alfred Dickens ended up as a colonial emigrant after failing an examination to become an army engineer. He went to Australia in 1865 at the age of twenty. In 1868, the sixteen-year-old Plorn followed. Of Plorn's preparation Dickens had written: "I am assured on the best authority that the practical knowledge of farming he requires is, for Australian purposes, of a very limited nature."[59] Hence Plorn was sent to Cirencester Agricultural College for eight months before his emigration. In his farewell letter to Plorn, Dickens wrote that he was satisfied that Plorn was trying for the "life for which you are best fitted." He continued, "I think its freedom and wildness more suited to you than any experiment in a study or office would have been; and without that training, you could have followed no other suitable occupation."[60] When Plorn had trouble adjusting to life in Australia, Dickens wrote to a friend there that Plorn was "born without a groove": "If he cannot, or will not find one, I must try again and die trying." He lamented that Plorn "does not seem to understand that he has qualified for no public examinations in the old country, and could not possibly hold his own against competition for anything to which I could get him nominated."[61] Plorn, too, was a failure who could not qualify for the civil service, a great burden to the father determined to make him independent.

With the exception of his outrage at the Indian Mutiny and his defense of Governor Eyre in the Morant Bay rebellion controversy, Dickens did not display a colonizing, imperialistic agenda. As Grahame Smith points out, while he urged the emigration of his sons and of prostitutes, as well as presenting it as a solution for several of his characters, it "was clearly not an option for Dickens himself."[62] He desperately needed to find somewhere for his sons to go. His fiction is full of young men who are sent to make a career in the colonies or in foreign countries with colonial associations. Walter Gay is sent to Barbados, Martin Chuzzlewit to the United States, Allan Woodcourt to China and India, Arthur Clennam to China, John Harmon to the Cape, and Edwin Drood to Egypt. Many critics have written about Dickens and the empire, but his case is one, like those of Eliot and Trollope, which is enriched and complicated by an understanding of the biographical context. His attitude was less that the world needed to be colonized than that middle-class sons must be found a "groove" in accordance with their class. Grahame Smith asks whether his actions toward his sons constituted "a kind of suppression, the removal of sons who, however charming as babies and little children, became increasingly tiresome as their inadequacies became apparent under the eye of a stern, if loving, taskmaster."[63] Looking at Dickens in the light of his contemporaries, we see that the colonies were a solution to a larger "younger son question" than his alone.[64]

I will now look at what happened to Thornie and Bertie in the various parts of South Africa – Natal, the Orange Free State, and the Transvaal – in which they lived and traveled between 1864 (when Thornie arrived) and 1875 (when Bertie died). The texts are the surviving letters they sent to Eliot and Lewes. Written as a consequence of failure at home and failure to become a part of the imperial bureaucracy, the letters are part of an intertext, reflecting and repeating the versions of colonial experiences found in popular literature at mid-century.

### THE EMIGRANTS' EXPERIENCE: COLONIAL SOUTH AFRICA

Thornie's letters display striking parallels with the adventure fiction he read. Fred Ellice's activities aboard the whaling ship *Dolphin* in Ballantyne's *The World of Ice* seem to be relived by Thornie. For example, Fred publishes "an illustrated newspaper once a-week."[65] In 1863, on board the *Damietta* to South Africa, Thornie wrote that the passengers had "started a newspaper of which I was the subeditor." But after a conflict, he "revolted," and "started a rival paper: 'The Damietta Blunderbuss,' which gun explodes every Wednesday morning punctually at $8\frac{1}{2}$ a.m., tis extremely popular."[66] In the microcosm of the ship, dramas are acted on and off the stage. On Ballantyne's *Dolphin*, "a theatre was set agoing" in which Fred directs "Blunderbore; or, The Arctic Giant."[67] Like his fictional counterpart, Thornie participates in theatricals, writing home that "we performed Buckstone's farce of 'Shocking Events' to an enthusiastic audience, I taking the part of Mr Puggs (Keeley's original part) & sending the spectators into roars."[68] And like Fred Ellice he shoots birds from the ship, writing that we "have had some shooting at albatrosses, one of which I bagged along with several petrels & c."

A juxtaposition of *The World of Ice* and Thornie's letters creates the impression that Thornie enacted a script of how teenagers should conduct themselves on board a ship bound for adventure.[69] The colonial story does not end with the ship voyage, of course, though its performance becomes more improvisational. Unlike the novel's heroes, who triumph in slaughtering a mother polar bear and her baby, Thornie is prevented by mishap from shooting any game. On his first hunting trip, he saw "gnus, quagglus, springboks, blesboks, & c & c," but confesses that he "was unable to shoot, for the waggon had gone over my fowling piece, taking the cock off, & the revolving rifle proved a complete failure."[70] Disappointed but undaunted, he reports that, as a consequence, he has "no hunting adventures to relate this time." This is one of several instances in which the rhetoric of adventure coincides with an absurd image (the waggon running over his gun). And, in fact, Thornie never has any successful hunting adventures to relate which approximate to those found in the fiction that had helped to whet his appetite for colonial killing.

From the first letter sent from Natal, Thornie dehumanizes Africans. He responds to various bits of news in letters that had reached him, one involving the theft of Eliot's purse during the move to their new home, the Priory. Striving to make a connection with the comfort of life in London, he writes that his robbers "will certainly not be men, except perhaps a few Bushmen now & then, who are almost the same as Chims or gorillas, so that shooting them will not be as exciting as shooting your robbers." He concludes that "there is worse game no doubt, than Lions, Leopards, & Bushmen."[71] Eliot excerpted this letter in one of hers to Barbara Bodichon, choosing to exclude some less attractive passages such as this one. She wrote, "let us trust in the good omen of a good beginning" (*GEL*, 4:140) and thanked Bodichon for helping to find "this new starting point for our nineteen-year-older" (*GEL*, 4:143). In their journals and letters, Eliot and Lewes generally evade those aspects of Thornie's doings which might form the basis for moral censure of him or of the colonizing process, which in theory they knew to be demoralizing.

When Lewes wrote that Thornie had started for Natal to "shoot elephants instead of Russians"[72] and Eliot referred to his "very sanguine expectation of shooting lions," (*GEL*, 4:117), they made light of the violence they had wished him to avoid and of his fanciful adventures. When Lewes wrote that he was "shooting tigers and Basutos in Natal" (*GEL*, 8:366), he engaged in uncharacteristic callousness. In his more serious moments he considered the humanity of Africans and deplored the slaughter of animals in Africa, but his investment in his son's success as a settler silenced these opinions. Perhaps they believed that the compromise of going to Natal, where Thornie was free to shoot lions, tigers, elephants, Basutos, and Bushmen, was a better solution than his going to war in Poland. At the very least, they were able to reconcile such masculine outlets of energy (or of fantasy) with the humane, responsible life they had sent him to find.

While Thornie maintained a remarkable optimism throughout his brief life, his letters trace a downward spiral of defeats. He scouted out possible opportunities, giving some thought to coffee farming, but instead traveled to the Transvaal in an attempt to establish himself as a trader. To that end, he started a business with an Englishman named Cronin.[73] But by June 12, 1865, he was "bankrupt, or what in reality comes to the same thing" (*GEL*, 8:343). Like the sons of Trollope and Dickens, Thornie had spent the money given by his parents to get him started. He anticipated that it would take five years for him to raise the £200–300 he would need to try again, and a year and a half after arriving in Natal he finds himself "*working* here, as Kafir storekeeper and general Bottlewasher etc." (*GEL*, 8:343) – hardly the respectable career for which his parents had hoped. In July 1865, following this first failure, Thornie volunteered for the Natal Frontier Guard, a cavalry corps that was preparing to do battle with the Basutos.

Ironically, South Africa provided an arena for the type of fighting that Lewes had hoped to preempt by sending him there. Were the vigilantes of the Natal Frontier Guard any less "rough" than the "guerilla band" of Polish insurgents? He soon became involved in armed conflict, fighting beside settlers and drifters in a white allegiance that effaced national differences. He expressed the change that had occurred in his militaristic outlook between 1861 and 1865: "Who would have thought, that by my coming out here, instead of going to Poland, I should have fallen from the frying pan into the fire, and instead of fighting an enemy I hate, I should have to fight one I despise" (*GEL*, 8:345). This distinction – between hated Russian oppressors of Poles and Chechens and despised Basuto impediments to British and Boer expansionism – is emblematic of the ideologically inconsistent discourses that shaped Thornie's perceptions of an Englishman's part in warfare around the world.

Five months after joining the Natal Frontier Guard, Thornie wrote to Lewes and Eliot, enclosing a separate sheet with a dispatch on the battle of Plattberg from "Your Own War Correspondent." In the document, he adopts a mock-journalistic style, with retrospective embellishments, to describe a battle that had taken place on December 6: "Day had just broken, when the low flat top of Plattberg peeped up on the horizon, & just as the sun was beginning to appear, half a dozen rifle shots from the front told that the days work had begun."[74] He dwells on geographical detail to give his readers a precise sense of South African warfare, and his narrative and tone derive from the conventions of adventure fiction: "One Kaffir had sprung up from some rocks, & was instantly bowled over, the commander in chief, old Frick, demeaning himself by going up to the Kaffir as he lay, & giving him the contents of his 'Colt.'" This barbaric act, acknowledged as demeaning, calls up a moral sense in Thornie that is displayed against the grain of the narrative, which otherwise strives to affect a nonchalance about killing and to present war as a great game.

The heroic ideals of Thornie's early revolutionary fantasies were tested by the reality of colonial warfare. Vigilante cattle raids lacked the idealism of Polish resistance. Referring to an illustration he drew for his parents, he tells of joining some Boers who "had got two Kaffirs in a cave," and helping them try "to kill the Kaffirs & cut out the horses." The scene resembles a shooting gallery in which "we posted ourselves on commanding positions, & whenever the Kaffirs gun appeared at the opening a bullet went crack at it." He had aligned himself with a minority group (the Boers) and their military cause, but there was nothing noble in sniping at men just to take their cattle or horses, and Thornie could not claim the heroism he imagined for himself.

The lure of the colony – escaping the restrictive social conventions of England – was also its greatest threat to anyone seeking adventure, the threat of losing respect for humanity and life. When Thornie first arrived, he relished the freedom of "having to obey no man," writing to Eliot that "Pater's so far off that his authority is not worth much, so I ought to feel independent."[75] The distance from the law of the father translated for him into a kind of lawlessness, which was supported by the opportunities around him. While he grappled with paternal authority in letters justifying his actions, the danger for him was that to which he ultimately succumbed – a lack of direction and guidance that allowed him to waste his energy and money in schemes which seemed caught between his society's simultaneous promise of adventure and desire for orderly settlement.

2. Manuscript page from Thornton Lewes's letter to G. H. Lewes and George Eliot, December 26, 1865, Beinecke Rare Book and Manuscript Library, Yale University.

Thornie's letters describing the Basuto War and its aftermath suggest further parallels with the boys' fiction he had read. In *The World of Ice*, the captain of the *Dolphin* intends "to impress the Esquimaux with a salutary sense of the power, promptitude, and courage of Europeans."[76] After this, there can be cooperation and mutual respect. Likewise, after the truce between Boers and Basutos, Thornie goes good-naturedly to shake the hands of the various chiefs – Moshesh, Masoepa, Paulus Moperi – whom he had "despised" just months before: "My friend Moligani with whom we fought at Plattberg was not there for which I was sorry, as I have a respect for that gentleman." This civilized act of shaking hands with the defeated enemy recalls yet another convention of nineteenth-century boys' literature. In Ballantyne's popular *The Coral Island* (1857), for example, the hero Jack "stepped up to the savage and gave him a hearty shake of the hand" and later "terminated rather abruptly by seizing the chief's hand and shaking it violently."[77] The English ethos of acknowledging a "fair" fight demands that the rules be followed, even if the "Kaffirs" had earlier been seen as animals.

With this happy, novelistic ending to the "war," Eliot and Lewes were eager to send Bertie to join his brother. Bertie did not need to fail an examination to be marked as a failure. After Hofwyl, Eliot and Lewes decided on something practical rather than intellectual for Bertie, and something far away, rather than close to home. On April 18, 1863, Lewes wrote in his journal that they were thinking of sending Bertie "to Australia as a farmer in a few years, when he has learned enough and is old enough" (*GEL*, 4:83). Writing to François D'Albert-Durade in 1865, Eliot explained that Bertie was "better fitted for colonial than for English life, at least as far as the means of pushing his fortune are concerned," and further, that he was "not suited to any other life than that of a farmer, and in England farming has become a business that requires not only great capital but great skill to render it otherwise than hazardous" (*GEL*, 4:212). Just as Dickens had been told that Australian farming required very little preparation, so Eliot thought that managing a colonial farm required less skill as well as less capital than farming at home. Like Thomas Hardy's Angel Clare, the problematic son who was sent to learn dairy farming in preparation for a colonial career, and like Plorn Dickens, Bertie was sent to a farm near Glasgow, and then to another in Warwickshire to prepare for his emigration.

The decision to send Bertie to Natal was made with the vague expectation of spoils from the Basuto War in the form of land. Thornie believed that "by volunteering for the Free State I obtain a right to a

farm in that country and to a share in the booty" (*GEL*, 8:352). Eliot
wrote to D'Albert-Durade on December 17, 1865, that "Thornton has
had some calamities to encounter in Natal, owing to a monetary crisis
in the colony and a war with the natives. But he is well in health and
shows much spirit" (*GEL*, 4:211).[78] Considering the language she uses –
"calamities," "crisis," "war" – it is surprising that her tone here is so
detached and that similar references are so few in her letters. Lewes
wrote on January 1, 1866: "Thornie has been unfortunate in Natal.
Bertie must wait another 6 months before going out (to Natal or New
Zealand – uncertain which)" (*GEL*, 4:222). Shortly after, he recorded in
his journal that Bertie's departure had been "suddenly resolved on after
excerpt of Thornie's letter announcing his having got a grant of land."[79]
Eliot wrote to Blackwood that Thornie had a "grant of land," that Bertie
had been "thoroughly drilled" in farming, and that "it seems the best
thing we can do for them to set them going as partners by stocking their
farm" (*GEL*, 4:305). Bertie left for South Africa on a mail steamer on
September 9, 1866.

Bertie's letters are intriguingly different from those of his brother. They
lack Thornie's theatricality, and although Bertie frequently mentions
reading, he does not interpret his own life in terms of fiction and romance.
Bertie's concerns and reflections are more mundane, but no less revealing
of emigrant culture in the 1860s. Bertie traveled second class, and he was
extremely conscious of the distinction: "We second class passengers are
not allowed to go near the 1st class." This letter reflects the careful class
distinctions among emigrants: "They have a piano in the saloon, but of
course we 2nd may not touch it. The 1st class consists of missionaries,
Nuns or Sisters of Charity, Clergymen, Drapers, and Grocers, etc, a very
good collection. There are one or two very nice young fellows amongst
them, and they are the only ones who speak to 2nd class."[80] Bertie's
resentment of the behavior of the first-class passengers in a situation of
artificial division suggests the ambiguity of the Lewes boys' class position,
and also raises the question of what class status was preserved by sending
them to be farmers in Natal. Bertie's approach to the world around
him is gentler if no less appropriative than Thornie's. The blacks are
pretty and viewed in the light of exportable property. He never mentions
wanting to shoot them, but rather later expressed a fear of being shot by
them.

On November 5, 1866, Bertie wrote from Durban that "Thornton
has not received his farm and it is not very likely that he will get one
at all."[81] In his own letter, Thornie explains that "the Free State Govt.

has broken its promises, and *done* all the Volunteers out of the farms, to which according to Law, they were entitled" (*GEL*, 8:390). Upon receiving these letters, Lewes wrote in his diary: "The prospect of the farm seems to have been imaginary."[82] Lewes's skepticism about Thornie's claims illustrates an epistemological problem that Lewes had encountered in his reading of exploration literature but which now had immediate personal consequences. Was the grant of land part of a script, like the gentlemanly handshake with the native chiefs after war? Bertie's future rested on Thornie, whose claims of achievement appeared to be "imaginary." With no authoritative means by which to confirm Thornie's accounts of land distribution, Lewes gambled on the prospect of free land and was understandably distressed when he discovered that there was none. Thornie gave his father an elaborate explanation, which begins: "Following your advice of filling letters with facts rather than jokes, I will begin by giving you in detail my plans for the future."[83] By the time Lewes received the letter, the boys had purchased 3,000–4,000 acres for £100 in the Wakkerstroom district of the Transvaal and had begun to try their luck at farming.

The incident of the imaginary land grant is revealing of the predicament in which many families of emigrant sons found themselves. In contrast to those whose sons "went out" in the structured environment of the army or civil service, the parents whose sons went out on their own had only the testimony of the young men themselves. Thornie did not inspire confidence. The letters detailing their attempts to build a house on their new land and to plant crops provided a record of steady decline and failure punctuated by occasional disaster. No doubt alarming to Lewes and Eliot, one letter begins "Tremendous Catastrophe! Awful Conflagration!!" and continues with Thornie's familiar mock sensationalism: "We regret to state that the magnificent mud mansion of the Messrs Lewes of the 'Fall of the Assagai' was totally consumed by fire on Saturday the 22nd June."[84] There is no information about this particular disaster, but Thornie's account overplayed the trivial and downplayed the dangerous by joking, so that it is difficult to evaluate the severity of the event he reports.

Was he exaggerating in his first letter home when he described his physical condition after walking from Natal to Pietermaritzburg: "Headache, heavy eyes, tremendous boil on each side of my neck, one on my back, sprained right arm & swollen hip (from a fall from horseback), stomach out of order and a Natal rose on my right thigh!"?[85] His condition here was the result of failing to take precautions or advice about the unfamiliar environment and climate. It was an early sign of the wretched physical condition that would force him back to England to die in 1869. His accounts of his health are disturbing but also confusing. He first thinks he has sciatica: "I lie in agony from sundown till about 3 a.m., when the pain mitigates; & I go to sleep, & worst of all feel so weak in the day that I can't do a stroke of work."[86] There was no medical treatment for Thornie on the isolated farm, and in January of 1868 he traveled to Pietermaritzburg where he discovered his misdiagnosis, only to receive another – kidney stone. He then treated himself with a "homeopathic cure" and felt "infinitely better," adding ominously that he hopes to "get back the use of my loins & legs."[87]

The same letter tells of more hardships: "Our crops unfortunately have been a failure this year, the ground is too new, & one has not the time nor implements to give land the thorough breaking up it gets in England." After some details about the particular crops they had planted and lost, he writes: "We don't consider we do so very badly so don't lose heart tho we shall not make anything by our crops, which to a farmer is hardly satisfactory." Bertie had written that "There is still war in the Free State. I am very glad Thornton did not get a farm there for we should not have been able to stop on the farm for fear of being killed by the Basutos."[88] The effects of poor health and physical hardship curtailed Thornie's enthusiasm for war: "We, the glorious Republic, are at war again . . . But don't you think we'll go. Nothing of the sort. It pays better to shoot Buffaloes than Kaffirs."[89] By 1868, both Thornie and Bertie were overwhelmed by the difficulties of subsistence farming.

In October of 1868, Thornie described a new, ill-conceived venture to trade ivory, which enticed them to leave their farm, spend their capital, and exhaust themselves in trekking, only to be duped by cannier traders. He wrote "to ask you to *lend* us £200 for one year" (*GEL*, 8:433). In this last letter, Thornie informs his parents of the debilitating illness that would eventually kill him and of which he had previously given hints: "I am gradually wasting away," he wrote: "In fact if I were 50 instead of 24, I should have quietly walked some fine day over our waterfall; but while there is youth, there is hope" (*GEL*, 8:434). He continued by requesting permission from his father to return to England to consult physicians there. Concerned about the expense, he pleads, "It is my last chance in life, and you are the only person I can apply to, so I don't hesitate to make the application" (*GEL*, 8:434). Barbara Bodichon's friend in Natal, Barbara Buchanan, remembered that when Thornie came to her family on his way to England, "we grieved to see the once stalwart fellow hardly able to move about, but he was still bright and cheerful."[90] At this time, Thornie's bravery and stoicism emerge; it was in illness rather than in battle that he confronted physical pain and impending death.

In May 1869, Thornie, financially and physically broken, arrived home to be nursed. His illness is still baffling, and the diagnosis in England was not more satisfactory than those from Natal. Doctors speculated that the cause had been a fall or that it was a glandular disease. Eliot noted that the "case seems to be rather obscure" (*GEL*, 5:45).[91] On 19 October, Thornie died. Eliot wrote that he "went to Natal on the 17th of October, 1863, and came back to us ill on the 8th of May, 1869." His death, she reflected, "seems to me the beginning of our own" (*GEL*, 5:60).

After Thornie's death, Bertie married, sold the failing farm, and attempted to support his family by "riding transport" and raising sheep. If his parents thought he was fitted for nothing else, Bertie himself never felt suited to the life that was chosen for him. He seems to have had modest ambitions and early regrets: "I often wish that I had learned some trade. A man in a colony ought to have some trade, if he has not got enough stock to live on a Farm with" (*GEL*, 9:16). The fact that his parents never considered learning a "trade" as a "fair prospect" for Bertie highlights class issues that shaped the British view of the colonies as a potential means of "pushing the fortunes" of British sons. Like Plorn Dickens, Bertie was considered a slow learner; he never aspired to the position of civil servant that Charles attained and Thornie fatefully failed to attain. Perhaps Eliot and Lewes simply did not know that carpentry or watchmaking might have been more practical skills in a colony. Such professions certainly would have been less physically demanding for Bertie, who had been sickly as a child and was thought to have an inherited glandular condition. Perhaps they had their own fantasies that the absence of mental quickness in the youngest Lewes boy would not have to mean a fall in the social standing they had worked so hard to achieve. After a lingering illness strangely like that of his brother, Bertie died alone in Durban, where he had gone to seek medical care. He would never see his second child, born to his wife Eliza shortly before his death.

Bodenheimer writes of Bertie that "the silence about him in the Lewes letters to others" and "the extreme distance with which he is mentioned in the Lewes letters" culminated in the few private reports of his death, which are "almost drained of affect."[92] The question of culpability inevitably arose for Eliot. In writing about Bertie's death to her future husband, John Cross, she concludes:

He was a sweet-natured creature – not clever, but diligent and well-judging about the things of daily life, and we felt ten years ago that a colony with a fine climate, like Natal, offered him the only fair prospect within his reach. What can we do more than try to arrive at the best conclusion from the conditions as they are known to us? (*GEL*, 6:165)

Looking back on the personal decision to send Bertie to a "fine climate," Eliot's sadly self-justifying analysis belies a larger social pattern in which the colonies served as the last resort for failures. The conditions made known to Eliot by Thornie's letters at the time Bertie emigrated included the lack of economic opportunity and the prevalence of violent conflict, but the fantastical optimism of Thornie's letters encouraged Eliot and Lewes's hopes for the "diligent and well-judging" Bertie.

The Lewes boys, particularly Thornie, epitomize a conflict between the romance that characterized representations of South Africa and the hard realities of attempting to make a living in an unfamiliar and frequently hostile environment. However much they may have differed from the sons of Dickens and Trollope, Thornie and Bertie Lewes shared with them a disappointing, even fatal experience of British colonialism. If these boys established English dominance because they lived in an overseas colony and lapsed into a racism that was endemic to colonial life, their example nonetheless complicates our retrospective understanding of the way colonialism developed. It suggests that English sons could be victims of expectations at home and that preserving class status could entail physical danger.

With the arbitrary choice of Natal, which the Leweses judged to be an inexpensive, non-competitive, temperate environment for sons of uncertain talents, they placed Thornie and Bertie in a situation that required more intelligence, skill, and endurance than they would have needed at home. Colonial South Africa also encouraged a disregard for human life that was too great for Thornie at least to resist before the sobering responsibility of making a living and living through pain overtook him.

Eliot chose not to comment in letters on the moral toll that emigration took on her stepsons and not to place her fictional characters in situations which tested this particular temptation to power. Yet much of that fiction was written during years of sending and receiving letters from South Africa and following events there in the newspapers. The final "painful experience" of watching Thornie die "entered very deeply" into Eliot (*GEL*, 5:71), remaining with her as she resumed the writing of *Middlemarch*. News of Bertie's death came as Eliot was writing *Deronda*, and the story of young men in both these novels, as Bodenheimer has suggested, may represent a rewriting of their failures, a way to redeem the loss of her exiled stepsons.

After Thornie's death, Eliot and Lewes praised his character in terms that suggest compensation for the fact that they could praise neither his talents nor his accomplishments. Eliot wrote: "Through the six months of his illness, his frank impulsive mind disclosed no trace of evil feeling. He was a sweet-natured boy – still a boy though he had lived for 25 years and a half" (*GEL*, 5:60). Lewes wrote to Blackwood that "a sweeter purer nature than his can seldom be met with; and we look back with peculiar satisfaction at the fact that never once did we discern the slightest trace in him of anything mean or unworthy" (*GEL*, 5:66). These are fit and sincere eulogies, yet they show how far the violence in the South African letters was either denied or dismissed as fanciful. Both the young men died "struggling amidst the conditions of an imperfect social state," as had Dorothea. Daily words and acts – beliefs, mistakes, accidents, choices – prepared the lives of Thornie and Bertie Lewes, sons and bad colonists who were sacrificed to no cause at all, dying not in a heroic fight for freedom, nor even for an idea of empire.

After 1863, Eliot and Lewes were bound to South Africa more profoundly than to any other part of the empire. They were continually thinking of Natal, sending money, books, and letters. They had a personal investment in the well-being of the colonial settlers there, but not enough desire to see the colony develop to actually invest their money in its various companies and projects. The first railway in Natal, from the port of Natal to Durban, was opened shortly before Thornie's arrival in 1864, initiating the expansion of the colony and altering its social make-up through the first importation of Indian "coolies." In 1860, Eliot had begun earning enough money from her writing to begin investing in the stock market. The fact that they bought no shares in the Natal railway or in the Natal Land Company, which in 1862 was offering 6 percent debentures,[93] suggests that they could dissociate the daily lives of their emigrant sons and the domestic economy that was helping to provide money for their support, just as they could dissociate Thornie's sweet nature from the violence in which he participated.

In the 1860s–1870s, Eliot and Lewes did have one notable investment in South Africa, though not in the colonies to which Thornie and Bertie emigrated (Natal and the Transvaal). These shares were in Cape Town Rail. According to the pamphlet *Railway Extension in the Colony of the Cape of Good Hope, S. Africa*, this company boasted four lines, including one direct to the Diamond Fields in Kimberley.[94] The rush for diamonds and the consolidation of the South African colonies had begun. With all the schemes – farming, tanning, trading in ivory – mentioned by the Lewes boys, they never seem to have considered going after diamonds. First discovered in 1867, diamonds made the Cape a magnet for fortune hunters and speculators. The only reference to the diamond rush that would make so many whites so rich is in a letter from Bertie to Eliot in 1870: "I have no news to tell except, that everybody is diamond mad" (*GEL*, 8:491). In 1868, Edward Clarke, the son of her sister Chrissey, wrote to his Aunt Marian from New Zealand. He tells his story of arriving in Australia in 1861, where he experienced "many hardships" and "very little success." Moving to Auckland in 1864, he found work as a journalist and made money from the gold mines: "I purchased a share in one of the old Claims for £40 – now it is worth £600" (*GEL*, 8:424). Her nephew's success in the colonies, the outcome of her earlier wish that Chrissey and her children should emigrate, must have made a painful contrast to the experiences of Thornie and Bertie.

The clues to Eliot's thinking about a colonial economy that involved the export of sons and of capital to South Africa and other spots around the globe are to be found in her journals and letters. The general associations between managing children and managing money – two forms of investing in a familial and a national future – are displayed throughout her fiction. In the next chapter, I look at the specifics of Eliot's investments as recorded in her journals, and consider the implications for her fiction of this elaborate connection to the empire.

CHAPTER 3

# Investing in empire

Political and social movements touched him only through the wire
of his rental, and his most careful biographer need not have read
up on Schleswig-Holstein, the policy of Bismarck, trade-unions,
household suffrage, or even the last commercial panic.

*Daniel Deronda* (499)

In 1860, when Eliot was wondering what to do with a son who was not
wanted at home, she had another new worry: what to do with more
money than she could spend. On September 27, she wrote in her diary
that she was expecting Thornie home from Hofwyl on his way to study
in Edinburgh, that she had recently "written a slight Tale – 'Mr. David
Faux, confectioner,'" and that she had "received from Blackwood the
first cheque (£1000) for the 'Mill on the Floss'" (*Journals*, p. 86). At this
time, as we have seen, Thornie was destined for India – and so were the
profits from *The Mill on the Floss*. After leaving Thornie in Edinburgh,
Lewes visited a stockbroker in London "who undertook to purchase
95 shares in the Great Indian Peninsular Railway for Polly," adding
that for "1825£ she gets 1900£ worth of stock guaranteed 5%."[1] Eliot
recorded that she had "invested £2000 in East Indies Stock, and expect
shortly to invest another £2000" (*Journals*, p. 87).

Eliot's choice of "East Indies" railway stock was representative of a
trend in English investing. She joined a select but growing number of
middle-class investors who took advantage of high-yield colonial stocks.
A. K. Cairncross writes that by 1870 there were "just over 50,000 English
investors holding on an average nearly £1800" in Indian Guaranteed
Railway Securities. Daniel Thorner observes that "capital which moved
from England to India" under the guaranteed interest railway contract
of 1849 "formed the largest single unit of international investment in the
nineteenth century." Ian J. Kerr confirms that "£150 million of British
capital was invested in India's nineteenth-century railways, the single
largest investment within the nineteenth-century British empire."[2] Eliot's

first shares, then, were the same as those chosen by many middle-class investors.

When the narrator of *Daniel Deronda* observes of Henleigh Grandcourt that "Political and social movements touched him only through the wire of his rental" (499), Eliot raises the implicit question of what "political and social movements" might count for the "careful biographer." In this ironic, damning portrait of the aristocratic Grandcourt, she employs a distinctively modern version of the web metaphor employed in *Middlemarch*. Not only are international events communicated via the telegraph wire, but their vibrations are felt in the national economy, connecting English incomes and lives to the greater world. Eliot's own income was touched by the wire of her investments, which she followed more closely than her complacent character. Her life and writing were continuous with and influenced by nineteenth-century economic transformations that democratized the stock market and exported increasing amounts of British capital to the colonies, contributing to an infrastructure (particularly railways) that made the later phases of imperialism possible.

The guarantee that she was to enjoy from her first purchase of shares, for example, was the product of a hard-won system negotiated by the founders of the first two Indian railways in 1849, and illustrates the vibrations felt in India through the wire of British investors. Romesh Dutt writes of the guarantee: "If there was extravagance and waste in construction, the shareholders nevertheless got their guaranteed profit on all the money that was spent, wisely or unwisely."[3] He continues: "If traffic decreased and the earnings fell short of the guaranteed rate, the difference was made good from the revenues of India, i.e. from the taxes paid by the people." P. L. Cottrell writes that by 1869 "the Indian Government had paid £15m to the railway companies under the guarantee system of 1849."[4] Not until 1879 would Eliot comment on the financial burden shouldered by India for British construction and warfare. In the aftermath of the disastrous second Afghan War, she remarked that there would be a "black day of Indian finance, which means alas a great deal of hardship to poor Hindus" (*GEL*, 7:171). In 1860 she was merely pleased to receive her "guaranteed 5%" on profits from *The Mill on the Floss*.

As shown in chapter 1, Eliot came to know the British colonies through published accounts about which she was skeptical. Her distrust of unverifiable information in colonial travel writing together with her disdain for inaccurate, unrealistic fiction contributed to the initial formulation of her realist aesthetic. In chapter 2, we saw that Thornie and Bertie's letters brought Eliot an intimate awareness of conditions in South Africa, but that their accounts were infused with romantic discourses that obscured the reality of their colonial life. The difficulty of seeing the situation in South Africa contributed to Eliot's self-consciousness about the distinction between the real and the imagined – particularly the susceptibility of the English at home to myths about the colonies. The slippage between the real and the imagined became a theme in her fiction. This further connection to the empire – the investments which made her domestic security dependent on colonial expansion – is also important to our understanding of the context in which she wrote. Writing, money, children, and empire were inextricably associated in Eliot's life and fiction.

In the first part of this chapter, I argue that the circumstances leading to Eliot's recognition of herself as a wealthy woman and a colonial shareholder generated an anxiety about money and children that was distinctive to her fiction of the early 1860s. The complexity of her representations of Victorian finance increased in proportion to her involvement in the stock market. A mentality of measuring human value as an investment is represented in *The Mill on the Floss* when Tom Tulliver's education is called "an investment" – which will be "so much capital to him" (71). Tom makes successful speculations in trade, but the danger to widows and children of unscrupulous speculators is reiterated throughout Eliot's later works. Reflecting on the gambler Lapidoth in *Daniel Deronda*, the narrator comments wryly that "the liberty a man allows himself with other people's property" is "often delicately drawn . . . which is the reason why spoons are a safer investment than mining shares" (676). In *Impressions of Theophrastus Such*, Sir Gavial Mantrap's defrauding of investors in the "Eocene Mines" and "other companies ingeniously devised by him for the punishment of ignorance in people of small means" (129) is one of many examples showing that the culture of empire generated a "proprietor's anxiety" about both money and children that was familiar to Eliot's readers.

In the second part of the chapter, I examine Eliot's financial investments, specifically in India, to show the extent of her involvement and that of other middle-class shareholders in the public domains of investment capitalism and economic imperialism. I argue that she represented the nation to itself by recasting the colonial periphery in a domestic setting. Even as she invested in the extension of the empire, her fiction invests in the consolidation of Englishness within the bounds of England.

SONS AND MONEY

Eliot's fiction in the 1860s, like her diaries, exhibits a confluence of concerns about sons, money, and writing. "Mr David Faux," published in 1864 as "Brother Jacob," is the story of a young confectioner who steals his mother's guineas and heads for Jamaica. The day that Eliot recorded the financial milestone of her first Indian investments in her diary also marked a creative departure. She noted that she was "engaged now in writing a story . . . It is 'Silas Marner, the weaver of Raveloe.'" *Silas Marner* offers a version of the "Brother Jacob" plot when Dunstan Cass steals the miser's gold and disappears as completely as if he had gone to Jamaica. Rewriting David's story in *Silas Marner*, Eliot turns the loss of Silas's gold into the occasion for his coming to understand the value of human bonds, particularly those between parents and children. "Brother Jacob" and *Silas Marner* also offer metaphors of literary production – confectionery and weaving – that imply an ambivalent nostalgia for an era in which the economy was simpler than that in which Eliot was becoming involved. Both stories transform into a parable the moral issues that she was facing concerning the payment of money for work done, as well as the obligations of children to parents and of parents to children.

Just as she insisted on the morality of her "marriage" to counter the scandal of her adultery, Eliot insisted on her role as a responsible parent to justify her interest in the matter of payment for her work. She told John Blackwood on November 30, 1859, that because she was "in a position of anxiety for others as well as myself," it was her duty to "seek no less than the highest reasonable advantage from my work" (*GEL*, 3:219). True, she was a mother, or at least a stepmother, with a new obligation to children who were not her own, but she was far from the "destitute women" she had described in "Silly Novels by Lady Novelists" (1856), who "turned novelists, as they turned governesses" (Pinney, p. 303). She had moved into the very class of wealthy women whom she had mocked and criticized for thinking "five hundred a-year a miserable pittance" (Pinney, p. 303).

Not long after she wrote this essay she began earning an income that would make five hundred a year seem a miserable pittance to her. Her 1861 diary begins with a summary of literary earnings for 1860, adding up to £8,330 (*Journals*, p. 88). But of course literary income was unreliable and through her investments she sought to combine the independence of a single woman with the security of marriage. She played the role of mother to her business advantage by insisting that she needed money to help others. Yet she traded maternal for economic responsibilities when she subsidized the emigration of her stepsons. Her anxieties about becoming a wealthy investor and about displacing her assumed duty to parent Lewes's sons onto the obligation to finance their exile were peculiar to the early 1860s and are evident in her fiction of this period.

Beginning with *The Mill on the Floss*, but particularly in "Brother Jacob" and *Silas Marner*, a set of moral issues about how money is earned and how people are valued became central in her writing as she worked out her new position as a wealthy woman and mother. But the economic changes reflected in her fiction were not merely personal. They also represent the new possibilities of capitalism and colonialism that were altering the lives of her contemporaries, as well as her own. "Brother Jacob" and *Silas Marner* expose the corrupting power of money in its most literal, material form – gold – precisely when Eliot was learning about the stock market, which epitomized the complexity and abstract nature of modern finance. Eliot's new role of adoptive parent, like her new role as wealthy shareholder, brought her into contact with aspects of her culture – the civil service bureaucracy, emigration protocol, stockbrokers, and joint-stock companies – that had been obscure to her when she had no sons and no wealth about which to worry.

In the late 1850s, before she began earning enough money to transform her social position, essays such as "The Natural History of German Life" established her belief that an extension of urban middle-class sympathies to the unfamiliar world of rural England was needed in fiction. To correct prejudices about the ways of common English life, she sought to represent that life as realistically as possible. She relocated the theatre of her readers' imaginations in England. Yet her contribution to the expansion of the empire through her support for emigration and investment affected the way she conceived of the England about which she wrote.

By asking in *The Mill on the Floss*, "what grove of tropic palms, what strange ferns or splendid broad-petalled blossoms, could ever thrill such deep and delicate fibres within me as this home-scene?" (41), Eliot probed the relationship between the home "scene" and individual identity: we may be fascinated by foreign landscapes, but we do not feel about them as we do about our home. Elizabeth Helsinger argues that by contrasting "familiar England and her 'strange' imperial and colonial periphery" Eliot's novels "complicate the fiction of a single nation with a continuous history that those novels mean to help to create."[5] Taking up this figure of colonial difference, Theophrastus explains the principle of understanding the "queer" and "absurd" in others by "looking for something of the same type in myself" (104).

In "How We Come to Give Ourselves False Testimonials, and Believe in Them," he observes that "men's minds differ in what we may call their climate or share of solar energy":

[S]ome are like a tropical habitat in which the very ferns cast a mighty shadow, and the grasses are a dry ocean in which a hunter may be submerged . . . Still, whether fate commanded us to thatch our persons among the Eskimos or to choose the latest thing in tattooing among the Polynesian isles, our precious guide Comparison would teach us in the first place by likeness, and our clue to further knowledge would be resemblance to what we already know. (104)

Elaborating this insistence on knowing the foreign by knowing ourselves, Theophrastus goes on in the "Modern Hep! Hep! Hep!" to show that the English will only understand the Jewish culture by recognizing its sameness to English culture. This sentiment enables us to understand that aspect of Eliot's fiction that seeks to represent what Helsinger calls "the fiction of a single nation." Colonial otherness is compressed into her representation of the English past because it is a part of what makes the English past distinctive.

Eliot's descriptions of the migrations within England by which characters such as David Faux and Silas Marner attempt to escape their past – that make Lydgate a "new settler" (116) in Middlemarch and place Gwendolen's family in the "border-territory of rank" (17) – borrow the language of colonialism. In *Impressions of Theophrastus Such*, Theophrastus describes himself as an internal emigrant, a citizen of the "Nation of London," who sustains himself through memories of his Midlands home (26). English emigrants to the colonies were a dispersed people, like the "patriarchal Aryans," whose "exodus" and status as "voluntary exiles" (27) unify English and Jewish history. This language reflects a perceived connection between emigration to the colonies and internal migrations, such as her own from the Midlands to London, and was supported by a discourse describing the inhabitants of the English countryside as antiquated or anachronistic. As Gillian Beer writes of both Victorian travel writing and domestic fiction: "Remote tribes and, sometimes, country people, were believed to represent intact much earlier phases in the cultural development of humankind."[6] Eliot articulated the parallel between internal and external migration most explicitly in *Impressions*, but the colonial context is crucial to understanding her representations of internal migrations throughout her novels.

"Brother Jacob" and *Silas Marner* are nostalgic tales in which the materiality of gold reduces the opposition between monetary and moral worth to its most basic form. The closest her work ever came to fable, these two stories moralize about the fetishization of money in an uncharacteristically direct fashion. When considered in conjunction with the role she was fashioning for herself as an author who was not writing for money but needed to earn as much money as possible to support her dependents, these works appear consistent with the self-justifying tone of her letters. It is not surprising, then, that they exhibit so much hostility toward ungrateful sons, like David Faux and Dunstan Cass. This hostility culminated in the ungrateful foster son Tito in *Romola*, the work she had begun to conceptualize before she started work on *Silas Marner*. When Thornie and Bertie left for South Africa, they became exiled sons living on the colonial periphery. Thereafter, Eliot's novels represented situations in which sons found reasons to return or to remain at home: Felix Holt, Harold Transome, Fred Vincy, Will Ladislaw, and Rex Gascoigne are all examples of sons who overcome temptations to leave through the discovery of their place in England.

In *The Mill on the Floss*, Eliot concentrated for the first time on the commercial middle classes. Their economic troubles, in contrast to those of Amos and Milly Barton, for example, are connected to matters of finance as opposed to mere poverty. As part of her argument that Eliot's early novels "universalize the British middle class," Margaret Homans observes that the decline of Dorlcote Mill and rise of Guest and Co. "mark the passing of an apparently timeless, pre-industrial social formation, a distant precursor of the Victorian middle class, and its replacement by a newer middle class that would have been more recognizable to Eliot's contemporaries."[7] Looking back at a time when the exchange of money and its attendant moral obligations were less complicated than they seemed to be later, Eliot's narrator observes that the Tullivers' "narrow notions about debt . . . may perhaps excite a smile on the faces of many readers in these days of wide commercial views and wide philosophy," because now "the fact that my tradesman is out of pocket by me, is to be looked at through the serene certainty that somebody else's tradesman is in pocket by somebody else" (279).

Even with the emergence of Guest and Co., when there was "growing capital, and growing outlets for it," as Mr. Deane tells Tom, what really matters are the "men of the right habits" – "So it will always be, sir" (397). But it would not always be. From the narrator's historical perspective, "illuminating doubts" about integrity and honor have been introduced into modern thinking by a theoretical view that devalues face-to-face transactions. Readers "in these days" (*circa* 1860) hold the "wide philosophy" that their actions are part of a larger economy for which they have no individual responsibility; consequently, individual hardships ("that my tradesman is out of pocket") are depersonalized. Eliot had referred previously to such economic theories, possibly those of Adam Smith and David Ricardo. In "The Natural History of German Life," she disparaged the belief "that all social questions are merged in economical science, and that the relations of men to their neighbours may be settled by algebraic equations" as being untenable to anyone with "a real knowledge of the People" (Pinney, p. 272). That honor should be a question in the paying of a debt is seen as quaint because in a laissez-faire economy everything "rights itself" – an easy justification for dishonorable behavior.

Yet this apparent nostalgia for a simpler time is tinged with irony. The narrator of *The Mill* can expose the "present" view as less humane than the earlier understanding of economic exchange, but the novel as a whole shows the Tulliver code of honor to be obsolete. The Tullivers' "debt," as Neil Hertz has argued, is both literal and metaphoric. Attachments to place provide Eliot's characters "with an inexhaustible fund of emotional capital" and "lay on them an ineradicable debt."[8] So while Tom is engaging in the modern activity of investing – "the prospect of a speculation that might change the slow process of addition into multiplication" (311) – he is still bound by a primitive oath of revenge sworn on the family bible.

The writing of *The Mill* was itself the payment of personal debt, a memorial to a past, a place, and a self Eliot had left behind. With its completion, she freed herself of obligation to most of her blood relatives. Her next two works, "Brother Jacob" and *Silas Marner*, reflect obsessions with money rather than debts of honor, with the breaking of familial bonds and the erasure of the past. Eliot's life at this time suggests that obligations of blood might be transferred to adoptive kinship and measured in money. Her primary debts by 1860 were to people whose claims on her were not those of land, memories, or blood; they were rather voluntary bonds to Lewes, to his sons, and even to his wife Agnes and her children. Lewes's debts became her debts, and she accepted them as part of their relationship. Blood brothers in her fiction, like Jacob and Dunsie, become intolerable burdens, while the freely chosen relationship between Silas and Eppie is irreproachable and redemptive.

The plots of both stories are initiated by the theft of gold coins hidden in private spaces. David takes the guineas kept by his mother "in the corner of a drawer where her baby-linen had reposed for the last twenty years" (231). He digs a hole in order to bury the money but is prevented from doing so by his "idiot" brother Jacob and is forced by his guilt to flee. Silas is accused of stealing a bag of church money that had lain "in the bureau by the departed deacon's bedside" (10). He did not steal the money, but rather was framed by William Dane, "with whom he had long lived in such close friendship that it was the custom of their Lantern Yard brethren to call them David and Jonathan" (8). The metaphoric configuring of this small dissenting community as a family and the men within it as "brethren" makes Silas and Dane into brothers, like David, Jacob, and Jonathan Faux, or Dunstan and Godfrey Cass. Dane marries Silas's fiancée, and the betrayal leads Silas to worship the money he subsequently hides in the hole beneath his cottage floor and from which it is stolen by Dunstan Cass – a repetition and realization of the original theft falsely attributed to Silas. Just as the bad brother has two identities in "Brother Jacob" (Faux and Freely), so he has two incarnations in *Silas Marner*, William Dane and Dunsey Cass, betrayers and thieves.

"Brother Jacob" and *Silas Marner* share a distinctive preoccupation with inside/outside dichotomies and the crossing of geographic and temporal boundaries, as well as with the related issues of labor and capital. Both have vague historical and geographic settings, which seem to epitomize rural England in the early part of the century. Each has an experimental but simple structure in which geographic exile spatializes the temporal division between past and present: both David and Silas leave their past identities behind when they migrate, David from his hometown to Grimworth and Silas from Lantern Yard to Raveloe. In *Impressions*, Theophrastus recalls his youth in the rural Midlands and his rides to "outlying hamlets, whose groups of inhabitants were as distinctive to my imagination as if they had belonged to different regions of the globe" (21). Likewise, in Eliot's novels, the distinction between domestic and foreign becomes internal to England, with the migrations from one part of the Midlands to another representing a cultural change as momentous as that between England and the "Indies." In the famous stagecoach ride that introduces *Felix Holt*, in which English geographical and temporal transformations are compressed, the narrator observes of the English shepherd that "his solar system was the parish; the master's temper and the casualties of lambing-time were his region of storms" (4).

In "Brother Jacob," Eliot refuses to represent Jamaica and reflects on the moral implications of deliberate misrepresentation. "Brother Jacob" explores the strains on credulity invited by the travel of Englishmen to places their neighbors at home have never seen. The story artfully integrates the theme of England's trade in West Indian sugar with a critique of fantastic and ignorant assumptions about "the Indies." David Faux the confectioner is already dependent on the steady supply of sugar at home when he imagines that in the "Indies," "a gullible princess awaited him" and "people would make him presents freely" (241). After six years of disappointing experience in Jamaica – represented by a gap in the narrative, the space between chapters – Faux returns to England with the new name Edward Freely and a fraudulent claim to "expectations" of a West Indian fortune that trades on the appetite for the exotic in his new home of Grimworth.[9]

Silas Marner is one of many "emigrant[s] from the town into the country" and an "alien" (4) who is "transported to a new land" (14). This migration from town to country reverses the pattern of movement in nineteenth-century England and represents an anachronistic movement back in time. Silas is out of sync, like David Faux, who seeks his fortune in the decaying colonial economies of the West Indies, rather than in, for example, the more promising opportunities of America.[10] Eliot invokes the psychology of a distant past to describe the townspeople of Raveloe:

[E]ven a settler, if he came from distant parts, hardly ever ceased to be viewed with a remnant of distrust, which would have prevented any surprise if a long course of inoffensive conduct on his part had ended in the commission of a crime; especially if he had any reputation for knowledge, or showed any skill in handicraft. (3)

Silas the weaver (with his "protuberant eyes" and "pale face") and Faux the confectioner (who has a "sallow complexion" and is "pale-faced") provoke the suspicion of their neighbors. Marner is protected from persecution because of the "vague fear" that he has knowledge of witchcraft. With a sideways glance at Brother Jacob, the idiot brother, he is likened to the "Wise Woman at Tarley," who had the power to prevent the birth of idiot children (17). And Faux/Freely is suspected on the grounds that he is "uncommonly knowing." "Dreadful suspicions" gathered round his green eyes, while his bow-legs had "a criminal aspect" (268). In contrast to Maggie Tulliver, suspicious because of her darkness, Faux and Marner are paler than their new neighbors, displaying physical signs of difference – a whiteness that suggests weakness and depravity rather than the superiority and power it would signify in a colonial context.

The tissues of superstition and ignorance that cloud the vision of both the Grimworth and the Raveloe townsfolk recall the ignorance of which Eliot's essays complained: "How little the real characteristics of the working-classes are known to those who are outside them" (Pinney, p. 268), and this because the "painter is still under the influence of idyllic literature, which has always expressed the imagination of the cultivated and town-bred, rather than the truth of rustic life" (Pinney, p. 269). "Brother Jacob" thematizes a similar principle – unrealistic representation that feeds ignorance – but in this case it is the working or peasant classes that are ignorant of colonial life. The story cautions against the storyteller's power to deceive but shows as well the complicity of the listeners in their own deception.

In the interweaving of writing, money, and empire, "Brother Jacob" implicitly connects linguistic and monetary systems of representation. David Faux fools others, and his story comments directly on the morality of financial dealings and indirectly on the morality of realism. The narrator observes:

> David's devices for getting rich without work had apparently no direct relation with the world outside him, as his confectionery receipts had. It is possible to pass a great many bad halfpennies and bad half-crowns, but I believe there has no instance been known of passing a halfpenny or a half-crown as a sovereign. A sharper can drive a brisk trade in this world: it is undeniable that there may be a fine career for him, if he will dare consequences: but David was too timid to be a sharper, or venture in any way among the mantraps of the law. He dared rob nobody but his mother. And so he had to fall back on the genuine value there was in him – to be content to pass as a good halfpenny, or, to speak more accurately, as a good confectioner. (257–8)

Considering the moment at which it was written, it is reasonable to see "Brother Jacob" as a manifestation of Eliot's ambivalence about making money in ways other than directly from genuine work – that is, from investments. Catherine Gallagher writes that in the theories of nineteenth-century laissez-faire economists, a "marketplace not directly bound to production, the value of a commodity wildly incommensurate with the value of the labor embodied in the commodity, is almost universally regarded as a bad thing."[11] Gallagher has in mind the hostility towards groups that represent a realm of exchange divorced from production, primarily prostitutes and Jewish usurers, two figures also "ubiquitous in nineteenth-century writing about authorship."[12] In the simplified economy of "Brother Jacob," getting rich without work would involve stealing (what David does to get to Jamaica) or blackmailing (what he does there), but in a more complex economy it would certainly include that sophisticated form of gambling – speculation on the stock market. Because he is too timid to take real risks, David inadvertently relies on honest labor, even if that labor produces a product (confections) of dubious social value. The monetary metaphor becomes personal when we realize that David fails in his attempt to pass a halfpenny (David Faux) as a sovereign (Edward Freely, heir to a West Indian fortune).

*Silas Marner* differs from the more cynical "Brother Jacob" in its presentation of a moral that would persist in Eliot's fiction: money is not an end in itself; there is a higher good that humans can attain – a good illustrated through the renunciation of money. The concern expressed in *Silas Marner* about the fetishization of money initiates what would become a pattern in Eliot's fiction after 1861. Loss has to be suffered before the appreciation of the greater value – the "love and tenderness" which, as she wrote in 1860, transcend "more material vulgar matters," such as money (*GEL*, 3:360). This higher good will come to be appreciated by Eliot's female characters: Romola, Esther, Fedalma, Dorothea, and even Gwendolen. At the same time, restitution always comes for those whose material property has been taken, and there is a price, monetary or moral, to pay for those who take what does not belong to them.

The moral of the miser tells against saving and hoarding as much as against fetishism. Silas is wayward in his love of gold for itself, but he is also guilty of letting his money sit idly, of removing it from circulation and from the local and national economies. The narrator tells us that "the love of accumulating money grows an absorbing passion in men whose imaginations, even in the very beginning of their hoard, showed them no purpose beyond it" (18). Investing (i.e. not hoarding) is also a habit, and when we consider that this passage was written in a climate of increasing middle-class investment, and within a year of Eliot's investing for the first time at least £2,000 of her own earnings, we can see that *Silas Marner* is a transitional text in the story of how she began to perceive the moral relationship between people and their money. Money must be given up, or at least fiction must teach the relative value of love to money by showing money's renunciation.

Such a moral lesson was familiar in Victorian fiction. Dickens's *Our Mutual Friend* (1863–5) famously derided the "traffic in shares": "Have no antecedents, no established character, no cultivation, no ideas, no manners; have Shares."[13] Mary Poovey reads the novel in relation to developments in the economic sphere of English society in the 1860s. She writes that after his fourteen years in the Cape Colony, John Harmon turns Bella into an investment. His plot is "specifically formulated as a speculation intended to convert Bella's lust for literal wealth into an appreciation of more emotionally substantive gratification, the 'true golden gold' of domestic affection."[14] Thus, like many of Eliot's plots, *Our Mutual Friend* works to "exchange the false currency of literal money for the 'true,' metaphorical coin of love." Such a romantic moral lesson was of course far from the reality of either author's life, but the discomfort Eliot felt in betraying that she might be writing fiction for money (rather than for the true golden coin of artistic accomplishment) is evident in her protestations to Blackwood.

Christina Crosby observes that the "impossibility of distinguishing with certainty between legitimate trade (in which wealth is derived from the making and exchange of useful goods) and the vice of speculation (devoted to nothing but money) haunted nineteenth-century writers, especially after the Joint Stock Companies Act of 1856."[15] This legislation opened up the stock market to less wealthy investors, and in so doing presented more temptations for both the gulls and the sharps. With general limited liability came the "era of modern investment" from which Eliot began to profit in 1860. And the Companies Act of 1862 followed. Less risk meant the establishment of more joint-stock companies and the rise of small investors and investment bankers to serve them. Swindles and dramatic bankruptcies are treated in Gaskell's *Cranford* (1851–3) and *Ruth* (1853), Thackeray's *The Newcomes* (1853–5), Dickens's *Little Dorrit* (1855–7), and Trollope's *The Way We Live Now* (1875) and *The Prime Minister* (1876), as well as in numerous minor novels by authors such as Margaret Oliphant and Mrs. J. H. Riddell.[16]

By setting her fiction (with the exception of *Deronda* and *Impressions*) in the early nineteenth century, Eliot avoided some of the complications of late nineteenth-century economic realities. She evaded the moral issues attending her own reliance on a system by which money generated money ("getting rich without work") and in which the value of stocks and shares differed from the "genuine value" of her own labor. The distinction was perhaps troubling for novelists in the same sense that the difference between fiction and lying had to be glossed by giving fiction a moral aim. One of the tasks of realist fiction was to identify the corruption of the economic system. Whereas the social-climbing Lady Monogram of Trollope's *The Way We Live Now* "had but a confused idea of any difference between commerce and fraud," Trollope certainly thought he knew the difference between sensible investing and irresponsible speculation.[17]

With the lines drawn between past and present economies and between gambling/speculating and investing, we might ask whether or how Eliot and her contemporaries evaluated the companies in which they invested. Were the two extremes of loving money for itself (and hoarding it like Silas) and speculating for the thrill of the game, which provokes Deronda's moral objection to making our gain from "another's loss" (284), the only abuses of money that required censure? One thing we can determine from looking more closely at Eliot's low-risk investments is that they were not exempt from the moral transgression of gaining from an "other's" loss, but that the loss was not direct, as it was to the British widows and children ruined by speculators.

Responsibility for the human cost of capitalist gain was not individual; it was dispersed among a nation of investors, and the relationship between British investors and Indian laborers, for example, was easily obscured by the investor's abstract way of thinking about where her money went or how her dividends were produced. Crosby claims that by the 1820s the "long process of the dematerialization of money" had begun, and that proliferating forms of credit "steadily erode[d] the significance of face-to-face, interpersonal credibility."[18] By the 1870s, however, the changes by which Eliot characterized her own generation in *The Mill on the Floss* had become entrenched: confidence in bankers as paternal figures, personally responsible for the well-being of their customers, faded with the professionalization that distinguished the second half of the nineteenth century. In "Brother Jacob," economic fraudulence and misrepresentations of the colonies are explicitly associated. For Eliot, as for Trollope and other authors, the cultural challenges of negotiating credit capitalism and colonial representations increased the moral value of realist fiction. As she wrote in *Adam Bede*, "Falsehood is so easy, truth so difficult" (176).

With so many members of Victorian families living in colonies and such a significant portion of the nation's wealth invested in colonial projects, the need for accurate representation to those at home became particularly urgent. Eliot's investments tied her to the national and colonial economies in ways that raise new questions about the individual and collective responsibilities to colonists and colonized people. Eliot lent her money to companies undertaking colonial projects and reduced those companies to the domestic "familiars" of stock certificates and to her own "incipient habit" of receiving quarterly checks. To understand the domestication of the foreign in her representations of England we need to explore the specifics of her economic dependence on the colonies, which has been suppressed in the tradition of biography and criticism, resulting in an incomplete picture of the biographical and cultural context of her fiction.

## GEORGE ELIOT AS SHAREHOLDER

The seventh volume of Gordon Haight's *The George Eliot Letters* (1955) includes two appendixes: "GE's Literary Earnings, Extracts from Journal" and "GHL's Literary Receipts." The latter was taken from Lewes's book of "Personal Expenses," but Haight omits the first nine pages, in which appear "a list of stocks and bonds in GHL's hand" (*GEL*, 7:365). What editorial principle led Haight to publish the record of every penny earned by Eliot and Lewes from their published works, but to exclude any sign of the work that money did for them when it was invested in the stock market? Why is it more interesting, for example, that Eliot earned £200 for the Australian reprint of *Middlemarch* in 1872, than that she earned just over £100 on bonds and debentures in New South Wales and Victoria in the same year?[19] Perhaps because the means of acquisition were not literary, such profits were irrelevant to a literary biography. Whatever the reason, the result is that Eliot appears less interested in her investments than she actually was.

Developments in the study of literary and cultural history since 1955 have made apparent the ways in which even those cultural texts and artifacts that are not strictly literary can have relevance for literary and biographical interpretations. Eliot received £50 for the German reprint of *The Spanish Gypsy* in 1872, but she earned more, £232.28.6, from "Berlin W.W." (Water Works) in the same year. Her income from publications is relevant to our knowledge of the nineteenth-century literary marketplace and to the economic value of the author's labor – the value to which Trollope famously reduced literary production in *An Autobiography* (1883). But Victorian authors, like other professionals, increased their income from their writing and became wealthy as a consequence of their investments in the domestic and colonial companies, projects, governments, and banks that comprised an important stratum of the world they represented in their fiction.

Yet the records of Eliot's investments are still neglected. They were not considered significant enough for inclusion in *The Journals of George Eliot*.[20] Editors Margaret Harris and Judith Johnston argue that "the journals form a substantial addition to the canon of George Eliot's work" (*Journals*, p. xvii) and that the "publication of the journals entire restores George Eliot as the speaking subject" (*Journals*, p. xxv). Their edition, however, does not present the journals entire. After Lewes's death on November 30, 1878, Eliot assumed the task of keeping her accounts. After she had passed through her intensive period of mourning Lewes's

3. Manuscript page from G. H. Lewes's diary for 1872, Beinecke Rare Book and Manuscript Library, Yale University.

death and had revised both his *Problems of Life and Mind* (vols. IV and V) and the proofs of her last book, *Impressions*, her money became the focus of her attention. Along with her letters and diaries, her financial accounts constitute the corpus of her writing during this period. Her duties and responsibilities to servants, bankers, relatives, charities, and to the entity she designated "self," are reflected in these entries. Harris and Johnston concede that while "information about her investment income and various expenditures has a certain interest, these extensive financial memoranda have not been reproduced in the text of this journal, nor have shorter records of dividend income and the like been annotated" (*Journals*, p. 149). Without the lists of stocks and investment receipts, we are unable to see Eliot's extensive holdings, the value she attached to them and the attention she gave them. Furthermore, by not annotating the dividend income that is reproduced in the daily entries, the editors imply that the names and numbers speak for themselves, when in fact these references are mysterious to modern readers and need to be deciphered.

Overall, the effect of omitting some and failing to identify other dividend income is to obscure Eliot's activities as a shareholder. These activities were important to Eliot and are important to us as a means of reconstructing the public and private manifestations of the Victorian culture of investing in which she took part. Eliot's financial records provide insights into her priorities, decisions, and actions. It is impossible to consider Eliot – the author and woman – "in context" without uncovering these private and hitherto effaced traces of her ties to international and colonial economies. They show, among other things, her determination to manage her grief by taking on her own business affairs. Like Silas Marner, she discovers the consoling power of counting her money, or rather of adding up numbers – the representation of her capital – perhaps made less abstract by their placement next to the names of cities, countries, and colonies of which she had some knowledge. And like Silas's counting, hers is private, relegated to personal diaries, which are also repositories of intense emotional suffering, primarily in the words of other poets.

Eliot's diaries during the last two years of her life are remarkable for the coexistence and juxtaposition of words and numbers on their pages. Each number, like each of the names punctuating her daily entries, constitutes an autobiographical fragment with a context and a story waiting to be revealed. For example, the 1879 diary begins with a note about South Africa, "Direct Packet to Natal, 6th of each month."[21] This reminder to send money to Bertie's widow, Eliza, is followed by several business addresses – including "Colonial Bank" and "Sambre et Meuse Railway" – and then by a line of poetry that might serve as a "motto" for the entire diary: "Here I and Sorrow sit," from Shakespeare's *King John*. Before beginning the daily record, Eliot copied additional epigraphs on the theme of sorrow from Heine, Shelley, and Goethe. Her early entries, interspersed with more poetry, include: "Cheque from East India Railway" (January 2); "Cheque from Continental Gas Co." (January 4); "sent Colonial and Sambre et Meuse to the Bank" (January 14).[22] At the end of the year, shortly after the first anniversary of Lewes's death, she copies a complete poem from Emily Brontë ("Remembrance"), an apt and painful poem of loss, which includes the stanza:

> No later light has lightened up my heaven
> No second morn has ever shone for me;
> All my life's bliss from thy dear life was given
> All my life's bliss is in the grave with thee. (*Journals*, p. 188)

Eliot's sorrow found expression in the words of other poets rather than in her own. Soon afterward her diary resumes its mundane entries of guests entertained and business transacted, for example: "Gas Light & Coke shares sold £1200 for 2260" (December 17–22). While there is something anti-poetic about the juxtaposition of Brontë's "No later light" and the sale of "Gas Light & Coke," these apparent incongruities constitute the value of the journals as a register of despair, counterbalanced by calm and business-like proceedings.

The numbers in her diaries, like the frequently cryptic words – "mental conflict" (March 28), "inward struggles" (April 3), "mental crisis" (April 7) – signify the numerous ways in which Lewes's death transformed her life. In 1878, she was legally still a "spinster." From the time she began to live with Lewes in 1854, she chose to call herself "Mrs. Lewes" and to act as if she were married. With the publication of her first works of fiction in 1857, she began to out-earn her "husband" (one of the facts we can see from Haight's presentation of their literary receipts), though to disguise her authorial identity her money was placed in his bank account. Later, in affirmation of the marriage fiction, the stocks were also held in his name. Lewes's will, which he made in 1859, left his estate to "Mary Ann Evans of Holly Lodge South Fields aforesaid Spinster." The will was proved on December 16, 1878, by "Mary Anne Evans Spinster his sole executrix."[23] For all their careful planning and Lewes's ill health, the will did not provide for the transfer of Eliot's money from his possession to hers. After his death, Eliot could access her own money and take possession of her own stock holdings only by changing her name to Marian Lewes. Thus she accomplished by the impersonal "deed poll" what she never could through marriage. As part of the case, she made notes of Lewes's earnings from 1855 until his death: "I make these memoranda to show that the property extant is far below the results of my work, and is therefore justly to be pronounced as placed out in trust for me." She recorded that by the beginning of 1873, the interest on money invested from her earnings was £1,500 (*GEL*, 7:383).

Eliot's investments in colonial as well as foreign and domestic stocks produced income that played a crucial part in the circulation of colonial interests throughout her personal and professional life. The income from her published work was invested in colonial ventures; the income generated from these investments facilitated Thornie and Bertie Lewes's emigration to South Africa. Bertie's widow Eliza and her children, when they came to England from South Africa, were supported by Eliot, and after her death they inherited substantial trust legacies. In her will, Eliot wrote that £12,500 should be invested "in or upon any of the Public stocks or funds or Government securities of the united Kingdom or in or upon any stock or securities of the Government of India or in the stock of the Bank of England" in trust, with the income to be paid to Eliza and to her children when they came of age.[24] At the time of her death, these stocks included shares in Cape Town Rail – Eliot's own contribution to the process of developing South Africa, in which Eliza's family, as well as the Lewes boys, participated.

As I have noted, in purchasing shares in Indian railroads, Eliot became typical of middle-class investors at mid-century. And she was not alone among her author contemporaries in taking advantage of the monetary gains offered by colonial railroads, land development, and banking. Trollope held colonial shares, including some in the Standard Bank of South Africa, and Dickens "invest[ed] throughout his career in steady Government, Russian, and Indian stock, railway paper and property."[25] Lewes had been involved in the earlier "railway mania," recording income in 1845 of £150 from "Railway Shares" (*GEL*, 7:367). The Brontës, too, had caught railway fever. In 1845 Charlotte Brontë wrote to Margaret Wooler:

Emily has made herself mistress of the necessary degree of knowledge for conducting the matter, by dint of carefully reading every paragraph & every advertisement in the news-papers that related to rail-roads and as we have abstained from all gambling, all 'mere' speculative buying-in & selling-out – we have got on very decently.[26]

Brontë makes the typical moral distinction between careful investment and speculative gambling. Yet her shares in the York and North Midland Railway, following the crisis of 1847, had by 1849 become "virtually worthless."[27] She was subsequently advised by George Smith to place her money in the Funds "where it would earn an unspectacular but safe dividend."[28]

The examples of Eliot and the Brontës raise questions about the largely neglected historical question of what role women played in the expanding nineteenth-century stock market. In a section of her 1854 pamphlet *Laws Concerning Women* entitled "Legal Condition of Unmarried Women or Spinsters," Eliot's closest female friend, Barbara Bodichon, wrote:

Women are occasionally governors of prisons for women, overseers of the poor, and parish clerks. A woman may be ranger of a park; a woman can take part in the government of a great empire by buying East India Stock.[29]

Bodichon's illustrations are intended to show the ways in which a woman might acquire some legal authority despite those laws dispossessing her of her money and prohibiting her from participating in a representative government. Since 1848 she had held a portfolio of stocks and shares given to her by her father, Benjamin Leigh Smith, which "yielded between £250 and £300 a year according to the market."[30]

Her comments touch upon the provocative issue of how much political power investments gave to the middle classes and especially to women. She assumes that by owning stock in the East India Company a woman's power to affect Indian politics was as direct as it was when she took domestic authority within prisons or institutions overseeing the poor. According to James Mill, to have any share in the power of the East India Company's Court of Proprietors it was necessary to be the owner of "500*l*. of the Company's stock."[31] In 1852, half of the 1,765 voters were women. The motives and powers of East India Company shareholders changed throughout the nineteenth century. Sometimes shareholders' interests were an impediment to reformers, such as Thomas Malthus and Thomas Macaulay, who hoped to reform the administration of India. Timothy Alborn has examined the way the board of proprietors used their power to effect change and struggled against the use of that power for patronage. He writes that while "Malthus had been able to count on support from middle-class radical shareholders who had bought stock in order to vote against the Company's monopoly," Macaulay faced a "proprietary for whom the sole motive for buying shares was now the prospect of patronage."[32]

In 1854, Bodichon argued that if a woman's investments were profitable, she would have some financial power at home as well as overseas. For Bodichon, who lived part of every year in French colonial Algiers with her husband, Dr. Eugene Bodichon, women's financial autonomy and the empire were interrelated. As suggested by her involvement with Maria Rye's Female Middle Class Emigration Society in 1861 and by her articles in the *English Woman's Journal*, she wished to facilitate the emigration of educated middle-class women to the colonies, where she believed they would have opportunities for employment and independence unavailable to them at home. Her observations about investing in the East India Company reveal her belief that the empire could provide an unmarried middle-class woman at home with an independent income and a role in the management of Indian men and women – the very privileges enjoyed by women who emigrated to the colonies.[33] Investing and emigrating were two separate but related forms of gaining from the empire, comprising Eliot's double interest in the economic advancement of emigrants and dividends from shares in colonial companies.

In addition to the Great Indian Peninsular and Madras Railways, Eliot owned stocks and bonds in Australia, Africa, Canada, and South America. These include: New South Wales, Victoria, Cape Town Rail, Colonial Bank, Oriental Bank, Melbourne and Hobson's Bay, Great Western of Canada, Scottish-Australian Investment Co., Buenos Ayres Great Southern Railroad, and Egyptian Bonds. At the time of her death, the colonial stocks made up just under half her total holdings. Other stocks directly connected to colonial trade (East and West India Docks, London Docks), domestic stocks (the Consols, Regents Canal), and foreign investments (Sambre and Meuse, Continental Gas, Pittsburgh, and Ft. Wayne) complete the portfolio.[34]

By the time she wrote *Daniel Deronda*, Eliot was fully invested and particularly sensitive to the risks of the stock market, from which she was protected by her disinclination to take risks and later by the advice of her investment banker, John Walter Cross. In her fiction women were not always so fortunate in their education about financial matters or in their male advisors. *Deronda*, in particular, examines the financial vulnerability of women. Eliot's concerns about her own money – as "spinster," "stepmother," breadwinner – are translated into the financial pressures experienced by her female characters. The money that Gwendolen would have inherited from her grandfather's Barbados estate is lost when Grapnell and Co. fails, perhaps representing the sensational

4. Manuscript page from George Eliot's diary for 1880, Beinecke Rare Book and Manuscript Library, Yale University.

collapse of the firm Overend and Gurney in 1866. The image suggested by Grapnell of a multipronged hook or anchor seems to emphasize the menace to vulnerable women who sink their fortunes in a risky market. This ensnaring imagery would be repeated in Theophrastus's character sketch of Sir Gavial Mantrap, an unscrupulous speculator who has fallen into disgrace "because of his conduct in relation to the Eocene Mines, and to other companies ingeniously devised by him for the punishment of ignorance in people of small means" (129).

Mrs. Davilow introduces the family's misfortune in a letter to Gwendolen which combines moral censure with second-hand knowledge of "Mr. Lassman's wicked recklessness, which they say was the cause of the failure" (10). Later, Gwendolen takes a literal view of the problem, asking whether Mr. Lassman has run away with the money, a question consistent with her experience of men, particularly the father she hardly remembers and the stepfather she rarely saw. Her mother attempts to explain: "There were great speculations: he meant to gain. It was all about mines and things of that sort. He risked too much" (199). Gwendolen's understanding of her own financial situation is as vague as her mother's, and as incomplete as her knowledge of what her West Indian grandfather did or of what it means to emigrate (199). It never occurs to her "to inquire into the conditions of colonial property and banking, on which, as she had had many opportunities of knowing, the family fortune was dependent" (51).

From the fragmented history Eliot gives us, we can piece together a typical mid-century economic pattern in which money amassed in the West Indies in the previous generation is sunk in domestic, foreign, or colonial mines, a plight reminiscent of Mrs. Pipchin in *Dombey and Son*, whose husband broke his heart "pumping water out of Peruvian Mines... Not being a Pumper himself, of course ... but having invested money in the speculation."[35] In Dickens's comic rendering, speculation kills the man, depriving the woman of a husband, and, as a woman, Mrs. Pipchin points to the literal/metaphoric confusion over the notion of "pumping" money into mines. The loss of a husband through speculation is an echo of Mr. Dombey's loss of his son and emotional estrangement from his daughter, which lasts until his money is lost, so that again we see the exchange of material for emotional rewards. In *Deronda*, Gwendolen's loss of capital drives her to a literal and primitive form of exchange that stands in contrast to the abstract and sophisticated workings of the modern stock market – selling herself in marriage for the financial security it will bring to her family.

Such a catastrophe would never befall Eliot or her dependents. Sophia Andres argues that the Davilow family misfortune was "representative of prevalent fears and hopes fueled by the bizarre and unstable practices of colonial investing" and that the British Empire could not "safeguard its own internal economy from the rampant forces that govern colonial ventures."[36] There is no evidence in the novel that the mines referred to by Mrs. Davilow are colonial, and Eliot's own colonial investments in the 1860s–1870s appear to have been quite stable. Her money was safe. The names of her investments, written on checks or in her journals, were familiar in their regularity, and like Silas's gold "familiars" (until they are stolen) provided comfort and stability. I will now look specifically at Eliot's investments in Indian railroads. As her interests in the empire expanded from their beginnings in 1860, she continued her fictional project of consolidating colonial expansion into a coherent Englishness, and her late works are increasingly self-conscious of the displacement.

### EAST INDIES STOCK

Eliot purchased her first shares of East India stock in 1860, shortly after the governance of India had passed from the East India Company to the British Crown in 1858. We saw in chapter 2 how this event had implications for the democratization of the Indian civil service. It was also a significant turning point that had implications for the notion that anyone owning private, commercial stock actually participated in ruling the Indian Empire.

The Great Indian Peninsula Railway line between Bombay and Thana opened on April 16, 1853. The company that built it was one of the first Indian railway companies. Its founder was John Chapman, "the foremost pioneer of railways in western India."[37] According to Haight, he was the cousin of the publisher John Chapman, for whom Eliot edited the *Westminster Review*. The articles he published in the *Westminster* during Eliot's editorship were "The Government of India" (April 1852), "India and Its Finances" (July 1853), and "Our Colonial Empire" (October 1852). In pamphlets such as *Principles of Indian Reform* he tried to negotiate the volatile issues of shareholder control and government reform – the interests of the British capitalists and the welfare of the Indian people. While he helped to sink British political and financial interests deeper into India through massive railroad construction projects, Chapman nonetheless rejected the notion of Britain's right to rule. He argued "that a handful of men from a distant land should rule for ever 150,000,000 people, is not to be expected." Notably anti-colonialist, he continued: "We are not lords of India in any other than a present practical sense. We do not and cannot rule it by force. We cannot colonize it nor ought we."[38] The railway itself and the commerce he hoped it would stimulate would be advantageous to the British and Indians alike, as he argued in *The Cotton and Commerce of India*.[39]

Thorner observes an irony in the fact that to introduce private enterprise the government guarantee was required, and that the enterprise of Indian railway construction "was called private but the risk was public."[40] He concludes that "the demand for 'private enterprise' in the making of India's railways marched hand in hand with the struggle for sweeping public aid."[41] Chapman's joint support for laissez-faire capitalism and public works may have been representative of this particular period in the history of the empire. But his views would not become the dominant ones. He died in 1854, before the Mutiny and the transition to British rule, and before the impact of railroad construction on the Indian economy and Indian society could be perceived.

In an unusual move, the *Westminster* republished "Our Colonial Empire" in its January 1870 issue, with an introduction written by the publisher John Chapman about the author's sudden death from cholera in 1854. The introduction begins by explaining that in 1852 the article had appeared "too early to excite any great and general interest in the subject" but that now its views are "likely to attract the attention of a large number of thoughtful readers."[42] The conjectured prematurity of the article may account for Eliot's referring to it merely as "a great, dreary article on the Colonies" (*GEL*, 2:54). Yet its reprint in 1870 suggests how far public investment and interest in Indian railways had developed since the 1850s. Others, moreover, praised Chapman's work and writing. In an article for *Household Words* entitled "Indian Railroads and British Commerce," Samuel Sidney, the author of the book on Australia that Eliot sent to her sister Chrissey, wrote of Chapman's *The Cotton and Commerce of India*: "The grand instrument for effecting a peaceful, profitable, social, commercial and agricultural revolution in India, will be the railroad – that divining rod of the nineteenth century – which not only discovers treasures, but creates them."[43]

Far from encouraging the cooperation and independence of the Indian people, railroads and British investment in them developed into a justification for continued British rule. In a pro-colonial *Westminster Review* article from 1870, "The Future of the British Empire," John Robinson challenged Gladstonian opposition to the consolidation and growth of the empire. He asked whether "the confidence which these investors have in colonial securities and investments" would continue if the colonies were "forced to become small and petty republics, the scenes of party warfare and political anarchy, for the prey of some rapacious and unscrupulous foreign power?"[44] Investment depends on confidence, which depends in turn on stability, which is guaranteed by British rule in India and throughout the world. In other words, without strong British rule the moral distinctions between safe investments and speculation in "petty republics," like those in South America, disappear.

*Middlemarch* combines issues of reform, economic development, and social stability with the narrative of a wayward son. The narrator explains that the "infant struggles of the railway system entered into the affairs of Caleb Garth, and determined the course of this history with regard to two persons who were dear to him" (451). The coming of the railway is part of the larger tapestry woven from the various threads of progress throughout the novel: the push for the Reform Bill of 1832, Lydgate's fever hospital and other medical reforms, and Dorothea's workers' cottages. The resistance of the locals to the construction of the railway through Lowick parish, true to conditions in England in 1831, also carried the cultural weight of later forms of railway construction. Kerr describes the effect of the 1857 "mutinies" on railway construction in India: "Work was generally halted, work gangs dispersed, station works and some bridge works destroyed, Europeans in the field forced to flee for safety or to stand and defend themselves."[45] From the 1850s, railway construction in India was attended by the same rhetoric of trade, investment, and progress that had characterized the connecting of the provinces to London. In the novel, London is to the country as England to India. One of the local workers, for example, has "a dim notion of London as a centre of hostility to the country" (453).

The clash between the locals and the railway surveyors in *Middlemarch* stages colonial conflict on English ground. The language Eliot uses to describe Fred's intervention in the conflict over the railway suggests that the event is colored for him by romantic images of adventure and heroism of the sort that further associate him with Thornie Lewes. His future is about to be decided, not by emigrating or participating in colonial warfare, but rather by staging a colonial battle safely in his own neighborhood. The chapter opens with Fred riding his horse along the lanes by the village of Frick, "worried by unsuccessful efforts to imagine what he was to do." Obliged to make a life decision, he asks himself "what secular avocation on earth was there for a young man (whose friends could not get him an 'appointment') which was at once gentlemanly, lucrative, and to be followed without special knowledge?" (454) – precisely the kinds of questions Thornie Lewes and his parents were asking in 1860. Presumably one of the "appointments" that Fred could not get by patronage was an appointment in the colonies. But just as Will Ladislaw will neither take the "post" that Chettam imagines getting for him in the colonies (397) nor carry through his scheme of settlement in the "far west" (654) because he wants to be close to Dorothea, Fred would accept no appointment that would take him away from Mary.

Fred's thoughts are interrupted when the "smock-frocks with hay-forks" make an "offensive" toward the "coated men," or railway agents. As the "coated men" run, Fred "covered their retreat by getting in front of the smock-frocks and charging them suddenly enough to throw their chase into confusion" (454). He threatens the aggressors: " 'You'll every one of you be hanged at the next assizes, if you don't mind,' said Fred, who afterwards laughed heartily as he remembered his own phrases" (455). The imagery of the scene is that of battle, complete with uniforms (reminiscent of red coats), weapons, and sacrifice. Caleb's young assistant is knocked down and needs saving because he had "snatched up the spirit-level at Caleb's order" (454), as if he were a standard-bearer and the spirit-level the colors of his regiment. Fred reinforces the military imagery when he proudly remarks to Caleb: "No knowing what might have happened if the cavalry had not come up in time" (455).

In this chapter (56), debates about railroad construction in the provinces are interrupted by the dramatic cavalry scene, which provides a solution to Fred's problem of not seeing the right career path and "determined the course of this history," that is, the narrative of *Middlemarch*. As a war hero, allied with Caleb in returning the surveyors to their work, Fred is able to realize his potential as a surveyor and farmer, and his reeducation begins. Fred looks back with humorous satisfaction on his imperious superiority in threatening the mutinous "smock-frocks," but the penal threats to the local rebels are not confined to the moment of Fred's quick-thinking heroism. Both the young soldier and his mentor/commander are implicated in the kind of imperial authority that brings progress to England and its empire.

Like a colonial administrator, Caleb sees that the illiterate, beer-drinking laborers will not accept progress. They call up the dictatorial side of his character. He tries to convince the men of their mistake: "Now, my lads, you can't hinder the railroad: it will be made whether you like it or not. And if you go fighting against it, you'll get yourselves into trouble" (456). And he is specific with his threats, warning them that they will "have to do with the constable and Justice Blakesley, and with the handcuffs and Middlemarch jail." The narrator compares Caleb to an orator, noting that he paused, "and perhaps the greatest orator could not have chosen either his pause or his images better for the occasion" (456). One of the laborers, Timothy Cooper, objects that times have only got "wusser" for the poor man: "An' so it'll be wi' the railroads. They'll on'y leave the poor mon furder behind" (457). But the narrator makes clear that Timothy Cooper is a relic, "a type lingering in those times – who had his savings in a stocking-foot" (457).

The eschewing of financial progress in the form of savings banks is associated with the superstition and ignorance of such anachronistic types, destined to be left behind by the advances of the railroads, an extinction for which the novel, in this episode, shows minimal regret, as the orator Caleb (with his strong arm Fred) successfully puts down the rebellion and advances the railway. Later, Caleb takes on Fred against his wife's wishes, but "where Caleb's feeling and judgment strongly pronounced, he was a ruler" and "everyone about him knew that on the exceptional occasions when he chose, he was absolute" (460).

Eliot had reason to associate reform in England with events in India and oratory with the platform of Indian reform. On January 1, 1869, she listed the many tasks she had set herself for the year, beginning with "A Novel called Middlemarch" (*Journals*, p. 134).[46] On January 23 she was reading "Bright's Speeches" to Lewes, specifically his "4th Speech on India" (*Journals*, p. 134). In his third speech (1858), John Bright, member for Manchester from 1847, addressed the British governance of Oude province (primary site of the Mutiny). His fourth speech (1859) took up the subject of Indian debt. Eliot was reading these speeches in 1869 because they had been collected and published in 1868. She and Lewes were interested in Bright's role in political reform throughout the 1850s and 1860s, and socialized with him in the 1870s, Lewes noting in 1877 that Eliot had been "talking with Bright about woman's suffrage" (*GEL*, 6:394).

Like the railroad founder John Chapman, Bright was interested in India's potential for producing cotton, in part because it was felt that England should decrease its dependence on the slave-holding states of the American South. As a member of the India Reform Society, he wanted to see the government take a greater role in encouraging British investment in transportation and other public works projects in India.[47]

In his fourth speech, Bright charged: "And so the government of India goes on; there are promises without number of beneficial changes, but we never hear that India is much better or worse than before."[48] And in an eloquent and prescient flourish, which we should imagine Eliot reading aloud, he concluded:

I hope that no future historian will have to say that the arms of England in India were irresistible, and that an ancient empire fell before their victorious progress, – yet that finally India was avenged, because the power of her conqueror was broken by the intolerable burdens and evils which she cast upon her victim, and that this wrong was accomplished by a waste of human life and waste of wealth which England, with all her power, was unable to bear.[49]

Bright shows the inseparability of private capital and political reform, aspects of the Indian empire with which Eliot was associated through her investments and her fiction. His speeches were part of the reading Eliot did in preparation for *Middlemarch*, and they provided a context for the history of reform – the perspective from which her narrator looks back on the events of 1829–32. They offer one clue to the way she might have been thinking about parallels between the coming of progress to India – encouraged by her own investments – and the coming of reform to Middlemarch.

In the second chapter of *Impressions*, Eliot's Theophrastus reflects on the visual and social effect of railroads on foreign and domestic land-scapes. As if echoing Bright's prediction that future historians might say that "an ancient empire fell before their victorious progress," the far-seeing Theophrastus wonders what it signifies that "a petty cloud of steam sweeps for an instant over the face of an Egyptian colossus im-movably submitting to its low burial beneath the sand" (25). Egypt and other past civilizations absorb the changes of modern times, and the vast expanses of sand evoked in this image are indifferent to a "petty cloud of steam." In contrast, the English landscape, which shaped the memories and aesthetic sense of both Eliot and Theophrastus, shows the "more or less delicate (sometimes melancholy) effects from minor changes." He continues with a scene recalling *Middlemarch*:

Then comes a crowd of burly navvies with pickaxes and barrows, and while hardly a wrinkle is made in the fading mother's face or a new curve of health in the blooming girl's, the hills are cut through or the breaches between them spanned, we choose our level and the white steam-pennon flies along it. (25)

The railroad has its subtle beauty, assimilated to the English countryside as a product of English labor, and carving only a minor, if melancholy, scar on the landscape. For the modern observer, these changes can and must find their way into both realistic fiction and the poetic lyricism of Theophrastus's reflections.

The landscape crossed by Indian railroads conjured images of both a lost civilization buried under slow sands and cultivated English farmland. Hills were cut and the breaches between them spanned to construct the Great Indian Peninsular Railroad, and the white steam-pennon flew along the Indian landscape, representing British technological progress and British control. The shadowy investors behind early British rail-roads, as represented in *Middlemarch*, were willing to force "a bit of harm here and there, to this and to that" in the interest of bringing a greater good to those able to survive its changes. Eliot did not profit from the initial cutting up of the English landscape (although she later held shares in the Midlands Railway), but anachronistic types – like the indigenous laborers and farmers in India and in the British colonies – still lingered in 1872, at a geographical distance as remote from her life in London as the English past she recreated in her fiction. No longer the center of her fictional narrative, the "common, coarse people" for whose representa-tion in art she had argued in *Adam Bede* (178) had become marginalized in her history of England, eliminating one crucial aspect of her "realism."

The distances that depersonalized suffering – of the Lewes boys in South Africa, for example – discouraged Eliot's consideration of the consequences (beyond the payment of dividends) of investing her money in colonial projects. There is an answer to the material question of what role Eliot played in reinforcing and encouraging colonization: she was one of many private investors in the 1860s and 1870s whose money bankrolled major colonial projects. If social/moral interests entered into her investment decisions, she might have believed, like John Chapman or John Bright, that she was investing in progress and civilization, even as her primary concern was the well-being of herself and her adopted family. And if Eliot, considered one of the period's great moralists, had no reservations about investing in the empire, how might *we* view her economic involvement in colonial expansion?

In the late twentieth century, many people began thinking about in-vestments as moral choices reflecting political opinions and supporting or undermining specific corporate actions. The strategy of "divestment," emerging from Vietnam War resistance and succeeding Vietnam as the central issue of American student protests in the 1980s, grew in the 1990s into the phenomenon of ethical, or "socially responsible investing" (SRI). Funds screened according to various sets of criteria have become an

accepted part of individual portfolios and pension plans.[50] Conceptions
of shareholder power – like that expressed by Barbara Bodichon about
the East India Company – have changed. Being a voting shareholder is
no longer thought to address the larger questions of a company's purpose and identity. This represents a transformation in thinking about the
relationship between individual principles and money. Just as the moral
terms by which we judge the historical motivations and consequences of
colonialism and imperialism have reversed Victorian moral categories
(the good of bringing "progress" becomes the bad of imposing it), so the
stark moral contrast between investing and speculating has been atten-
uated, and a new form of responsible acting with respect to the stock
market has arisen, though embraced by a minority of investors.

If we were to judge Eliot's colonial investments from a twentieth-
century perspective, we would have to say that her diversified portfolio reflected Britain's economic imperialism around the world, with
British citizens benefiting from the construction of railroads in Canada,
Australia, Africa, and India. We would make a blanket indictment of
nineteenth-century imperialism comparable to that made in the 1980s
of Apartheid, the very result of the colonial conditions in South Africa
that Eliot helped to create when she invested in the Cape Town Rail,
or when she provided money for her stepsons' farm in South Africa.
As I have been arguing throughout, however, any assertion on our part
that Eliot could have made similar connections would falter on the assumption that imperialism, as a totalizing term applying to the British
colonies, existed as a concept which anyone in the mid-Victorian period
could recognize or criticize.

There were moral concerns about different aspects of colonialism,
such as what responsibility England had to its colonial emigrants. In
1853, John Chapman wrote about Britain's revenue from the opium
trade with China: "morals have their value even here: for that which
is unjust or immoral is necessarily unstable and unsafe."[51] But in 1860
Indian railways seemed unrelated to the decaying Jamaican society alluded to in "Brother Jacob" or to the prospects of sons who emigrated to
South Africa or Australia. What we see is rather that the very process of
investing in discrete colonial projects contributed to the emergence of a
more unified concept of imperialism in the last quarter of the century as
continued investing became a reason to maintain and expand the empire.

In a period before British colonialism became the New Imperialism,
Victorian analysts believed that their empire had developed unevenly,
and by 1870 increased investment was both a cause of and a justification

for its continuation and expansion. In his evaluation of the colonial situation in 1870, John Robinson expressed the common Victorian belief that "England has colonized with no set political purpose – on no settled principle of action."[52] He notes further that few people have a "fair idea of what our colonial empire has become in a commercial and material sense."[53] Robinson touches on the very aspect of empire building in which Eliot was most involved:

Nine millions sterling are now paid by India and the colonies yearly upon the funds advanced by British investors on their bonds and debentures. Every year adds to the amount borrowed, the recognition of British rule being the main element of security.[54]

Without articulating a pro-empire position, Eliot had a British investor's interest in British rule, and the interests of the investors were spoken for in explicitly political terms during this transitional period prior to the ascension of the Tory party.

John Walter Cross saw that the "wire" of investments connected the British to the rest of the world, specifically the New World, and to the future. In "On the Extension of Railways in America" – first published in *Fraser's Magazine* in 1873 – Cross writes that "a curious characteristic of the ordinary British investor is that, as a rule, he will take very little trouble to acquaint himself with the true condition of his purchases."[55] Through him Eliot came to know more about her own holdings than the ordinary British investor.

In the next chapter, I argue that Eliot did not view the empire as a monolithic evil to be protested or economically undermined. Such a view was being forged during this period. Her actions, like those of many others, contributed to the formation of this view, and her opinions were affected in turn when she began to see the injustice of colonial enterprises in a new light. In Eliot's diaries, letters, and late fiction we can see that the concept of "imperialism" was emerging. In *Deronda* and *Impressions* there is a new self-consciousness about the imagined community of England and the colonial "other" by which the nation knows itself. For Eliot, collective self-knowledge meant self-criticism, hence the scourging of English society in both of her last works.

# CHAPTER 4

# Daniel Deronda, Impressions of Theophrastus Such, *and the emergence of imperialism*

> ... not only towards the Jews, but towards all oriental peoples with whom we English come in contact, a spirit of arrogance and contemptuous dictatorialness is observable which has become a national disgrace to us.
>
> George Eliot to Harriet Beecher Stowe (*GEL*, 6:301)

In recent years, *Daniel Deronda*, once Eliot's least appreciated novel, has received a disproportionate share of critical attention. The reasons for this are fairly evident. "The Jewish half," as F. R. Leavis famously defined it, is concerned with the notion of transforming a religious tradition of "return" into a modern Jewish nationalism. Its themes of unknown parentage, disinheritance, and cultural transmission acquired new appeal for late twentieth-century critics preoccupied with issues of national and racial identity. Its prescience about the establishment of a Jewish state has attracted critics who write about the immorality of British imperialism. Because criticism of Eliot's fiction relating to imperialism and colonialism consists primarily of post-colonial readings of *Deronda*, this chapter addresses a set of meta-critical issues about *Daniel Deronda* and the British empire.[1] It demonstrates the fallacy of arguments that claim that *Deronda*, as Susan Meyer writes, displays "a disquieting continuity with imperialist ideology."[2]

For some critics, not merely the subject matter but the novel form itself makes all novels complicit in imperialism. Meyer believes that "most of the domestic fiction of nineteenth-century Britain ultimately affirms imperialist ideology."[3] Suvendrini Perera argues that "imperial ideology, far from being an incidental intrusion of the late Victorian period, was throughout a major factor in the English novel and had, in fact, a crucial, shaping role in the development of the form itself."[4] Perera and other post-colonial critics have avoided discussion of Eliot's fiction, except in so far as it represents nineteenth-century realism. The argument about "imperial ideology" is based on the work of theorists such as Terry

Eagleton and their ideological critique of realism. Eagleton has claimed that *Daniel Deronda* marks "one major terminus of nineteenth-century realism – a realism now buckling under ideological pressures it is unable to withstand."[5]

Assuming *Deronda* to be Eliot's last piece of fiction, Eagleton and others have ignored Eliot's most experimental work, *Impressions of Theophrastus Such*, and have failed to address the ways in which it problematizes arguments for the relationship between imperialism and literary form. In *Impressions*, Eliot self-consciously fragments the realist novel and its authoritative narrative voice. Her striking last literary effort coincided with the emergence of a new, coherent conception of British imperialism, which is reflected in her correspondence, her investment practices, and her fiction. By integrating analyses of the form, the content, and the context of Eliot's fiction, including *Impressions*, this chapter complicates our understanding of the relationship between form and empire.

Initiated by Edward Said's claim that the Jews in the novel are "European prototypes so far as colonizing the East is concerned," the rhetoric about *Deronda*'s imperialism has escalated.[6] The novel's indefinite conclusion, which sends Daniel and Mirah on an unspecified mission to "the East," has come to be accepted as a plot resolution that is complicitous in a general European imperialist ideology. After Said, critics have discovered a more specifically British imperialist ideology not only in the novel's conclusion, but in details of its domestic plot. For example, because Gwendolen is the granddaughter of a "West Indian" who owned a plantation in Barbados, Meyer sees her as one who "thoughtlessly benefit[s] from imperialism."[7] This reading borrows from Said's more recent methodological approach of giving "emphasis and voice to what is silent or marginally present or ideologically represented" in European fiction.[8] Said has argued that when reading Jane Austen's *Mansfield Park*, we need to fill in the colonial context of Sir Thomas Bertram's estate in Antigua, even though Antigua is not represented and his activities there are shadowed background to Austen's domestic plot. Meyer takes further the imperative to emphasize what is not represented by condemning Gwendolen on the basis of the actions of her grandfather, who not only is not a character in the novel but remains an indistinguishable figure whom the character Gwendolen has never known. His silence in the novel is certainly rich with implications, but how are we to read that silence?

Judgments such as Meyer's are typical of a kind of analysis which, by concentrating on ideology, ignores the colonial connections to everyday Victorian life that Eliot sought to represent when she created Gwendolen's familial history. With these details, Eliot revealed the conflicting motivations for, and fragmented knowledge about, British colonialism. Her emphasis is on what Gwendolen and her mother do not know about their inherited income, and thereby implicitly criticizes the ignorance in which women are kept by the men who control their money. Furthermore, by situating these briefly mentioned colonial activities a generation earlier than the action of her novel, she called attention to the ambiguities of complicity in the legacy of colonialism with respect to both the social condition of middle-class women and the abstractions of modern finance. The money that Fanny Davilow inherits, made during an earlier colonial era in which the West Indies were a thriving part of the British economy, has been transferred into a modern economy. No longer tied to land in Barbados, the fortune is now fungible and vulnerable to speculations in "mines and things" that put dependent women at risk.

The spectacular loss of Fanny Davilow's income resulting from the failure of Grapnell and Co. is just one of the many ways in which the novel represents the general shift from a land-based economy and social hierarchy to a market-driven capitalist society. In contrast to her other English novels, all of which are set during or before the early 1830s, *Deronda* (which is set in 1864–6) represents the long-term effect of social and political changes, such as the abolition of the slave trade (1807) and of slavery in the British colonies (1833), on the descendants of West Indian absentee planters. Mr. Armyn, Fanny Davilow's father, can be figured as a contemporary of Sir Thomas Bertram. He was a "West Indian," but his daughters, like the Bertram girls, were never in the West Indies. The implication is that he was or became an absentee plantation owner who sold out his interest, as did many such planters, after their plantations ceased to be profitable. Mrs. Davilow is twice a widow, and her paternal inheritance reverted to her upon the death of her husband Captain Davilow (Gwendolen's stepfather). Her sister Nancy Gascoigne's portion of the estate belongs, of course, to her husband and is also lost. This suggests that it was the Rev. Henry Gascoigne who oversaw the finances of both sisters after Mrs. Davilow and her daughters came under his care at Offendene.

Traced backwards, these details are part of a broad social history of the liquidation of the landed interest, both at home and in the colonies, and the assumption of control by the upwardly mobile middle classes. These changes are represented in the ambitions of Captain Gaskin/Rev.

Gascoigne and the break-up of the Mallinger estate, as well as in the dispersion of the West Indian fortune. The latter is lost through bad investments overseen by Gascoigne but blamed vaguely on the "wicked" Mr. Lassman. Gwendolen, for her part, after learning about her mother's dramatic loss, engages in a more archaic form of exchange, pawning her father's symbolic legacy of a turquoise necklace in the hope of obtaining cash and perhaps gambling her way to replacing her now-lost maternal inheritance. At the same time as Mrs. Davilow is being persuaded that the Jewish-sounding Lassman has robbed her, Gwendolen is feeling resentment towards the Jewish pawnbroker, Mr. Wiener, for making his living by cheating Christians who want to get rich by turning their material wealth ( jewels, land) into capital with which they gamble or speculate. Together, these ill-informed assumptions create an aura of Christian vulnerability to perceived Jewish financial power, part of an anti-Jewish attitude the novel as a whole undermines.

This flagrant scapegoating of Jews in the modern forms of financial exchange parallels Daniel's awakening to the history of Jewish suffering through his meeting with Mirah. In redeeming Gwendolen's turquoise (itself a possible symbol of British plunder), Daniel misunderstands her situation. As a wealthy Englishman, he cannot know or imagine the total loss of her income and security. Believing himself to be the illegitimate son of an unknown mother, he cannot imagine disregarding the value of inheritance. The episode is the novel's plot in miniature: Daniel steps in where other men have failed – to safeguard women and restore losses. His incapacity to see her need to liquidate her material inheritance sets up the chain of miscommunications between them, culminating in Gwendolen's incomprehension of why he embraces Jewishness at the end of the novel. Daniel's presumptive overvaluation of tradition and material wealth – heightened by the pain of unknown parentage – conflicts with the landless Gwendolen's irreverent and speculative spirit.[9] His conservatism may appear to reflect a superior moral sense, but Gwendolen's position is distinctly that of a powerless woman striving for power and one with which Eliot is sympathetic. Daniel, who has recently saved Mirah from suicide, enjoys the role of savior to women, but his returning the necklace fails to address Gwendolen's more immediate need of money to help her mother. Daniel is not prepared to understand why a woman might take the extreme measure of cutting herself off from her familial treasures in order to achieve financial independence, and in this respect his misunderstanding of Gwendolen foreshadows his incomprehension of his mother when he finally comes to learn her story.

In a novel that raises questions about the taint of material inheritance – in the diamonds that Grandcourt forces Gwendolen to wear and in her partial inheritance of his estate – the originally West Indian fortune and its loss are thematically relevant. Yet the novel invites an exploration of the complicated moral problems attendant upon such inheritance, rather than a wholesale condemnation of the women whose livelihood depended on it.[10] In "Brother Jacob," David Faux steals his mother's money, some of which he expected to inherit, in order to speculate on his chances for success in Jamaica. In that story, Eliot reduced the issue of monetary inheritance to the straightforward moral transgression of theft. Her experiences with money and colonialism between 1860 and 1876 contributed to her presentation of more shaded moral pictures. When examined closely, and in the light of her own involvement, such references to British colonialism complicate the "imperialist ideology" that many critics are eager to expose. Criticism of *Deronda* that searches for an ideology to condemn has narrowed the notion of context to a morally blameworthy imperialism, distorting our understanding of the text's mimetic and moral subtleties.

## SAID'S INFLUENCE

In the earlier chapters of this book, I argued that Eliot's reading in colonial literature influenced the formulation of her realism and that the roles of stepmother to colonial emigrants and wealthy investor in colonial stocks, which she assumed simultaneously in the early 1860s, shaped the moral outlook of her fiction, particularly in relation to children and money. Given the overwhelming material evidence of Eliot's emotional and financial involvement in colonialism, it is surprising that neither biographers nor critics addressing the relationship of *Deronda* to "imperialist ideology" have taken these facts into account. A cultural critic interested in reprimanding Eliot for her role in facilitating colonization and its attendant injustices might profitably look to this material complicity. Straining to see what is invisible, or "ideologically represented" – as if the characters were living people whose unrepresented activities could be known – critics have been blinded to the visible. An unquestioned, self-perpetuating critical tradition about *Deronda* has emerged since Said's initial pronouncement of the novel's complicity in European imperialism. Reading within this critical tradition and beyond the ending of the novel, many critics seem to assume that Daniel took an active part in displacing Palestinians and raising an Israeli flag on Palestinian soil.

Bruce Robbins has perhaps been the most polemical in asserting the primacy of Said's reading of *Deronda*, arguing that the elucidation of the novel's Zionist context has become "common sense" within the profession.[11] He claims that to discuss *Deronda* "without considering Zionism as a continuing if also particular extension of European colonialism is not to be seriously historical but to be arrogantly antiquarian."[12] I disagree with the characterization of Zionism as the "context" for Eliot's novel, but I also want to address the implications for historical and literary scholarship of accepting the hegemony of any single reading, especially one so clearly political in its intention. The result in this case has been a seriously distorted representation of the text, authorizing irresponsible and anachronistic readings. For example, Meyer interprets the epigraph to chapter 23 of *Deronda* – "Among the heirs of Art, as at the division of the promised land, each has to win his portion by hard fighting..." – as a sign of the "imperialist ramifications of proto-Zionism": "The plot of *Daniel Deronda* rather ruthlessly sends off Mirah and Daniel to be the ancestors to such a struggle."[13] In Eliot's metaphor about what it means to be an artist, Meyer sees a "ruthless" embracing of twentieth-century violence – that is, of future events about which Eliot could have had no knowledge.

I will not be contributing to the exercise of guessing what the fictional characters Daniel and Mirah might have done between 1866, when they leave England, and 1896, when Theodor Herzl published *The Jewish State*.[14] Instead, I want to enlist the facts about Eliot's life that have been established in previous chapters to clarify the complexities of the Victorian culture of empire as evident in *Deronda*. In considering Eliot's letters, journals, and financial records to be relevant intertextual material for the illumination of her fiction, I ask how these particular facts relating to her life, and therefore to her culture, might be important to inquiries about the role of the colonies in everyday Victorian life. My analysis of the local details in Eliot's life and writing suggests that "imperialist ideology" is a term that not only fails to describe but actually misdescribes the complex relationship between nineteenth-century authors, their works, and the British empire.

Said's work has, of course, been influential, not merely in interpretations of *Deronda*, but in the reading practices that have come to define post-colonial studies. *Culture and Imperialism* is a prescription for reading colonial texts. His chapter on *Mansfield Park* is a model for the type of reading that attempts to see the invisible. He assures us that we need not jettison *Mansfield Park* because of its "affiliations with a sordid history," if we take seriously our intellectual and interpretative vocation to make connections, to deal with as much of the evidence as possible, fully and actually, to read what is there or not there, above all, to see complementarity and interdependence instead of isolated, venerated, or formalized experience that excludes and forbids the hybridizing intrusions of human history.[15]

These "affiliations" are more evident to today's critics than they would have been to Jane Austen and her readers. Said is primarily concerned with the way post-colonial readers with a knowledge of subsequent colonial events see colonial references differently from previous generations. Yet there is a limitation on his imperative to "deal with as much of the evidence as possible," because his exploration of the place Antigua holds in *Mansfield Park* excludes Jane Austen's knowledge of, and connections to, the British empire. As of 1760, Jane Austen's father was a trustee of a plantation in Antigua, a fact that Claire Tomalin sees as a "link with slavery," which may explain Austen's choice to make Sir Thomas an absentee landlord in Antigua.[16]

I want to challenge two primary aspects of Said's method of reading. The first is the erasure of the author's life from the cultural evidence that counts as relevant in the contextualization of literary texts. The second is the anachronistic imposition of knowledge about later events – and the systems of value arising from such knowledge – on texts that are as historically situated in the beliefs and daily practices of an earlier time as they are in a teleological history of disparate colonial atrocities, culminating in a present, enlightened view.

My critique has implications not only for our assessment of Said's work, but for post-colonial criticism of nineteenth-century literature in general. In post-colonial studies, biographical facts have counted only in the study of texts by authors who had direct colonial experiences. Biographical history has not signified in the readings of works by authors who did not either live or travel in the colonies. For example, in her foundational post-colonial reading of *Jane Eyre*, Gayatri Spivak opposes earlier feminist criticism, which was naively concerned with women's "subjectivity," and dismisses a deconstructive approach which would "loosen the binding of the book." She proclaims: "I need hardly mention that the object of my investigation is the printed book, not its 'author.'"[17]

Susan Fraiman has resisted this trend by arguing that Said isolates Austen from her position in late eighteenth-century/early nineteenth-century English society. She points out that Said acknowledges such experience in his chapters on Conrad and Kipling in *Culture and Imperialism.* Calling Austen "a contradictory figure neither pretty nor little, with widely engaged interests and independent views," she contends that Austen was far from representative of the hegemonic Englishman.[18] Insisting on biographical and cultural contextualization to counter Said's picture of Austen "as an English national in the period preceding colonial expansion," she argues for her "more precise status as an unmarried, middle-class, scribbling woman."[19] As an unmarried and financially dependent woman, Austen was "a kind of exile in her own country."[20] Fraiman uses these biographical facts to emphasize the ironic distance that Austen kept from her characters. In *Mansfield Park*, Fanny Price is marginalized from the wealth and status of her uncle's estate, and this distance signals a critical rather than approving attitude toward Sir Thomas's colonial interests.

Fraiman's critique of Said has implications for his treatment of Eliot. The same case that she makes for Austen's "incompletely realized citizenship"[21] applies to Marian Evans Lewes, also a disenfranchised, unmarried nineteenth-century woman. Because she earned enough to be financially independent, Eliot entered more fully than Austen into the economic sphere of her male contemporaries, but even at the height of her success her fiction did not lose its concern for the displaced and marginalized. Fraiman shows that Said had to overlook a set of facts about Austen's life in order to turn her into a type of colonizing Englishman. In writing about *Deronda*, Said must similarly turn Jewish characters into "European prototypes," inseparable from English Christians in their role as colonizers. Daniel Deronda is like Fanny Price: adopted by a landed aristocrat, he enjoys the advantages of wealth but explicitly and crucially feels his outsider status. Before he learns that he was born a Jew, and especially afterwards, he allies himself with the marginal minority. His sympathies are presented in such a way as to preclude his status as a model, prototypical European colonizer.[22]

Said argues that we must "take stock of *Mansfield Park*'s prefigurations of a later English history as registered in fiction."[23] Sir Thomas's Antigua connections take on a "greater density" only when we "think ahead" to later novels. He wants us to look forward to texts as late as *Heart of Darkness* (1902) and *Wide Sargasso Sea* (1966) when reading Austen. The colonial context of earlier fiction may help track historical developments as represented in later works, but do works like *Wide Sargasso Sea* really help us to understand *Jane Eyre*, much less *Mansfield Park*? This aspect of Said's way of reading, I think, defines anachronism. While he articulates his methodology most clearly in *Culture and Imperialism*, this reading backward from present circumstances is also the basis for his earlier criticisms of *Deronda*. His reading of *Deronda* as a novel that is complicitous in imperialist ideology depends on the assumption that Jewish nationalism, or Zionism, is a form of British imperialism. This interpretation looks back from the consequences of twentieth-century Zionism to find its roots in British imperialist and Jewish nationalist impulses in the nineteenth century.

Deronda's idea of helping the Jews who were already living in various Eastern countries is vague, as much philanthropic as nationalistic. Eliot had no wish to align herself with the efforts of certain Jewish and non-Jewish Englishmen, such as Moses Montefiore, Charles Warren, and Lawrence Oliphant, to establish colonies in Palestine, perhaps because of her reservations about philanthropy in general or perhaps because of the aggressive Christianity that inspired men such as Warren and Oliphant.[24] Oliphant, who was born in South Africa and was a regular contributor to *Blackwood's Magazine*, became involved in a project to settle Jews in Palestine after Eliot published *Deronda*. John Blackwood wrote to Eliot in 1879 about Oliphant's activities: "There is a cry H.E.P. to Jerusalem and I imagine that Oliphant is in some manner the forerunner of work in these parts" (*GEL*, 7:108). But she replied evasively: "There is a great movement now among the Jews towards colonising Palestine, and bringing out the resources of the soil. Probably Mr. Oliphant is interested in the work, and will find his experience in the West not without applicability in the East" (*GEL*, 7:109). Blackwood persisted in the comparison, writing that he thought that she, Benjamin Disraeli, and Oliphant were all "working to one end" (*GEL*, 7:192). Eliot did not respond to this observation. She has often been taken as an advocate of the colonization of Palestine based on isolated readings of *Deronda*, but her reluctance to celebrate early signs of its actual occurrence suggests that she distinguished between the idea of Jewish nationalism and the practices of religious (mostly Christian) colonizers.

*Deronda* is more difficult to reduce to a Zionist novel than Said's rhetoric would suggest, and his reading depends on a number of logical slips that undermine his argument. He begins with the assertion that the novel's "main subject is Zionism."[25] Anachronistically, her characters become Zionists, and "approbation for her Zionists derives from her belief that they were a group almost exactly expressing her own grand ideas about an expanded life of feelings."[26] To follow the logic of this sentence, we must accept that Eliot approves of "her Zionists" because she "believes" that they "were a group" "almost exactly expressing her own grand ideas." Is Said suggesting that Eliot believed these characters expressed her ideas independently of her creation of them, that she discovered and then approved them because they supported what she believed independently? Or, are "her Zionists" a historical "group" that Eliot is merely representing in her fiction?

Mordecai's guiding vision concerns the restoration of the Jews to the Holy Land, lost to them centuries earlier, a dream frequently interpreted by critics of the novel as a form of Anglo-Jewish imperialism. Far from being Eliot's call for Europeans to take what does not belong to them, the idea of the restoration of the Jews engages her sense of justice and reparation for wrongs committed, a view consistent with much of her fiction. Said argues that Eliot was "indifferent to races who could not be assimilated to European ideas."[27] He sees her "gentile Zionism" as sharing with European imperialism a view of the Holy Land as "essentially empty of inhabitants."[28] His objections raise the question of whether restitution was for Eliot a euphemistic justification for an imperialist intention. According to Said, Eliot knew that the Arab inhabitants of Palestine existed, but like her contemporaries she participated in the denial of their "status as sovereign and human inhabitants."[29] It is worth asking whether Said's notion of "sovereignty" was not, at the time, a Western notion.

Mid-Victorian British travelers to Palestine, often motivated by Christian sympathies, complained about the living conditions of Christian communities under Turkish rule and about British foreign policy. For example, in his *Syria and Palestine in 1851 and 1852* C. W. M. van de Velde voices strong opposition to the British support of the "Turkish empire": "Not a book do we find written upon Palestine that does not lament over the violence of its oppressors!"[30] Eliot's growing sympathy to other peoples is evident in a letter to Harriet Beecher Stowe in which she directly criticizes the English on the grounds that "a spirit of arrogance and contemptuous dictatorialness is observable which has become a national disgrace to us" (*GEL*, 6:301). Defining a national trend, Theophrastus argues: "That any people at once distinct and coherent enough to form a state should be held in subjection by an alien antipathetic government has been becoming more and more a ground of sympathetic indignation" (160). The Turkish rule of the Holy Land defined imperialist oppression for the English. Eliot wanted sovereignty for indigenous peoples – freedom from an "alien antipathetic government."

Did Eliot approve of making Arabs the "superseded proprietors" to which she refers in *Deronda* (507)? Was this her intention in sending Daniel to learn about and help the long-established but often destitute Jewish communities in Jerusalem and elsewhere in the Middle East? No one actually settles in the East. Mordecai dies without ever seeing the Holy Land, which remains a construction of his imagination based on ancient and religious texts rather than on a grounding in contemporary information. His comments about the contemporary "East" are limited to the discussion of the Philosopher's Club at the Hand and Banner, and while they inspire Deronda to adopt aspects of his vision of restoring a Jewish nation, we cannot be sure that his beliefs were Eliot's own or that she was without skepticism as to their practical application. In contrast to her other novels and to novels by other Victorian writers, there is no postscript to tell us what Daniel and Mirah saw and did in the East: think of Mr. Peggotty's return from Australia in *David Copperfield*, of the letter telling of Hetty's death in *Adam Bede*, or of the Finale to *Middlemarch* in which the fates of "young lives" are detailed, for who could quit them and "not desire to know what befell them in after-years?" (677). In *Deronda*, that curiosity has abated, perhaps because the projected future is lived in a land Eliot did not feel she could represent.

Just as "Brother Jacob" is directly critical of myths about the British colonies that are perpetuated by ignorant Englishmen, so *Deronda* criticizes the very myth of empty land Said attributes to it. Early in the novel, myths of empty land in actual British colonies are exposed as immature and uninformed. Rex Gascoigne, in attempting to persuade his father that Canada is his future, reasons that "There are plenty to stay at home, and those who like might be allowed to go where there are empty places" (72). Eliot emphasizes the error and childishness of such fantasies when her narrator observes that Rex lacks the knowledge to distinguish among colonies: "Rex thought the vagueness of the phrase prudential; 'the colonies' necessarily embracing more advantages, and being less capable of being rebutted on a single ground than any particular settlement" (72).

Rex's fantasy is limited to his building a hut and escaping to a "great wide quiet" – images out of boys' adventure romances of the sort read by Thornie Lewes prior to his emigration to South Africa. His sister Anna has her own fantasy of freedom from the social constraints on women, but significantly they remain "secret" and unspoken when she says to herself that in the colonies "I should have done with going out, and gloves and crinoline, and having to talk when I am taken to dinner and all that!" (74). As discussed in chapter 2, Rex and Anna's fantasy of "playing at life over again" epitomizes a particular British attitude toward emigration to the colonies as a flight from home, problems, and "civilization." This mentality of escape coexists with other aspects of colonialism, represented by their brother Warham's preparation for the Indian civil service examination, and Deronda's departure from England with a nationalist mission. Fantasies of escape, practical concerns about career choices, and nationalist ideals coexist and contend in Eliot's life and writing.

Eventually Rex studies law. As if commenting on his earlier susceptibility to boys' adventure fiction, Rex remarks that "law rubbish" is "not so bad as the rubbishy literature that people choke their minds with" (604). Rejecting the romance of the colonies for the more literal-minded legal profession, Rex distinguishes himself in the eyes of his father, who has replaced him as the romantic of the family. He looks to Rex's success within England, all but dismissing the prospects of his other son: "Warham, who had gone to India, he had easily borne parting with, but Rex was that romance of later life which a man sometimes finds in a son whom he recognizes as superior to himself" (605). The superior son rejects the unreal "rubbish" that had marked his youth and is resolved to stay at home in order to continue the social climb begun by his father. The son's colonial romance of youth becomes the father's domestic romance of age, while the actual colonial son, Warham, is anything but romantic – cramming for exams and easily parted with – gone out to India and out of his family's mind.

Eliot's awareness of the English habit of constructing foreign and colonial spaces from literary representations is evident in the theme of misguided romanticism, together with her own refusal to participate in such practices. She turned her wit on Orientalism in "Brother Jacob," and most famously in the character of Mr. Casaubon in *Middlemarch*. In *Impressions*, the chapter "How We Encourage Research" offers a satire on contemporary Orientalist scholarship in which "the masters of those who know on oriental subjects" (34) are presented as a school of territorial whales with "Grampus" at their head. The point of this story about an interloper's challenge to hegemonic discourse is a critique of the self-referencing, closed system of Orientalist knowledge.

Reinforcing an insider/outsider dichotomy that runs throughout *Impressions*, Theophrastus describes how the upstart amateur Proteus Merman is pilloried for attempting to contribute to European scholarship on the "comparative history of ancient civilisations" (29). Describing his treatise on the Magicodumbras and the Zuzumotsis, Theophrastus recounts that "a new idea seized him with regard to the possible connection of certain symbolic monuments common to widely scattered races" (30). Merman's theory is discredited through ridicule by the authorities in his field, and Merman himself is transformed from a mere outsider into a pariah.

Said's critique of Orientalism does not take into account such Victorian anticipations of his own post-colonial insights – their self-consciousness about the constructedness of knowledge in general and of the Orient in particular. "How We Encourage Research" reveals a contemporary critique of this "vast yet microscopic knowledge" (32). Grampus and the authors of works such as *"L'orient au point de vue actuel"* (33) enshrine their narrow authority by debunking a scholar who, as a "merman," is metaphorically not of their cetaceous kind. Merman, caught up in their rhetoric, perpetrates comparably blinkered visions when trying "compendious methods of learning oriental tongues," which got at "the marrow of languages independently of the bones" (34). Yet he is also a victim of more powerfully situated authorities, and his egoistic attempts to storm the fortress of European knowledge about the Orient result in his financial and psychological ruin. As the final insult, Grampus incorporates Merman's insights without acknowledgment, effectively erasing his presence from the dominant perspective on the Orient. Ultimately, Orientalism emerges as one of several forms of knowledge that construct places and people with an arrogant disregard for "the truth." The chapter demonstrates absolutely that in the case of *"L'orient"* there is no object of study, but merely a stream of self-referential language constructing what may or may not have some external, empirical referent (Magicodumbras and Zuzumotsis).

*Impressions* complicates Said's claims about nineteenth-century Orientalism because it represents a critical counter-discourse to the dominant norm, just as *Deronda* incorporates a critically self-conscious attitude toward the myth of empty land. The importance of *Deronda* in the larger argument of Said's *The Question of Palestine* (and "Zionism from the Standpoint of its Victims") is minimal, and its use in the essay is polemical. Said's is not a close or careful reading of the novel. Yet his brief comments, despite their shaky syntactic/literary ground, have been reaffirmed in the readings of other critics. Said has authorized a post-colonial tradition of reading *Deronda*, and within that tradition the fallacies and oversimplification of his remarks have been perpetuated rather than examined. These need to be redressed, particularly as they relate to Eliot's presumed "ideology of imperialism."

The search for evidence of imperialist ideology in *Deronda*, as inspired by Said, has influenced readings of the domestic plot as well as the ending of the novel. Deirdre David, for example, focuses on metaphors of imperialism to analyze Gwendolen, whom she writes "is busy at her psychological colonising, establishing human territories for domination . . . while her class is at work building up the actual empire which, in part, determines and permits her exercise of domestic, psychological imperialism."[31] David's generalizations about the "actual empire" and about Gwendolen's "psychological imperialism" are vague and do not clarify the relationship between the two. How does the colonization by Gwendolen's "class" (itself ambiguous) permit her to bully her mother and sisters or her cousin Rex? Such criticism is representative of a view that assumes a conception of imperialism so coherent that it needs no explanation. "Psychological" and other metaphoric forms of imperialism are conflated with British colonial activities during the 1860s. The connection between the two is asserted rather than analyzed, with little concern for how colonial activities might actually illuminate the text. Imperialism is simply bad, and all forms of power – psychological, financial, physical – may be explained by it.

Such equations of political and domestic power have served those looking for an alignment of proto-feminist and anti-colonial sentiments in Eliot's work. Several critics see the Jewish nationalism of *Deronda* as an imperialist aspect of an anti-imperialist novel. Reina Lewis writes: "Whilst *Daniel Deronda* criticizes the ethos of imperialism, it does not relate it to Mordecai's plans in the East."[32] By first finding a critique of imperialism, then defining Mordecai's vision and Daniel's journey as imperialistic, these critics create a duality in the novel that has a moral shock-value for readers today: we can both excuse and blame the author for the apparent contradictions in her novel. Katherine Bailey Linehan, for example, sees "an ideological tension – between Eliot's feminist critique of imperialism on the one hand and her embrace of nationalism, racialism, and patriarchy on the other."[33] Carolyn Lesjak remarks that "Eliot's critique of imperialism, with its resultant vision of an alternative nationalism via Zionism, bears within it the very structure of the object of its critique."[34] In other words, Eliot tried to criticize imperialism, but unknowingly failed because she could not see that Daniel's plan of helping the Jews in the East, inspired by Mordecai's vision of a reconstituted Jewish nation, replicated the imperialist ideology she meant to criticize.

When they argue that Eliot provides a "critique of imperialism," these critics refer to a moral critique, instead of, say, an economic one. Metaphors of domination are prevalent in *Deronda*, with references to the "breaking" of animals and to physical torture. In Genoa, Gwendolen thinks that Grandcourt "tyrannizes" her, seeking to gain "domination" and "mastery." She feels imprisoned, as if she were on the rack (581–2). Eliot's most explicit reference to colonial rule comes in her narrator's hypothesis that if Grandcourt,

this white-handed man with the perpendicular profile had been sent to govern a difficult colony, he might have won reputation among his contemporaries. He had certainly ability, would have understood that it was safer to exterminate than to cajole superseded proprietors, and would not have flinched from making things safe in that way. (507)

Although Grandcourt represents a bred-out type of the morally decaying aristocracy, he is nonetheless an anomalous moral monster. There is little evidence to suggest that the critique of him extends to patriarchy or even to men generally. In this sense, critics have been too quick to jump from Eliot's numerous analogies to physical violence to the conclusion that she was providing a blanket condemnation of colonialism or of a coherent ideology of imperialism that did not yet exist.

### THE NOVEL

Some critics are not concerned with the author's consciousness, but look to unconscious structures to find what we now call imperialist ideology. The post-colonial critique of the nineteenth-century realist novel goes beyond the simple claim that individual characters are imperialists and beyond critics who identify imperialist ideology in individual texts. It holds that the novel, as a genre and in its very form, is imperialist. This belief seems to have emerged without any distinctive argument of its own. It has transcended the need for proof, and is a conclusion reached by various methodological paths. For example, there is the straight-forward claim that the Western genre has "colonized" other non-Western narrative forms. Mary N. Layoun discusses the consequences of the imperialist legacy for late twentieth-century non-Western novels, the "imposition of the dominant form of the modern, realist, bourgeois novel on 'non-Western' narrative genres and forms that preceded the 'immigrant' genre of the novel."[35] She points out that this imposition was both literal – colonial officers promoting the novel over other forms – and (primarily) metaphoric: "[T]he modern *Western* novel – its formal characteristics, its structural framework, not to mention its content – is crucially and complexly linked to an expansive and decidedly imperialist ideology."[36] The form of the novel is imposed externally (subordinating indigenous forms to it) and internally (closing down non-realist possibilities in its narrative).

For Layoun, form, content, and social circumstances conspire: the novel's complicity in imperialism is multiply determined. Other critics mix and match their methodologies to make comparable claims. The assertion that the novel is an imperialist genre conflates the arguments of Marxist, post-structuralist, and post-colonialist theories, as well as theories of the novel's "rise." It has separate but related parts, only some of which involve content or representation. Others rely on sociological observation, and still others concentrate on ideology. As Layoun suggests, the imperialist claim depends on certain assumptions about the novel's realist and bourgeois nature. These analyses date to Georg Lukács's *The Meaning of Contemporary Realism* (1958) and, in a liberal but non-Marxist tradition, to Ian Watt's *The Rise of the Novel* (1957), which laid a foundation for subsequent histories of the novel.

Watt argued that the term "formal realism" applied to "a set of narrative procedures" so distinctive that "they may be regarded as typical of the form itself." Formal realism is the "narrative embodiment" of a "premise, or primary convention, that the novel is a full and authentic report of human experience."[37] The novel's documentary aspirations, its "more immediate imitation of individual experience set in its temporal and spatial environment," distinguish it from other forms, and its representation of colonial activities appears to legitimate those activities as part of a social order. Defoe's *Robinson Crusoe* serves as initiator of the novel tradition. Defoe's realism "expresses some of the most important tendencies of the life of his time."[38] The originality of *Robinson Crusoe* lies in the fact that "profit is Crusoe's only vocation, and the whole world is his territory." In other words, economic imperialism and colonization are part of the novel's content from the start. The realist novel, as opposed to Pope's couplets or Swift's satires, prevailed, together with the second stage of British colonialism, to become predominant in the nineteenth century, and criticism has tended to focus on the simultaneous "rise" of the novel and imperialism.[39]

Lennard Davis attempts to negotiate between Marxist theory and Watt's historicism by explaining the novel's historical relationship to theoretical understandings of ideology. He is interested in the problem of the novel's fictionality in light of its claims to be factual: "The novel's fictionality is a ploy to mask the genuine ideological, reportorial, commentative function of the novel."[40] And this brings him back to a more theoretically articulated version of Watt's earlier claims about realism.

Davis writes that "realism can be seen as a function of ideology and ideology can be seen as embodying the same processes as are used in the realistic novel."[41] This view allows us to applaud or condemn individual novels, depending on whether they resist or perpetuate bad ideology. As Davis concludes, novels "must be seen as both embodying and counteracting ideology."[42] Applying his views about the novel and ideology to the colonial context in a review of Margaret Anne Doody's *The True Story of the Novel*, Davis accuses Doody of trying to "hijack" the anti-imperialist, pro-multicultural agenda of post-colonial novel studies, which has tended to see that "the novel" was brought to the colonies "as a way of creating compliance with an imperialist ideology rather than giving us a universal narrative form to contain human wishes."[43]

Critics have looked to breaks with eighteenth-century economic, political, and cultural forms to establish what is unique about Victorian, realist novels. Eagleton, in his chapter on ideology and literary form in *Criticism and Ideology*, gives specificity to the relationship between socio-economic structures and literary form. He attributes the form of Eliot's fiction in particular to an increasing "corporatism" between 1846 and 1876, which found itself in conflict with the individualism Watt described as a hallmark of eighteenth-century novels. Eagleton's notion of corporatism includes "the growth of capitalist partnerships and joint-stock enterprises, the railway amalgamations, the gradual emergence of an increasingly centralised state bureaucracy in such spheres as education and public health."[44] Like a giant railway company, the novel, he concludes, "attempts to subordinate other modes of discourse," its form adapting and mutating under capitalist pressures.[45] For Eagleton, the novel's discursive domination reflects capitalist hegemony with its attendant class oppression and imperialist expansion.

Outside Marxist circles, it has also become popular to claim that not just individual texts but all novels are imperialist. Patrick Brantlinger's *Rule of Darkness* makes the case for content, seeking to show how "early and mid-Victorians expressed imperialist ideology in their writings."[46] He looks not only at novels, but at poetry, essays, and travel writing. His is not a formalist argument, and he cares about the authors' views. His introduction discusses Trollope's personal opinions without reference to his fiction, concluding that Trollope was indeed an "imperialist." Brantlinger's later work *Fictions of State* leaves the author behind to explore the nationalist, imperialist nature of representation in general and novels in particular. Addressing post-structuralist theories of culture and discourse, he presents the notion that the "inevitable fetishism of representation is, moreover, imperialistic."[47] He argues, by way of Benedict Anderson, that "the ideological sublimity (including darkness, terror, superstition, and fetishism) of the nation state forms the invisible subtext, context, or horizon of *every* 'English' novel."[48] So an anti-nationalistic novel may still embody the nation state in an "invisible subtext" reminiscent of Fredric Jameson's "political unconscious." The political formations of nation-state and empire become inevitably part of the discursive formation, the novel, regardless of the novel's author, subject matter, or self-conscious politics.

While most arguments for the imperialist ideology of the novel form avoid Eliot's works, many explanations for late nineteenth-century trans- formations in realism invoke them. George Levine argues that *Deronda*, with its non-linear chronology, mystical visions, and an ending in which the hero emigrates to "some other country that the novelist's hand – bound by the demands of realistic representation – could not describe," displays an adulterated realism that has been discussed in terms of ro- mance and allegory.[49] *Deronda* represents a "crisis" in realist form because "fictionality" is "becoming incorporated as a level of signification within the text itself."[50]

These critics are all interested in establishing the relationship between texts and their sociopolitical contexts. Few, after the advent of post- structuralist theory, are willing to include the author's experiences or consciousness in their definition of that broader cultural context – what Spivak would call a naive interest in "subjectivity." Their attempts to ac- count for formal variations as manifestations of ideology raise questions about how we might understand Eliot's transformations of the realist novel in relation not only to the actions that constituted colonial expan- sion but also to her own consciousness of "imperialism" as an emerging political concept. Mary Poovey has established that "ideology" devel- oped unevenly in nineteenth-century England.[51] Taking off from her claims about gender, I am arguing that what we call imperialist ideol- ogy was unrecognizable until imperialism was embraced as a political position. Conceptual historians such as Ian Hacking have shown that the naming of a concept creates new effects on those who begin to ac- knowledge its existence. Elsewhere, I have argued that Eliot was writing about anti-Jewish prejudice just prior to the moment of its naming as "anti-Semitism."[52] Just as "anti-Semite" became a name that jew-haters adopted as an identity, so "imperialist" emerged as an identity for pro- expansionist Englishmen at the time Eliot was writing her last work.

While the uneven development of imperialist ideology may be traced throughout the nineteenth century, we must ask how Eliot reacted and contributed to "imperialism" as a concept that Victorians could approve or oppose. A related and equally complex problem is that of the way her realist vision fragmented, even as she maintained her belief in the moral imperative of realism.

Locating ideology in a single genre eliminates considerations of the author's production across genres. It is difficult to generalize about the author and the form simultaneously, though this does not prevent many critics from writing about what George Eliot thought and believed, as it suits their needs. If the novel is an imperialist genre, then all novels will be imperialistic, regardless of the author's views; similarly, if a form (say, the drama, which could be said to have declined as the novel rose) is not inherently imperialist, then even an imperialist author's contributions to that form may not be imperialist. We need to examine all forms – not just novels – in historical context, truly including "as much evidence as possible."

### IMPRESSIONS OF THEOPHRASTUS SUCH

Eliot's most explicit criticisms of British colonial activities came in response to the Anglo-Zulu War (1879) and may be taken as evidence that her notion of British imperialism (though she never used the word) had begun to cohere at the same time that her art began to change in dramatic ways she would not live to pursue. These criticisms came in the form of letters, but were anticipated by *Impressions of Theophrastus Such*, in which Eliot's character Theophrastus makes a more direct, historical critique of British colonialism than had appeared in any of Eliot's previous works. *Impressions* is a fictional experiment that both departs from and comments on the formal realism of her novels. It exposes the seams of its fictional pieces, the separate parts linked through the voice of Theophrastus, the ancient Greek writer of "characters" turned contemporary Victorian author/character and created by that authorial persona George Eliot. It takes further what Eagleton identifies as the modernist characteristics in *Deronda*, specifically a "constant oblique meditation on its own fictive status."[53]

In *Impressions* there is a narrative voice, but its controlling power is compromised by the absence of a sustained story and by the unreal nature of the "characters." Literary characters are imported from other texts, as suggested by allusive names such as Glycera, Merman, Ganymede,

Clarissa, and Euphorion. The fiction is that these are real, contemporary people. The fact is that they are drawn from literature rather than from life, as if the world the author wanted to represent, indeed the world that s/he knew, was textual. By narrowing what is known about the outside world and representing instead other texts, *Impressions* foreshadows those allusive later works by Stein, Woolf, Joyce, and T. S. Eliot, which we associate with modernism.[54]

Allusion, fragmentation, and reflexivity are among the formal characteristics of *Impressions*, linking it with later developments in fiction. How might we examine "external" or social conditions to help explain the pressures that produced such variation? Whereas Eagleton looks at "corporatism" to explain the realist novel's demise, Fredric Jameson postulates that the break-up of the realist novel was attributable to the emergence of late imperialism, a view that seems to contradict the more popular, Marxist-influenced notion of the nineteenth-century realist novel as an agent of imperialist ideology. He suggests that authors were conscious of the British colonies as a part of the nation that was geographically removed and inaccessible; this consciousness led to the fragmentation of literary form, conventionally called modernism.

Jameson argues that "the structure of imperialism also makes its mark on the inner forms and structures of that new mutation in literary and artistic language to which the term modernism is loosely applied."[55] His notion of imperialism is inseparable from capitalism and he elects 1884 for its starting point. In his model, something is lost in the representational art produced in the metropolis after 1884:

[F]or colonialism means that a significant structural segment of the economic system as a whole is now located elsewhere, beyond the metropolis, outside of the daily life and existential experience of the home country, in colonies over the water whose own life experience and life world – very different from that of the imperial power – remain unknown and unimaginable for the subjects of the imperial power, whatever social class they may belong to.[56]

He argues further that literature "will now henceforth always have something missing about it . . . it is only that new kind of art which reflexively perceives this problem and lives this formal dilemma that can be called modernism."[57] In this speculation, an extension of Lukács's understanding of the relationship between nineteenth-century class structure and the realist novel, Jameson implicitly raises the question of what effect the presence of the colonies had on the consciousness of realist novelists prior to his watershed of 1884.[58]

*Impressions* is a valuable text to consider in light of Jameson's comments on modernism and form. It exhibits many modernist characteristics in a way that is unexpected (and unrecognized) in Eliot's work. Its form is related to its content, and both can be illuminated by our awareness of her new consciousness of British colonialism past and present. Just as her best-known chapter "The Modern Hep! Hep! Hep!" invokes both the continuity and the historical specificity of anti-Jewish attitudes, *Impressions* as a whole presents an English tradition of colonization while insisting that its audience take note of the specific contemporary manifestations of the English colonizing impulse. Just as she had begun to do in *Deronda*, in *Impressions* Eliot shows a state of continuity between past and present that makes possible new categories and identities for individuals and communities: the Jews are urged to form a modern nationality based on the memories of their collective history; the English are urged to scrutinize and remake their national character by recognizing a history of colonization, aggressive greed, and complacent superiority. In *Impressions*, we begin to see a critical awareness on Eliot's part of what might today be called "imperialist ideology."

In *Impressions*, Eliot assumes a pose in relation to English history, positioning her English character/narrator Theophrastus as simultaneously inside and outside English culture. As an Englishman he criticizes the English. At the same time, as an ancient Greek he has a sweeping historical perspective. Theophrastus is the first of Eliot's characters to speak of the English and of English history in terms of colonization, as a nation "secure against invasion and able to invade other lands when we need them, though they may lie on the other side of the ocean" (150). Theophrastus's view of the English and England is mixed. He notes that historically the English have needed to "consider who are the stifled people and who the stiflers before we can be sure of our ground" (160), yet he defends the "glorious flag of hospitality" (159) held up by England to its immigrants. He exposes the hypocritical application of rhetorical slogans, such as "sympathy with the injured and oppressed" (161), and urges that the English compare their attitudes toward immigrants to their history of emigration, "for we are at least equal to the races we call obtrusive in the disposition to settle wherever money is to be made and cheaply idle living to be found" (160).

In "A Half-Breed," Theophrastus describes the character Mixtus, whose name reinforces the chapter's racial metaphor to characterize an intellectual and social hybrid, a man who has lost sight of early ideals by devoting himself to commerce, and who "knows the history

and theories of colonisation and the social condition of countries that
do not at present consume a sufficiently large share of our products
and manufactures" (79). Mixtus has turned away from his earlier altruistic motives, and now "continues his early habit of regarding the
spread of Christianity as a great result of our commercial intercourse with
black, brown, and yellow populations" (79). Mixtus, a particular type of
Englishman, translates a reforming enthusiasm into a justification of his
middle-class life. His character embodies the inseparability of colonialism, the English economy, and middle-class complacency. Furthermore,
Mixtus makes internal the notion of "half-breeds" which became familiar to Victorians through colonialism, as Eliot's own much-discussed
references to "half-breeds" in *Deronda* suggest. In a dinner-party episode,
a Mr. Torrington observes that "the blacks would be manageable enough
if it were not for the half-breeds," leading Deronda to comment that "the
whites had to thank themselves for the half-breeds" (279).[59]

In "Moral Swindlers," Theophrastus addresses the contemporary understanding of morality and its hypocritical application in the public and
private spheres. The chapter begins with a discussion of the activities of
Sir Gavial Mantrap, who has fallen into disgrace "because of his conduct
in relation to the Eocene Mines, and to other companies ingeniously devised by him for the punishment of ignorance in people of small means"
(129). Theophrastus portrays Sir Gavial as the ultimate "immoral" man.
He defines immorality. He is a Gavial (an alligator, like Grandcourt)
and a "man trap" (like *Deronda's* Grapnell), enticing people with lies and
destroying them with his swindling. The Eocene Mines themselves are
evoked in the notion of a man trap, but in this essay about the word
"moral" and the ways it should be applied the emphasis is not on those
who work in the mines but rather on "the widows, spinsters, and hard-
working fathers whom his unscrupulous haste to make himself rich has
cheated of all their savings" (129).

Theophrastus's position in this chapter is that "our habitual phraseol-
ogy" needs to reflect a higher sense of morality than merely the "relation
of the sexes." He connects the "informal definitions of popular language"
(131) to a larger system of knowledge, and relates this knowledge specifically to money and empire:

[K]nowledge, navigation, commerce, and all the conditions which are of a
nature to awaken men's consciousness of their mutual dependence and to make
the world one great society, are the occasions of selfish, unfair action, of war
and oppression, so long as the public conscience or chief force of feeling and
opinion is not uniform and strong enough in its insistence on what is demanded
by the general welfare. (132)

Knowledge, navigation, and commerce were essential elements of colonialism and of what Eliot saw as the transformation of the world into "one great society," a global state of mutual dependence with positive as well as negative potential. If unchecked by public opinion (which she suggests can be misguided in its morality), knowledge, navigation, and commerce become excuses for "war and oppression."

But because colonialism has so often produced violence and oppression, Theophrastus prefers nationalism as an antidote to European racialism and capitalist greed. Developing the theme of Jewish nationalism introduced in *Deronda*, "The Modern Hep! Hep! Hep!" incorporates a much stronger critique of anti-Jewish attitudes among the English within the context of English colonial history. In a broad historical survey of British colonialism, Theophrastus comments first on "the Red Indians": "their opinions did not signify, because we were able, if we liked, to exterminate them" (146). On India and the Indian Mutiny, he observes that "though we are a small number of an alien race profiting by the territory and produce of these prejudiced people, they are unable to turn us out; at least, when they tried we showed them their mistake" (146). He sees an analogy between the Jews and the Irish, "also a servile race, who have rejected Protestantism though it has been repeatedly urged on them by fire and sword and penal laws" (155).

Eliot's perspective on colonialism – in the sense that all of English history is the history of colonialism – is illuminated by Theophrastus's reflection on his own Englishness. Theophrastus writes unambiguously of English identity as bound up in the colonizing project, including himself in the description: "We do not call ourselves a dispersed and a punished people: we are a colonising people, and it is we who have punished others" (146). Salvaging what is admirable in English culture despite this harsh view of English motives and habits, *Impressions* challenges the notion that all Victorians shared the same attitudes toward their empire. Their views, as suggested by Eliot's attempt to capture the various types of Englishman in the 1870s, were ambivalent, diverse, and self-conscious. And the form of *Impressions* reflects these fractures, as if the novel, which began to crack with *Deronda*, broke open with *Impressions*, just as imperialism was emerging as a concept.

## THE EMERGENCE OF IMPERIALISM

Even at the political level Victorian views were mixed, as suggested by the division between the Liberals and the Tories at the time Eliot wrote her late fiction. Between 1868 and 1874, prime minister W. E. Gladstone held to an isolationist policy and had wanted gradually to reduce Britain's responsibilities to and for the colonies. Gladstone's government was the target of attack by Benjamin Disraeli, who took a pro-empire stance as part of his Tory agenda. In his famous "Crystal Palace Speech" of 1872, Disraeli deplored the political divisions within the country on the question of empire:

If you look at the history of this country since the advent of Liberalism – forty years ago – you will find that there has been no effort so continuous, so subtle, supported by so much energy, and carried on with so much ability and acumen, as the attempts of Liberalism to effect the disintegration of the Empire of England.[60]

In appealing to national pride, he was tapping but also shaping the nation's mood. His election in 1874 marked a transition to a more aggressive official policy of imperial expansion, and he is traditionally credited with fueling a new enthusiasm for the empire.[61] Gladstone countered with anti-imperialist moralism, denouncing the Second Afghan War (1878–80) and the Zulu War (1879) in his successful 1879 "Midlothian" campaign, claiming that the Zulus has been slaughtered "for no other offence than their attempt to defend against your artillery with their naked bodies, their hearths and homes, their wives and families."[62] Despite Gladstone's success and the partial appeal of a newly evolving moralism, Disraeli had pushed the anti-empire Liberals to the right, altering the political spectrum and helping to create a new breed of pro-empire Liberals who began in the 1880s to identify themselves as "imperialists." By the end of the 1870s a more coherent imperialism was emerging, both to embrace and to oppose, and Gladstone would preside over the African land grab during the 1880s, a period of increasingly international competition for imperial supremacy.

In general, Eliot did not object to Disraeli. While writing *Deronda* in 1874, she wrote to Barbara Bodichon: "Do you mind about the Conservative majority? I don't" (*GEL*, 6:14). She defended him to Edith Simcox, who as a Liberal and labor organizer opposed the Conservative agenda. Simcox wrote in her diary for December 26, 1879, that Eliot "scolded me much" for calling Disraeli unprincipled and "was disgusted with the venom of the Liberal speeches from Gladstone downwards."[63] Later, partly as a result of her involvement with the emigration of Thornie and Bertie Lewes and her continuing connection with South Africa through Bertie's widow and children, Eliot became a critic of colonial policy in the last years of her life. But she never pronounced on imperialism as a national policy.

In the 1870s, a new aggression in South Africa foreshadowed what would become the "scramble for Africa." This was the context in which Eliot wrote *Middlemarch, Deronda*, and *Impressions*, published between 1871 and 1879. South African politics and the Zulu War reflected and influenced changing attitudes toward imperial expansion. Anthony Nutting, writing about the history of South African consolidation, claims that the 1870s "undoubtedly marked the most significant turning point in South African history since the arrival of the 1820 settlers heralded the era of British colonisation."[64]

Events in South Africa prior to the late 1870s had been virtually ignored by the British press and its reading public. John Davidson writes that in 1877, "during a lull in the Eastern Question, the English newspapers discovered S. Africa."[65] The news of the battle of Isandlwana on January 22, 1879, shocked the home country into an awareness of the Zulu situation – shocked, because it was a British loss. Conditions in South Africa polarized the British reading public. A *Blackwood's* article argued that after conquering the Zulus, "we shall have placed the native question upon a firmer basis, and reached the end of those little wars, which so unsettle the minds of our colonists, impede their prosperity, and burden the revenues of the mother country with expenses."[66] In contrast to this view, Eliot followed the opinions of liberal intellectuals and condemned the Zulu War. Evidence of Eliot's emerging critical position on the actions of the government can be found in her letters relating to the Zulu War, which brought the earlier minor skirmishes into the realm of the world-historic, turning isolated incidents into war and a cause that few could support and many were roused to condemn.

Blackwood sympathized with Eliot because the conflict would remind her of "poor Thornton and Natal," adding: "What a state Lewes would have been in" (*GEL*, 7:108). In response, Eliot expressed doubts about British colonial policy: "I don't know what you think of Sir Bartle Frere's policy, but it seems to me that we cannot afford either morally or physically to reform semi-civilized people at every point of the compass with blood and iron" (*GEL*, 7:109). By "policy," she probably meant the demands for the "reform" of Zulu society made by Frere's administration as a pretense for invasion. Frere's beliefs, as well as his actions, were severely criticized in the *Fortnightly Review*. For John Morley, who took over the editorship of the *Fortnightly* from Lewes, the nature and definition of British colonialism were at stake in the popular and government responses to the Zulu War. His comments reveal some of the divisions on the question of colonialism between political right and left in 1879, differences about methods and responsibilities. The ultimate issue was Englishness: what kind of colonizer will England be? How would England's colonial policies shape its national identity? Significantly, even the liberal *Fortnightly* offers no radical critique of colonialism *per se*, although the moral objection to expansion grew louder after the Zulu War. Morley writes:

I believe in England's civilising power too, but only on condition that every maxim which Sir Bartle Frere's school think capital, shall be finally condemned by English opinion as infamous. His despatches abound in phrases of edification about our obligations as a civilised and Christian government, about our national guilt in sanctioning elements antagonistic to civilisation and Christianity, and so forth. When I come across such phrases in a blue-book, I shudder; they always precede a massacre.[67]

Frere is portrayed as a renegade colonial administrator whose actions defied public opinion. By the next issue of the *Fortnightly*, Morley's rhetoric had escalated: "It is for the people of England to decide whether . . . they are content to be taxed for the pleasure of men who unite the mean avarice of hucksters to the lawless violence of buccaneers; and whether the old realm which was once the home of justice and freedom, is to be transformed into a Pirate-Empire, with the Cross hypocritically chalked upon its black flag."[68]

Ongoing personal connections to South Africa heightened Eliot's awareness of events there. Bertie Lewes's widow Eliza wrote plaintively about life in Natal just prior to the war: "Just fancy dear Pater," read an ill-timed letter, arriving shortly after Lewes's death, "these nasty dirty black creatures" (*GEL*, 9:241). Eliza and her two children emigrated to England, "terrified away by the image of a Kafir irruption" (*GEL*, 7:127). Blackwood wrote: "We shall doubtless slaughter those wretched Zulus in any number but that is no satisfaction. One is ashamed to look at the illustrated papers and see the portraits of the ourang outangs with whom we are fighting" (*GEL*, 7:112). The Zulu War was the leading story in the *Illustrated London News* for most of 1879. It is easy to see from its drawings where Blackwood got his image of "ourang outangs."

*Blackwood's Magazine* saw the Zulu War as an issue of British power and prestige, doubting whether "our *prestige* was felt to have suffered such an indignity as it has now sustained at the hands of a horde of savages."[69] In a strikingly different perspective from that of the *Fortnightly*, Alexander Allardyce urged that the British must "punish," "avenge," and "subject" the "enemy." The story told in the pages of *Blackwood's* exonerates Sir Bartle Frere, placing exclusive blame on the Zulu Chief Cetywayo. The political left and right had very different conceptions of what the British "people" wanted. It is clear that Eliot disagreed with some of the accounts in *Blackwood's*. Her letters show that her own views on the Zulu War were much more sympathetic to the moral objections as expressed in the *Fortnightly*.

Writing on April 10, 1879, to Harriet Beecher Stowe, she lamented: "The hopes of the world are taking refuge westward under the calamitous conditions, moral and physical, in which we of the elder world are getting involved. This wicked war in S. Africa (I mean wicked on *our* part) is sending to England our widowed daughter and two grandchildren" (*GEL*, 7:132). She also refers to "that wicked war" in writing to Cara Bray (*GEL*, 7:124). To David Kaufmann, with whom she corresponded about her representation of Jews in *Deronda*, she wrote that "the best part of our nation [is] indignant at our having been betrayed into an unjustifiable war (in South Africa)" (*GEL*, 7:138).

Even Blackwood could not defend the Zulu War. In April 1879 he wrote of the "telegraphic news from Africa": "In the main the intelligence is satisfactory but there is heavy loss to ourselves and no satisfaction in killing these savages" (*GEL*, 7:141). Despite Blackwood's use of the term "savages," the journalistic rhetoric frequently represented the Zulus as a mighty warrior nation, justifying British losses and the ongoing war in general. With the Zulu War came the sense that nothing was to be gained from the expense of blood. On June 29 Eliot wrote: "Does not this Zulu War seem to you a horribly bad business?" (*GEL*, 7:174). To which Blackwood replied on July 15: "The Zulu war is emphatically a useless and miserable business" (*GEL*, 7:181–2).

The situation in South Africa called forth new and distinctive moral objections to British colonial activities. J. A. Froude, the editor of *Fraser's Magazine*, spent time in South Africa as a special government envoy. In October 1879 he wrote an article for the *Fortnightly*, placing the Zulu War in the history of the British empire. He admitted: "The spread of the English race over the globe has been attended with a stain which will cling to us through all coming time. In every country to which we have gone, except India, the coloured man has been degraded and destroyed before us."[70] Yet for Froude, such a disgrace did not diminish the larger project of empire, nor its benefits for white sons. In his book *Oceana* (1885) he argued that emigration was rejuvenating, and that in "the fairest spots upon the globe . . . the race might for ages renew its mighty youth."[71] The Native Question is suspended while the moral and physical good of fresh colonial air is proclaimed as an antidote to the ills of industrialization at home.

Froude took the path of the future, writing of the Zulu War: "To condemn Sir Bartle Frere, to condemn the Colonial Office or the Colonists, or anybody concerned, may be reasonable; but it will be certainly unprofitable; and it may be easily unjust."[72] Trollope expressed paternalistic views toward Natal: "I myself can well remember how unwilling we were to have Natal, and how at last it was borne in upon us that Natal had to be taken up by us, – perhaps as a fourth rate Colony, with many regrets, much as the Fiji islands have been taken up since."[73] He added a chapter on Zululand to the 1879 abridged edition of his *South Africa* in which he directly responded to the new outbreaks of violence by criticizing government policy.

Eliot's most explicit critique of colonial expansion came in the years 1879–80, after Lewes's death and after she had written her last book. At this time, she could neither condone nor overlook new acquisitiveness on the part of the English. We cannot know whether the effects of her response to the Zulu War and other events during the politically volatile final two years of her life might have found expression in her creative work. But as she began responding to changes in British colonial policy and rhetoric that marked the era of a "new imperialism" she would not live to see, she stressed the interconnectedness of foreign events.

We can see in *Deronda* that Eliot continued the project of representing the increasing permeability of English society, its Englishness leaking out while other influences seeped in. *Deronda* registers the forces, not always great and noble, that were penetrating and altering both her consciousness and English society. The rootlessness of the middle classes, cosmopolitanism, and emigration meant that England and Englishness were not to be found on native land alone. English culture was reconfiguring in conjunction with an emerging concept of imperialism, and *Impressions* reflects this fragmentation in its form at the same time that it seeks to define an inclusive English culture that could preserve English identity in the wake of these changes.

In *Deronda*, both Daniel and Gwendolen emerge from isolation and egotism into an awareness of the greater world. Each mediates for the other a set of new connections to a hitherto unknown world beyond self and England, connections to which complacent aristocrats like Grandcourt, attentive only to the "wire of his rental," were indifferent. Deronda is conscious of the imbalance in his relationship with Gwendolen. Waiting to meet his mother and learn simultaneously his past and his future, he reflects that his "far-reaching sensibilities" were "hardly more present to [Gwendolen] than the reasons why men migrate are present to the birds that come as usual for their crumbs and find them no more" (533). The image of migration is transferred from birds to men and suggests both Jewish immigration to England and the English emigration to the colonies that forms the contemporary context of the novel. When she learns of his plans, Gwendolen experiences an epiphany:

There comes a terrible moment to many souls when the great movements of the world, the larger destinies of mankind, which have lain aloof in newspapers and other neglected reading, enter like an earthquake into their own lives – when the slow urgency of growing generations turns into the tread of an invading army or the dire clash of civil war, and grey fathers know nothing to seek for but the corpses of their blooming sons, and girls forget all vanity to make lint and bandages which may serve for the shattered limbs of their betrothed husbands. (689)

Gwendolen's awakening is likened to the violence of invasion, civil war, and social crisis that calls for sacrifice and an elevation above self. Deronda is not going to war, but his new-found connection to the "larger destinies of mankind" makes him as remote to Gwendolen as the civil war in America or life in "the colonies."

In the 1870s, Eliot was looking out to a landscape beyond the domestic. A set of realities about the colonies had entered her life, less like an earthquake than like a series of tremors that shook her consciousness and affected the form and content of her last two works. How this growing personal awareness affected her aesthetics is related to the larger question of colonialism and form. Theophrastus's argument for realism in art holds to the same principle as Eliot's early essays. Eliot still believed, as she wrote in "The Natural History of German Life," that the "picture of human life such as a great artist can give, surprises even the trivial and the selfish" into attention to "what is apart from themselves" (Pinney, p. 270). In "How We Come to Give Ourselves False Testimonials, and Believe in Them," Theophrastus affirms that a "fine imagination" is based on "a keen vision, a keen consciousness of what *is*, and carries the store of definite knowledge as material for the construction of its inward visions" (109). *Impressions* articulates clearly the moral implications of the "habitual confusion of provable fact with the fictions of fancy and transient inclination" (110), suggesting that Eliot remained constant to the notion that art extends sympathies. *Impressions* also comes closer than any of her other works to defining British history and culture as imperialist.

The renewed argument for realism in *Impressions* coexists with a self-conscious critique of colonialism, and the fragmented, unrealistic form of the work parallels the emergence of a coherent concept of imperialism. Said and others who believe that the novel is an imperialist genre would argue that Eliot's novels, in their very realism, reproduce and affirm an unconscious imperialist "ideology." Jameson would argue that the fragmentation in realist form that came to be called modernism resulted from the author's consciousness of a dispersed national economy and daily life. I would argue that Eliot's particular experiences with British colonialism fragmented her sense of English identity. In *Impressions*, the author multiplies, and is present as Marian Evans Lewes, George Eliot, and Theophrastus. Theophrastus's attempts to hold himself together represent Eliot's conscious attempts to impose coherence on a culture that was dispersed geographically and divided internally on the question of political and moral issues surrounding colonial expansion.

In *Impressions*, we see a blurring of self and other, of author and character. For Eliot the boundary between art and life was becoming blurred. Perhaps this is why the form of *Impressions* strains against its advocacy of realism, spoken after all by a fictional character. *Impressions* affirms a moral and aesthetic commitment to realism at the same time that it challenges the conventions of realist fiction. The work as a whole attempts to represent the contradictory elements comprising English national character in the 1870s – a liberal humanism that is both sincere and rhetorical, iridescent yet somehow stable, nationalistic yet encompassing multiple cultures, dispersed yet centralized. A similar balance is proposed by Theophrastus as an aesthetic ideal. Here Eliot most clearly establishes the relationship between the real and the ideal in artistic representation.

One of the fundamental mistakes made by critics of *Deronda*'s "Zionism" is the confusion of author with character, particularly of Mordecai's views with Eliot's. Eliot admires these visionaries, but their views should not be mistaken for hers. Mordecai's visions, drawn from poetic and religious texts, are transmitted to Deronda, but remain separate from his determination to ascertain the condition of Jews living in the East. Deronda's sanity is stressed through his attempts to separate his own understanding of his relationship with Gwendolen from her fantasies about his role in her fate.

Dramatized in *Deronda*, and presented more explicitly in *Impressions*, is the connection between the moral limitations of egoism and the aesthetic failures of false representation. At the moment Gwendolen is shattered by a consciousness of external events, she becomes aware of Daniel as a person with a life beyond her imaginative constructions. In *Impressions*, a clear distinction is made between the "cheaper substitute" of a "glorifying imagination" and the "fundamental power of strong, discerning perception" (109). The moral and aesthetic stakes defined by Theophrastus go to the heart of Eliot's realism, "for apart from this basis of an effect perceived in common, there could be no conveyance of aesthetic meaning by the painter to the beholder" (110). Our imagination must come of "susceptibility to the veriest minutiae of experience, which it reproduces and constructs in fresh and fresh wholes" (110). If we confuse "provable fact" with "fictions of fancy," the culture as a whole risks a kind of madness.

In "Moral Swindlers," Eliot anticipates the aestheticism movement and the "negation" of moral sensibilities represented by the "gauzy mental garments with their spangles of poor paradox" which are the "self-crowning" of "mental alienation," a "glorifying of swinishness" (136). In an apparent reference to symbolist poetry, Theophrastus seeks to reconnect morality and art, even before the *fin-de-siècle* attempt to sever them. In his dual capacity as late nineteenth-century Englishman and ancient Greek contemporary of Aristotle, he speculates: "suppose it had been handed down to us that Sophocles or Virgil had at one time made himself scandalous in this way: the works which have consecrated their memory for our admiration and gratitude are not a glorifying of swinishness, but an artistic incorporation of the highest sentiment known to their age" (136).

This concern with separating the moral "scandal" of the author from the admired and consecrated works may be read as Eliot's attempt to prepare the way for her own association with the likes of Sophocles, Virgil, Dante, and Shakespeare. By the time she wrote *Impressions*, she had outlived the scandal of her relationship with Lewes, but after his death she moved toward a new, ambiguous social position as the wife of John Walter Cross. Their courtship was conducted through readings of *The Divine Comedy* and through discussions of her investments. In marrying Cross, her personal life became at once scandalous (because he was younger than she) and respectable (because the marriage was legal). Significantly, by giving her legal married status Cross had already begun the project of securing her personal and artistic reputation, which would culminate in his editing of her letters and journals after her death and the invention of the highbrow "George Eliot," whose moralism the next generation would reject.

In the conclusion to this study, I look at the mutual influences of her fiction on his writing about finance and of his knowledge about colonial investments on her late writing and life. This excavation of the "structure and attitude of reference" in two disparate forms of Victorian discourse – fiction and financial analysis – would be meaningless without our knowledge of biographical details which provide a crucial context for understanding Victorian culture. Only through a combined examination of form, content, and authorial experience can we employ the method-ology of taking into account "as much evidence as possible," which Said advocates but does not fully realize. With a method of historical cultural studies that includes the author's experiences as they are known to us, we can better see the tensions that complicate the notion of a determining ideology.

# Conclusion

During these forty years we have, more and more, come to live and
move and have our being by the New World.

John Walter Cross[1]

Eliot's courtship with Cross revolved around two subjects: Dante and
finance. In her diaries for 1879, she recorded that Mr. Cross came "to
consult about investments" (*Journals*, p. 165); "to discuss investments"
(*Journals*, p. 166); that he brought "account of sales and purchases of
stock" (*Journals*, p. 167) and "came on business" (*Journals*, p. 168). Eliot
signed one love letter to Cross, "Beatrice" (*GEL*, 7:211–12), and another,
"Your obliged ex-shareholder of A and C Gaslight and Coke" (*GEL*,
7:234–5). Cross recreated this unusual marriage of literature and finance
in writings. As if recalling *Impressions of Theophrastus Such*, his first book
was titled, *Impressions of Dante and the New World, with Some Thoughts on Bi-
Metallism*. His second volume, *A Rake's Progress in Finance* (1905), once again
joined literature and finance, dealing with a range of issues, including
South African emigration. Recognizing that his yoking of literature and
finance was unusual, he wrote that it was "not an every day combination
as the person who studies the one does not often study the other."[2]

Money had always been important to Eliot, but she felt obliged to view
it as "vulgar." In 1859 she wrote to John Blackwood: "I don't want the
world to give me anything for my books except money enough to save me
from the temptation to write *only* for money" (*GEL*, 3:152). In 1860, she
introduced the subject of her first purchase of shares with an assessment of
her domestic situation: "my cup is full of blessings: my home is bright and
warm with love and tenderness, and in more material vulgar matters we
are very fortunate. I have invested £2000 in East Indies Stock, and expect
shortly to invest another £2000" (*GEL*, 3:360). The words "material,"
"vulgar," "blessings," and "fortunate" belie the conflict she felt about
her interest in money and the rewards for hard work that she knew were

more than fortunate. For Cross, money was anything but vulgar. In her relationship with him money became inseparable from love and from literature.

Cross's writing on Dante and bimetallism epitomizes the apparent incongruities that characterized their courtship. Throughout the 1870s, he published articles on investment, finance, and emigration in several prominent periodicals, including *Fraser's*, *Macmillan's*, and *The Nineteenth Century*. In them he invoked the works of George Eliot to authorize his own views. After meeting Cross, Eliot wrote more explicitly about finance, both literally and metaphorically – in *Middlemarch*, *Deronda*, and *Impressions*. Through an intertextual reading of Eliot's and Cross's writings, we see what Gillian Beer, in her discussion of money and gossip in *Middlemarch*, refers to as "an easy slippage between the discourse of narration and the discourse of finance."[3] Similarly, we see slippage in the notion of a New World, which refers to the spiritual frontier Cross described when he wrote of Dante that "the divine poet took us into a new world" and also to the economic frontier of North America, New Zealand, and South Africa.[4]

Catherine Gallagher ends her essay "George Eliot and *Daniel Deronda*: The Prostitute and the Jewish Question" with the claim that, when she married John Walter Cross in May 1880, "George Eliot, author, and Marian Evans Lewes, scandalous woman, went out of existence in the same instant."[5] Gallagher focuses on the trope of the author as prostitute and examines Marian Evans Lewes, the scandalous woman and highly paid author, in the light of representations of Jews, money, and women in *Deronda*. As I have argued, considerations of Eliot's relationship to her money, both in biography and literary criticism, have been limited to her earning-power as an author, and have not examined her position as a wealthy shareholder. Similarly, as in Gallagher's essay, interest in her personal relationships has tended to stop with Lewes, with whom she enjoyed twenty-four years of intellectual companionship, and whose writing was continuous with and influential for her own:

Eliot's transformation of a long-standing friendship with her banker "Johnny" Cross into an emotionally charged courtship and marriage does not appear to have comparable intellectual/literary relevance. Rosemarie Bodenheimer is correct in writing that marrying Cross "was the most practical step she could have taken."[6] Yet Bodenheimer also notes that Eliot presented her affair with Cross as a "miraculous romance tale, in which the heroine, rescued from death and restored to life at the last minute, is still too dazed to know quite what has happened to her."[7]

Cross himself and Haight after him contribute to this myth by playing up the Paolo and Francesca motif of their readings in Dante, as when Haight writes that in August 1879 "there came a day when in that book they read no more."[8] The combination of the literary/romantic and the practical/financial is striking.

Gillian Beer asks apropos of monetary metaphors in *Middlemarch*, "Is the novelist then the banker?"[9] Or, in this case, did the banker remake the novelist? Was her marriage to Cross, as Gallagher suggests, the end of "George Eliot" or a new beginning? Bodenheimer writes that Cross "read to perfection his function in George Eliot's life" – to repair the damage done by the "scandalous woman" and even to override the passions and ambiguities of her fiction by presenting the "autobiography" of a woman who was in effect his own creation.[10] Born in 1840, Cross was of a new generation, and in examining his union with Eliot we can go beyond the biographical implications to consider the union of literature and finance their marriage represented. I have been arguing that by studying aspects of Eliot's everyday life we establish new contexts that more accurately explain the conditions under which she wrote and which open her fiction to new interpretations. Her marriage to Cross reveals the overlapping Victorian discourses of literature, finance, and empire that signified a future about which *Impressions* in particular shows Eliot to have been pessimistic and uncertain.

Cross has become popularly known in the twentieth century as the man who jumped from a window of a hotel in Venice into the Grand Canal on his honeymoon. This mysterious, anecdotal event has come to stand as a sign of his insanity, his sexual insecurity, and his mismatch with the great woman author, twenty years his senior, and its disturbing, comic anomalousness has lent itself to fictional treatment.[11] I redirect attention to Cross in his primary capacity as Eliot's financial advisor, as someone knowledgeable and thoughtful about what he termed the "New World," and whose writing about the British empire influenced Eliot during the 1870s, long before their marriage.

She even began to use the term. For example, she wrote to Johnny's younger brother Richard James Cross in New York, inviting him to England with his wife, "to give her a sight of this Old World, groaning and travailing with sorrows but also rich with memories of which the New knows nothing except by report" (*GEL*, 7:292). Because she knew the New World only "by report," she saw it in an unreal, symbolic light, like other places she had not seen – the Jamaica of "Brother Jacob," or the East of *Daniel Deronda*. In contrast, Cross had lived in the United

States, working for his father's investment firm, Dennistoun, Cross, and Co. He had also traveled to Australia to sell a sheep station owned by his company. Like all British travelers, he reflected on what he saw and about the future of the colonies. Writing to his mother from Melbourne in 1872, he observed that the Australians were inferior to the English – there was a "distinct want of individuality" about them: "I wonder whether they would improve by being left to themselves."[12] In asking such questions about the improvement and evolution of colonial populations, Cross echoed other authors concerned specifically with the character of the empire, rather than with practical matters of business. In 1869, Charles Wentworth Dilke wrote that in Australia, "a national character is being grafted upon good English stock": "What shape the Australian mind will take is at present somewhat doubtful."[13]

Cross's writings about investment and the colonies demonstrate a pragmatic optimism. But like Eliot in *Deronda* and *Impressions*, he worried about the future of the Old World, specifically in economic terms. Cross attempts to assess the likely future of trade and commerce, observing that the temptation "to project imagination into the future" is "almost irresistible."[14] Yet he also qualifies this imaginary projection by quoting his future wife as a kind of sage – an early beginning to his later construction of her as "George Eliot" in his 1885 *George Eliot's Life*. He writes: "'Among all forms of mistake,' says George Eliot, 'prophecy is the most gratuitous. Man must always carry a threatening shadow under full sunshine.'"[15] With this kind of invocation, he not only introduced George Eliot's words into contemporary financial writing, he also participated in the project, initiated by Alexander Main's *Wise, Witty and Tender Sayings*, of transforming her into a moralist and purveyor of maxims. In this sense, Cross created Eliot's image and piloted her reputation into the next generation. During the years of his most intensive contact with the Leweses, Cross's experience in the colonies and knowledge of British finance relative to the New World economies had an impact on Eliot's life.

When Cross returned to England in 1872 he pursued the friendship with Eliot and Lewes which had begun in Rome in 1869. In 1875, he started his own company, Cross, Benson, and Co., and took on the responsibility of overseeing Eliot's investments. The Leweses' fondness for "nephew" Johnnie was linked with their reliance on him as a knowledgeable ally in business dealings that ranged from his finding their summer home in Surrey to his purchasing diverse railway shares with Eliot's increasing literary earnings. The profits from *Middlemarch*, for example, went directly into American railroads. In 1873, Lewes and Cross negotiated the best strategy for investing Eliot's earnings: "I would rather concentrate the 2250 on *five* than on 10 railways – to be selected by you."[16] American railroads, as Cross wrote in "The Extension of Railways in America," represented the future of English investment, and Eliot's portfolio came increasingly to reflect his views. Railroads throughout the New World British colonies also offered profitable investments for English shareholders, and Eliot placed her money in these and other colonial ventures.[17]

Cross was an especially important advisor to Eliot after Lewes's death. One of the first financial arrangements he helped her to make was the provision for a memorial to Lewes in the form of a studentship at Cambridge, requiring an endowment from the money her investments produced. On March 11, 1879, she authorized the sale of "San Francisco Bank, Continental Gas, and the American coupons previously marked to the amount of £5000 – to be invested in L. and N. W. Debentures – also U.S. Funded which were about to be paid" (*Journals*, p. 166). The £5,000 worth of perpetual debentures of 4 percent stock in the London and North West Rail Road Company were transferred to the trustees of the studentship, and on September 2 Eliot recorded that "The Trust deed is now signed and the money transferred" (*Journals*, p. 180). The studentship and the support of various Lewes relatives caused her anxiety about her money, and financial consultations brought her into frequent and intimate contact with Cross.

In May 1880, Eliot and Cross married, to the surprise of everyone except Edith Simcox, whose jealousy of Cross is discussed by Beer: "The parental dyad of George Eliot and G. H. Lewes is augmented by these emulous sibling rivals, twenty years younger than Eliot and Lewes, and both desperate for George Eliot's attention and love."[18] The rivals also represented different political perspectives – Cross a liberal capitalism and Simcox a radical socialism, Eliot's sympathies clearly falling with the former. After Eliot's death, Cross selected and edited her letters and journals for publication, a job that had been coveted by Simcox. With his own comfortable income, he seems to have settled into his role as widower of George Eliot. In 1891, he approached William Blackwood, drawing on the George Eliot connection, and proposed collecting his previously published journal articles, together with some new reflections on Dante, whose writing he had studied with Eliot during their courtship and marriage.[19]

Looking at her fiction as a whole, we see evidence of her anxiety about the future and about the way individual lives will be perpetuated and remembered. If Eliot did not lament the fact of not having borne children, her fiction shows an awareness of the fears suffered by older women – from Mrs. Transome to the Princess Halm Eberstein – when looking ahead to their own deaths. In 1875, John Blackwood wrote of Eliot to his nephew William that Eliot seems to "feel that in producing her books she is producing a living thing, and no doubt her books will live longer than is given to children of the flesh" (*GEL*, 9:149). She also concerned herself with the futures of Lewes's family – the children of Charles and Bertie Lewes.[20] If the first generation of Lewes's children had been seen as potential investments which devolved into charities, then providing for the grandchildren became an investment in the future beyond her own life. She cared about her posterity and that of Lewes, including his textual progeny. She would leave her own future in the hands of Cross, but she applied herself to engineering Lewes's posthumous reputation by revising his *Problems of Life and Mind*.

After Lewes's death, she had an authority over his authorial identity that he himself no longer had. With the death of the author begins the life of the author as constructed from the surviving texts. The author then lives only within the words of the text. Once dead, he or she becomes more like a character in a fiction for whom no physical referent exists. She had scrutinized Mr. Casaubon's desire to have Dorothea complete his life's work, and Lewes had referred to his own research, which Eliot would finish after his death, as his "Key to All Psychologies." In a prophetic reversal shortly before Lewes died, Eliot created a character who speculated about the fate of his unpublished papers and about his posthumous reputation. The childless Theophrastus concludes his autobiographical first chapter with a reflection on the death of himself, the author:

I leave my manuscripts to a judgment outside my imagination, but I will not ask to hear it, or request my friend to pronounce, before I have been buried decently, what he really thinks of my parts, and to state candidly whether my papers would be most usefully applied in lighting the cheerful domestic fire. (12)

Theophrastus explains that someone "outside" his imagination is better prepared to judge his work than he is. He leaves himself – his "parts" – in the care of an unnamed friend. The attitude that Eliot created in her fictional character, she later had to imagine as belonging to Lewes – the willingness to trust someone else to arrange his writings in the manner which represents him best, or at least which best represents *him*. Theophrastus continues by conceding that he "will only ask my friend to use his judgment in insuring me against posthumous mistake" (13). And in the end it was Cross who was left to judge what parts of her letters and journals should be used in the constitution of the posthumous "George Eliot."

In the 1870s, both Eliot and Cross saw the nation's future in terms of literary and monetary representation. Issues like specie payments and bimetallism were among those preoccupying Cross, while Eliot wrote about "Debasing the Moral Currency" as a metaphor for cultural decline. The common use of other metaphors, such as evolution theory, to speak about finance suggests a further slippage in which finance is explained in terms of biological progress and race. In "The Future of Agricultural Labourers' Emigration," Cross writes of British emigrants to the colonies in evolutionary terms, contrasting organized emigration to former days – the days when the Lewes boys emigrated – when "only those as a rule emigrated who by a process of natural selection were among the strongest and hardiest and most self-reliant."[21] The irony of this attitude is heightened when he quotes "the noble words of the author of 'Romola'" to argue that emigration should not be taken lightly, for "the light abandonment of ties, whether inherited or voluntary, because they have ceased to be pleasant, is the uprooting of social and personal virtue."[22]

In a chapter titled "America Rediviva" (originally published in 1879), Cross favors Darwinian imagery again in talking about financial development and the suspension of specie payments. Addressing the emergence of new financial accommodations, he explains that for a while two currencies existed, "the bags of gold going round, as in primitive races; then, after some years, cheques; lastly, after some more years, clearing: a beautiful example for students of evolution!" (204). Published in the same year, *Impressions* uses similar Darwinian language to talk about the evolution of machines and the future generally in "Shadows of the Coming Race." Theophrastus writes that

there rises a fearful vision of the human race evolving machinery which will by-and-by throw itself fatally out of work. When, in the Bank of England, I see a wondrously delicate machine for testing sovereigns, a shrewd implacable little steel Rhadamanthus that, once the coins are delivered up to it, lifts and balances each in turn for the fraction of an instant, finds it wanting or sufficient, and dismisses it to right or left with rigorous justice. (137)

It was Cross who had taken Eliot and Lewes to the Bank of England in 1874 where they saw a machine for testing coins.[23] Theophrastus continues to describe his response to these advancements: "I get a little out of it, like an unfortunate savage too suddenly brought face to face with civilisation, and I exclaim – 'Am I already in the shadow of the Coming Race?'" (138).

In this essay, the "shadow" imagery itself suggesting a Dantesque vision, as well as the darkness of the "coming race," Eliot mingles biological and financial metaphors, just as Cross had done. In Theophrastus's dystopian projection of machines evolving to take over the world, he imagines mechanisms acting on each other, discharging volts of electricity to galvanize tools into life and "by this unerringly directed discharge operating on movements corresponding to what we call Estimates, and by necessary mechanical consequence on movements corresponding to what we call the Funds, which with a vain analogy we sometimes speak of as 'sensitive'" (139). Theophrastus plays on the contemporary language of finance, such as Cross's, which speaks of "Estimates" and "the Funds" in terms of living organisms. Most importantly, "Shadows of the Coming Race" worries in Darwinian terms that the "humbler kinds of work should be entirely nullified while there are still left some men and women who are not fit for the highest" (137). In "The Future of the Agricultural Labourers' Emigration," Cross insists that these are precisely the kind of men and women who should emigrate to the New World.

I end with a discussion of Eliot and Cross's relationship because his image of George Eliot made a tremendous impact on future generations, and, even more importantly, because Eliot's marriage to him and the points of overlap in their writings of the 1870s epitomize the connections between literature, finance, and empire that characterized British culture on the brink of a new, self-conscious, and aggressive imperialism that would transform the future in ways Eliot would not live to see. As Dilke wrote in *Greater Britain*, "Everywhere we have found that the difficulties which impede the progress to universal dominion of the English people lie in the conflict with the cheaper races." He observes that "miscegenation will go but little way towards blending races" and that the "dearer are, on the whole, likely to destroy the cheaper peoples."[24] Eliot used similar metaphors, but without such a confident assertion of English superiority. Financial and racial metaphors abound in *Impressions* in chapters such as "A Half-Breed," "Debasing the Moral Currency," and "Shadows of the Coming Race." These chapters associate financial and racial amalgamation, implicitly connecting both to British colonialism and to the New World – the future of rapidly changing English and international cultures. Theophrastus observes that the "tendency of things is towards the quicker or slower fusion of races" – a tendency which it is "impossible to arrest" (160).

Realistic representations of the past in Eliot's fiction made room toward the end of her life for speculations about the future, for national movements that she approved and for warfare that she abhorred. The colonies were places she would never see. Like the future, they maintained an imagined quality, pieced together from texts about which she was skeptical. Cross, for his part, had been to the New World and seen its potential, and was convinced that the future of the old world – its products, commerce, livelihood, culture – would and should be bound up with the new by which "we have, more and more, come to live and move and have our being."[25] In marrying him she embraced a particular kind of future for England and, perhaps unwittingly, secured a particular image of herself for posterity – ironically, the foundations of a biographical tradition that has ignored her connections to finance and to the empire.

Running through Eliot's fiction is a subtext of her intimate involvement with the empire. In this respect, despite the uniqueness of her life, she was typical of her nation and class: she had multiple investments in the future of England and its colonies. It is crucial to see the details and ambiguities of these investments in order to understand the contexts of the Victorian world in which she lived.

# Notes

## INTRODUCTION

1 Herbert Lewes to GE and GHL. While some of the Lewes boys' South African letters were printed in Gordon S. Haight's *The George Eliot Letters*, 9 vols. (New Haven: Yale University Press, 1954–5 and 1978), vols. viii–ix, I draw primarily on the letters Haight did not publish, now in the George Eliot–G. H. Lewes Collection at the Beinecke Rare Book and Manuscript Library, Yale University.

2 Rosemarie Bodenheimer, *The Real Life of Marian Evans: George Eliot, Her Letters, and Her Fiction* (Ithaca: Cornell University Press, 1994), pp. 193, 230.

3 Herbert Lewes to GHL and GE, October 14, 1866, MS Yale.

4 Richard Koebner and Helmut Dan Schmidt, *Imperialism: The Story and Significance of a Political Word, 1840–1960* (Cambridge University Press, 1964), p. 1.

5 Charles Wentworth Dilke, *Greater Britain: A Record of Travel in English-Speaking Countries during 1866 and 1867*, 2 vols. (London: Macmillan, 1869), vol. II, p. 380.

6 See Bernard Semmel, *The Liberal Ideal and the Demons of Empire* (Baltimore: Johns Hopkins University Press, 1993).

7 Margaret Homans argues that *Deronda* "supplies a biting summation of this negative image of queenliness in the expansive context of imperialism." See *Royal Representations: Queen Victoria and British Culture, 1837–1876* (University of Chicago Press, 1998), p. 233. On Eliot and the Governor Eyre controversy, see Tim Watson, "Jamaica, Genealogy, George Eliot: Inheriting the Empire after Morant Bay," *Jouvert* 1:1 (1997), 1–31.

8 Bodenheimer, *Real Life*, p. 5.

9 Recent biographies follow the general outline established by Haight. See Gordon S. Haight, *George Eliot: A Biography* (New York: Oxford University Press, 1968); Rosemary Ashton, *George Eliot: A Life* (London: Hamish Hamilton, 1996); Frederick Karl, *George Eliot: Voice of a Century* (New York: Norton, 1995); Kathryn Hughes, *George Eliot: The Last Victorian* (London: Fourth Estate, 1998).

10 Elizabeth Helsinger, *Rural Scenes and National Representations: Britain, 1815–1850* (Princeton University Press, 1997), p. 236.

11 Edward Said, *Orientalism* (New York: Pantheon, 1978), p. 94.

12 *Ibid.*

13 Firdous Azim, *The Colonial Rise of the Novel* (New York: Routledge, 1993), p. 30.

14 Edward Said, *Culture and Imperialism* (New York: Alfred A. Knopf, 1993), p. 75.

15 George Eliot, "*Evenings in My Tent; or, Wanderings in Balad Ejjareed, Illustrating the Moral, Religious, Social, and Political Conditions of Various Arab Tribes of the African Sahara* by the Rev. N. Davis," *Leader*, April 8, 1854, 330. On Eliot and the *Arabian Nights*, see Alicia Carroll, " 'Arabian Nights': 'Make-Believe,' Exoticism, and Desire in *Daniel Deronda*," *JEGP* 98:2 (April 1999), 219–38.

16 On the experiences of failed colonists, see Nicholas Thomas and Richard Eves, *Bad Colonists: The South Seas Letters of Vernon Lee Walker and Louis Becke* (Durham, NC: Duke University Press, 1999). Their methodology, which treats the letters of two South Seas colonists as important historical and anthropological artifacts, addresses a neglected facet of colonial studies: the experiences of "bad" or failed colonists.

17 Charles Dickens, *Dombey and Son*, ed. Alan Horsman (Oxford University Press, 1982), p. 2.

18 Edward Said, *The Question of Palestine* (New York: Vintage, 1979), p. 66.

## 1 IMPERIAL KNOWLEDGE: GEORGE ELIOT, G. H. LEWES, AND THE LITERATURE OF EMPIRE

1 "*Evenings in My Tent*," 330.

2 Reviewed by Ebenezer Syme, *WR* 59 (January 1853).

3 *The Letters of Charles Dickens*, eds. Madeline House, Graham Storey, and Kathleen Tillotson, 11 vols. (Oxford: Clarendon Press, 1965–99), vol. IV, p. 27.

4 Samuel Sidney, *The Three Colonies of Australia; New South Wales, Victoria, South Australia; Their Pastures, Copper Mines, and Gold Fields* (London: Ingram, Cooke, & Co., 1852), p. viii.

5 *Ibid.*, p. ix.

6 George Eliot, "John Ruskin's *Modern Painters*, vol. III" in *Selected Essays, Poems and Other Writings*, eds. A. S. Byatt and Nicholas Warren (Harmondsworth: Penguin, 1990), p. 368.

7 Among books reviewed in the *Leader* (1850–54) were: *Sir John Franklin and the Arctic Regions* by Peter Lund Simmonds, *A Visit to the Indian Archipelago* by Captain the Hon. Henry Keppel, *The Colonial History of Lord John Russell's Administration* by Earl Grey, *The Australian: Practical Hints to Intending Emigrants* by W. Crellin, *Victoria; Late Australia Felix, or Port Philip District of New South Wales* by William Westgarth, and *A Narrative of Travels on the Amazon and Rio Negro with an Account of Native Tribes, etc.* by Alfred R. Wallace. After 1855, Lewes recorded reading the following books (titles are given as they appear in his journals): Stephen's *Incidents of Travel*, Thomas Williams's *Fiji and the Fijians*, Petherick's *Travels in Central Africa*, Cook's *Voyages*, Humboldt's *Travels*, Kane's *Arctic Expedition*, Oliphant's *China and Japan*, Kohl's *Kitchi-Gami*, Bennett's

*Australian Natural History*, Trollope's *Australia*, Elphinstone's *History of India*, Wilson's *The Abode of Snow*, Baker's *Nile Expedition*, Edwards's *Up the Nile*, and Trollope's *South Africa* (GHL journals, July 1856–November 1878).

8 "*Evenings in My Tent*," 330.

9 *Ibid.*

10 *Ibid.*

11 Eliot, *Selected Essays*, eds. Byatt and Warren, p. 381.

12 George Eliot, "*First Footsteps in East Africa* by Richard Burton and C. J. Andersen's *Lake Ngami*," *WR* 66 (October 1856), 310.

13 *Ibid.*, 309.

14 *Lake Ngami; or, Explorations and Discoveries, during Four Years' Wanderings in the Wilds of Southwestern Africa* by Charles John Andersen [Karl Johan Andersson], ran through numerous editions in the 1850s. In it he contradicted information brought back by David Livingstone after his "discovery" of Lake Ngami in 1849. In fact, both men were right. The lake in what is now northwestern Botswana expands and shrinks according to season and rainfall.

15 See Patrick Brantlinger, *Rule of Darkness: British Literature and Imperialism* (Ithaca: Cornell University Press, 1988). For a recent study of Anglo-Indian literature, see Nancy Paxton, *Writing under the Raj: Gender, Race, and Rape in the British Colonial Imagination, 1830–1947* (New Brunswick: Rutgers University Press, 1999).

16 Harriet Ritvo, *The Animal Estate: The English and Other Creatures in the Victorian Age* (Cambridge, MA: Harvard University Press, 1987), p. 205.

17 Robert W. Jones, "'The Sight of Creatures Strange to our Clime': London Zoo and the Consumption of the Exotic," *Journal of Victorian Culture* 2:1 (Spring 1997), 5.

18 See John M. MacKenzie, *The Empire of Nature: Hunting, Conservation and British Imperialism* (Manchester University Press, 1988).

19 *Leader*, July 27, 1850, 423.

20 *Ibid.*

21 *Ibid.*

22 Lewes's objections were exceptional. MacKenzie writes that "Cumming was not condemned by his contemporaries, although some professed to find his exploits rather far-fetched and found the subsequent showmanship distasteful." *Empire of Nature*, p. 99.

23 MacKenzie, *Empire of Nature*, p. 36.

24 *Ibid.*

25 G. H. Lewes, "Life in Central Africa," *Blackwood's Edinburgh Magazine* 89 (April 1861), 452.

26 Cumming, Gérard, and Livingstone were major lion-hunting figures and are mentioned in a guide for visitors to the Regent's Park Zoo. See Jones, "'The Sight of Creatures,'" 24.

27 G. H. Lewes, "Lions and Lion Hunting," *WR* 65 (January 1856), 116.

28 *Ibid.*, 117.

29 *Ibid.*, 121.

30 *Ibid.*, 122.

31 *Ibid.*

32 *Ibid.*

33 Shortly after "Lions and Lion Hunting" appeared, Lewes wrote to Herbert Spencer, answering the charge of having a weakness for lions: "There's a young lioness in the Z. Gardens just now more *kissable* than the loveliest Circassian in the Sultan's harem" ( *GEL*, 8:151).

34 Rudyard Kipling, *"The Man Who Would Be King" and Other Stories*, ed. Louis L. Cornell (Oxford University Press, 1987), p. 269.

35 For a study of mid-Victorian discourses of discipline, including Kingsley's, and their relationship to imperial conquest, see James Eli Adams, *Dandies and Desert Saints: Styles of Victorian Manhood* (Ithaca: Cornell University Press, 1995). For an overview of "constructions" of masculinity in the Victorian period, see Joseph A. Kestner, *Masculinities in Victorian Painting* (Aldershot: Scolar Press, 1995).

36 Some exceptions include Eve Sedgwick, *Between Men: English Literature and Male Homosocial Desire* (New York: Columbia University Press, 1985), and Sharon Leah Kayfetz, "Counterfeit Coins and Traffic Jams: Rewriting Masculinity in *Adam Bede*," *New Orleans Review* 24:2 (1998), 62–72. For an excellent overview of feminist approaches to Eliot's writing as well as a contextualization of her life and work in terms of nineteenth-century gender issues, see Gillian Beer, *George Eliot* (Brighton: Harvester Press, 1986).

37 Bodenheimer, *Real Life*, p. 193.

38 See Beryl Gray, " 'Animated Nature': *The Mill on the Floss*" in *George Eliot and Europe*, ed. John Rignall (Aldershot: Scolar Press, 1997), pp. 138–55.

39 Susan Meyer sees in this passage a critique in which Eliot suggests that the "impulse towards imperialism is a lazy one, associated with vagrancy rather than with tools and the love of work." *Imperialism at Home* (Ithaca: Cornell University Press, 1996), p. 136.

40 G. H. Lewes, "African Life," *WR* 69 ( January 1858), 15.

41 Lewes's review of Barter's book forms part of a larger review of a number of different books under the heading "Literature" in the *Leader*, April 15, 1853, 67.

42 Robert James Mann, *The Colony of Natal. An Account of the Characteristics and Capabilities of This British Dependency* (London: 1859).

43 *Ibid.*, pp. 213–14.

44 *Ibid.*, p. 187.

45 *Ibid.*, pp. 208–9.

46 *Ibid.*, p. 222.

47 *Leader*, April 2, 1853, 330.

48 "African Life," 1.

49 *Ibid.*

50 *Ibid.*

51 *Ibid.*

52 *Ibid.*, 7.

53 For an examination of the imperial hero, see Daniel Bivona, *British Imperial Literature 1870–1940: Writing and the Administration of the Empire* (Cambridge University Press, 1998), and Graham Dawson, *British Adventure, Empire and the Imagining of Masculinities* (New York: Routledge, 1994).

54 Referring to Speke's "Journal of a Cruise on the Tanganyika Lake, Central Africa," *Blackwood's* 86 (September 1859), and to "Captain J. H. Speke's Discovery of the Victoria Nyanza Lake, the Supposed Source of the Nile, from his Journal," *Blackwood's* 86 (October–November 1859), Eliot wrote that "Excellent Captain Speke can't write so well, but one follows him out of grave sympathy" (*GEL*, 3:185).

55 Speke's bad writing was apparently the instigation for what became his dramatic break and subsequent rivalry with Burton. Eliot, Lewes, and Blackwood were inclined to take Speke's part, given their dislike of Burton. See *The Letters of George Henry Lewes*, ed. William Baker, 3 vols. (Victoria, BC: University of Victoria Press, 1995 and 1999), vol. II, p. 17. Explorers published in *Blackwood's* included Laurence Oliphant, Admiral Sherard Osborn, Captain Charles Hope, and Colonel J. A. Grant. See David Finkelstein, "Breaking the Thread: The Authorial Reinvention of John Hanning Speke in His *Journal of Discovery of the Source of the Nile*," *Text: An Interdisciplinary Annual of Textual Studies* 9 (1997), 280–96.

56 G. H. Lewes, "Uncivilized Man," *Blackwood's* 89 (January 1861), 29.

57 Richard Burton, *The Lake Regions of Central Africa* (1860; reprint, New York: Dover, 1995), p. vii.

58 Eliot, "*First Footsteps*," 310.

59 Lewes, "Uncivilized Man," 31.

60 *Ibid.*, 36.

61 *Ibid.*, 37.

62 Ritvo, *Animal Estate*, p. 22.

63 For an illustrated discussion of this exhibition, see Gail Ching-Liang Low, *White Skins/Black Masks: Representation and Colonialism* (New York: Routledge, 1996).

64 "The Zulu Kaffirs," *Leader*, May 28, 1853, 502.

65 Dickens also went to see the Zulu exhibit in May and incorporated his impressions in the vitriolic essay "The Noble Savage," *Household Words* 7:168 (June 11, 1853), 337–9.

66 Nancy L. Paxton, *George Eliot and Herbert Spencer: Feminism, Evolutionism, and the Reconstruction of Gender* (Princeton University Press, 1991), p. 202.

67 *Ibid.*, p. 224.

68 G. H. Lewes, "Hereditary Influence, Animal and Human," *WR* 66 (July 1856), 89.

69 *Ibid.*, 76.

70 *Ibid.*, 89.

71 See Lewes's "Mr. Buckle's Scientific Errors," *Blackwood's* 90 (November 1861). For Eliot's views on Buckle, see Neil McCaw, *George Eliot and Victorian Historiography* (Basingstoke: Macmillan, 2000).

72 GHL diary, February 14, 1859, MS Yale.

73 Lewes, "Hereditary Influence," 90.

74 For a survey of Eliot's views on war generally, see Nancy Henry, "George Eliot and Politics" in *The Cambridge Companion to George Eliot*, ed. George Levine (Cambridge University Press, 2001), pp. 138–58.

75 Mary Poovey, *Uneven Developments: The Ideological Work of Gender in Mid-Victorian England* (University of Chicago Press, 1988), p. 170.

76 *Ibid.*, pp. 165–6.

## 2 "COLLEAGUES IN FAILURE": EMIGRATION AND THE LEWES BOYS

1 Anthony Trollope, *The West Indies and the Spanish Main* (London: Chapman and Hall, 1859), p. 102.

2 Patrick A. Dunae, "Education, Emigration and the Empire: The Colonial College, 1887–1905" in *"Benefits Bestowed"?: Education and British Imperialism*, ed. J. A. Mangan (Manchester University Press, 1988), p. 196. See also Dunae, *Gentlemen Emigrants: From the British Public Schools to the Canadian Frontier* (Manchester University Press, 1981).

3 Trollope nominated Charles for a position, which he obtained after passing an examination. For Charles's career, see Rosemary Ashton, *G. H. Lewes: A Life* (Oxford: Clarendon Press, 1991), and Bodenheimer, *Real Life*. Blackwood's nephew Charles died within two years of joining the army. Dickens's son Walter died in India in 1863, as will be discussed below.

4 For Lewes's early life, see Ashton, *G. H. Lewes.*

5 *The Letters of George Henry Lewes*, ed. Baker, vol. II, p. 41. Call, an intellectual, poet, and clergyman who had renounced his orders, was the second husband of Eliot's friend Rufa Brabant Hennell.

6 Anthony Trollope, *The Three Clerks*, ed. Graham Handley (Oxford University Press, 1989), p. 82.

7 *Ibid.*

8 *The Letters of Charles Dickens*, eds. House, Storey, and Tillotson, vol. X, p. 53.

9 Trollope, *Three Clerks*, p. 556.

10 *Ibid.*, p. 561.

11 Timothy Alborn, *Conceiving Companies: Joint Stock Politics in Victorian England* (New York: Routledge, 1998), p. 41.

12 John William Kaye, "The Indian Civil Service: Its Rise and Fall," parts I–II, *Blackwood's* 89 (January 1861), 115–30; (March 1861), 261–76.

13 *Ibid.*, part II, 273.

14 Thornton Lewes to GE, March 3, 1861, MS Yale.

15 Thornton Lewes to GE, October 20, 1861, MS Yale.

16 Dunae, "Education," p. 199.

17 Bodenheimer, *Real Life*, p. 196.

18 See Alicia Carroll, "The Giaour's Campaign: Desire and the Other in *Felix Holt, the Radical*," *Novel* 30:2 (1997), 238.

19 Bodenheimer, *Real Life*, p. 221.

20 Eliot, "*Evenings in My Tent*," 330.

21 GHL journal, October 2, 1864, MS Yale.

22 Dickens, *Nicholas Nickleby* ed. Paul Schlicke (Oxford University Press, 1990), p. 145.

23 *Ibid.*, p. 147.

24 Thornton Lewes to GHL, December 20, 1857, MS Yale.

25 On the emergence of the colonial war hero, see Dawson, *British Adventure*, Bivona, *British Imperial Literature*, and Linda Dryden, *Joseph Conrad and the Imperial Romance* (London: Macmillan, 2000).

26 Thornton Lewes to GHL, June 15, 1859, MS Yale. In 1840, Lewes wrote a review article condemning the despotism of the Austrians and predicting revolution in Italy, Hungary, and Bohemia. "Social Despotism in Austria," *Monthly Chronicle* 5 (June 1840), 500–508.

27 In May of 1860, Garibaldi and his "Red Shirts" embarked on their conquest of Sicily in the name of Italian unification, which was achieved in 1861. Steven Türr (1825–1908) was a Hungarian who fought with Garibaldi against the Austrians.

28 Thornton Lewes to GHL, February 3, 1861, MS Yale.

29 In 1848, "Abd el Kader at Toulon or the Caged Hawk" was published in *Punch*. Other English poems on the Algerian hero were "The Liberation of Abd-el-Kader, an Ode" (Anonymous, 1856) and *The White Lily of the Great Sahara, a Romance of the Algerian Arabs under Abd-El-Kader*, published by the author of colonial romances Charles H. Eden in 1879.

30 Viscount Maidstone [Earl of Winchilsea], *Abd-el-Kader. A Poem in Six Cantos* (London: Chapman and Hall, 1851), p. 171.

31 Thornton Lewes to GE and GHL, November 17, 1859, MS Yale.

32 G. H. Lewes, "*The Caucasus* by Ivan Golovin," *Leader*, January 14, 1854, 42.

33 Thornton Lewes to GHL, December 11, 1860, MS Yale.

34 Important work on nineteenth-century boys' adventure fiction and its connection to the empire includes Martin Green, *Dreams of Adventure, Deeds of Empire* (New York: Basic Books, 1979), Brantlinger, *Rule of Darkness*, Joseph Bristow, *Empire Boys: Adventures in a Man's World* (New York: HarperCollins, 1991), and Andrea White, *Joseph Conrad and the Adventure Tradition: Constructing and Deconstructing the Imperial Subject* (Cambridge University Press, 1993).

35 *Leader*, December 23, 1853, 1243.

36 Also reviewed were *The Charm*, *Picture Pleasure Book*, Miss Martineau's *Playfellow and Feats of the Fiord*, Miss Edgeworth's *The Crofton Boys*, and others.

37 Mayne Reid, *The Young Voyageurs; or, The Boy Hunters in the North* (London: David Bogue, 1853), p. 3.

38 *Ibid.*, p. 74.

39 Richard Phillips shows Ballantyne's *The Young Fur Traders* (1856) to be typical of its genre in representing "white, middle-class masculine rites of passage" through the unexplored colonial spaces of western Canada. See *Mapping Men and Empire: A Geography of Adventure* (New York: Routledge, 1997), p. 56.

40 R. M. Ballantyne, *The World of Ice; or, Adventures in the Polar Regions* (London: T. Nelson & Sons, 1860), p. 2.

41 *Ibid.*, p. 28. In 1859, Thornie had written to his father from Hofwyl: "Picture to yourself a strong, muscular fellow of fifteen years, like I am, dressed in a thick great coat, and armed with a deadly never-failing pistol" (Thornton Lewes, juvenilia, n.d., Yale MS).

42 Ballantyne, *The World of Ice*, p. 93.

43 *Ibid.*, p. 94.

44 *Ibid.*, p. 49.

45 Aimard wrote fifty Cooperesque novels with titles such as *Loyal Heart; or, The Trappers of Arkansas, The Pirates of the Prairies,* and *The Gold Seekers,* which were very popular and which influenced R. L. Stevenson, among others. See Green, *Dreams of Adventure*, p. 381.

46 Gustave Aimard, *The Tiger-Slayer: A Tale of the Indian Desert* (London: Ward and Lock, 1863), p. 2.

47 *Ibid.*, p. 133.

48 *Ibid.*, p. 208.

49 *Ibid.*, p. 222.

50 Bodenheimer, *Real Life*, p. 224.

51 P. D. Edwards, *Anthony Trollope's Son in Australia* (University of Queensland Press, 1982), p. 62.

52 Anthony Trollope, *The Way We Live Now*, ed. John Sutherland (Oxford University Press, 1992), vol. I, p, 62. On Trollope and the empire, see J. H. Davidson, "Anthony Trollope and the Colonies," *Victorian Studies* 12 (March 1969), 395–430, Michael Cotsell, "Trollope: The International Theme" in *Creditable Warriors, 1830–1876,* ed. Michael Cotsell (London and Atlantic Highlands, NJ: Ashfield Press, 1990), pp. 243–56, Graham Handley, *Trollope the Traveller* (London: Pickering and Chatto, 1993), and Catherine Hall, "Going A-Trolloping: Imperial Man Travels the Empire" in *Gender and Imperialism*, ed. Clare Midgley (Manchester University Press, 1998), pp. 180–99.

53 *The Letters of Charles Dickens*, eds. House, Storey, and Tillotson, vol. VIII, p. 152.

54 Peter Ackroyd, *Dickens* (London: Sinclair-Stevenson, 1990), p. 785.

55 *The Letters of Charles Dickens*, eds. House, Storey, and Tillotson, vol. VI, p. 723.

56 *Ibid.*, vol. XI, pp. 362–3.

57 *Ibid.*, vol. IX, p. 71.

58 *Ibid.*, vol. X, pp. 195, 319.

59 *Ibid.*, vol. XI, p. 397.

60 *The Letters of Charles Dickens, Edited by His Sister-in-Law and His Eldest Daughter,* 2 vols. (London: Chapman and Hall, 1880–82), vol. II, pp. 402–3.

61 Quoted in Mary Lazarus, *A Tale of Two Brothers* (Sydney: Angus and Robertson, 1973), p. 46.

62 Grahame Smith, "Suppressing Narratives: Childhood and Empire in *The Uncommercial Traveller* and *Great Expectations*" in *Dickens and the Children of Empire* ed. Wendy S. Jacobson (Basingstoke: Palgrave, 2000), p. 50.

63 *Ibid.*, p. 44.
64 On Dickens's work in relation to colonialism and imperialism, see Jacobson, ed., *Dickens and the Children of Empire*, Deirdre David, "Children of Empire: Victorian Imperialism and Sexual Politics in Dickens and Kipling" in *Gender and Discourse in Victorian Literature and Art*, eds. Antony H. Harrison and Beverly Taylor (Dekalb: Northern Illinois University Press, 1992), pp. 124–42, and Suvendrini Perera, *Reaches of Empire: The English Novel from Edgeworth to Dickens* (New York: Columbia University Press, 1991).
65 Ballantyne, *The World of Ice*, p. 201.
66 Thornton Lewes to GE and GHL, November 14, 1863, MS Yale.
67 Ballantyne, *The World of Ice*, p. 127.
68 In 1855, when Thornie was eleven, Lewes had adapted *Buckstone's Adventures with a Polish Princess*, "a broad farce for the comic actor John Baldwin Buckstone to perform at the Haymarket." Ashton, *G. H. Lewes*, p. 161.
69 One difference is that Thornie was leaving rather than questing for his father, a recurrent motif in boys' adventure fiction. Only once does he imagine that he might see his father in Africa, telling him that "if we wake up some fine morning & see you driving a unicorn up to the door of the 'Fall of the Assagai,' I should shout out to the Kaffirs to cook breakfast for four with out expressing any astonishment." Thornton Lewes to GHL, June 16, 1867, Yale MS.
70 Thornton Lewes to GHL, August 29, 1864, MS Yale.
71 Thornton Lewes to GE and GHL, January 18, 1864, MS Yale.
72 *The Letters of George Henry Lewes*, ed. Baker, vol. II, p. 276.
73 Dr. James Mann wrote in 1859: "Nothing could be more unwise than for any individual to emigrate to Natal with the purpose of starting in *business* immediately upon his arrival." Mann, *The Colony of Natal*, p. 192.
74 Thornton Lewes to GE and GHL, December 26, 1865, MS Yale.
75 Thornton Lewes to GE, January 28, 1864, MS Yale.
76 Ballantyne, *The World of Ice*, p. 180.
77 R. M. Ballantyne, *The Coral Island* (London: Andrew Dakers Limited, n.d.), p. 232.
78 Natal experienced economic depression in the second half of the 1860s due to a combination of factors: bad weather, civil war in the US (which affected trade), war between the Orange Free State and Basutoland (in which Thornie took part), and sheep diseases. Many banks and companies in the colony failed at this time. See *Enterprise and Exploitation in a Victorian Colony: Aspects of the Economic and Social History of Colonial Natal*, eds. Bill Guest and John M. Sellers (Pietermaritzburg: University of Natal Press, 1985).
79 GHL journal, September 10, 1866, MS Yale.
80 Herbert Lewes to GE and GHL, September 16, 1866, MS Yale. A mail steamer from Southampton to the Cape took forty-two days and cost £47 for first class and £17–20 for second class. Thornie had crossed on a sailing vessel, which took eighty to ninety days and cost £17–35. See *The Colony of Natal. Compiled for the Use of Emigrants, from the Most Authentic Sources, by the*

*Natal Land and Colonization Society Co.* (London: Jones and Causton, 1861), p. 54.

81 Herbert Lewes to GE and GHL, December 25, 1866, MS Yale.
82 GHL journal, December 25, 1866, MS Yale.
83 Thornton Lewes to GHL, June 2, 1866, MS Yale.
84 Thornton Lewes to GE and GHL, July 12, 1867, MS Yale.
85 Thornton Lewes to GE and GHL, January 28, 1864, MS Yale.
86 Thornton Lewes to GHL, September 16, 1867, MS Yale.
87 Thornton Lewes to GHL, March 9–April 26, 1868, MS Yale.
88 Herbert Lewes to GE and GHL, October 27, 1867, MS Yale.
89 Thornton Lewes to GHL, April 26, 1868, MS Yale.
90 Barbara Buchanan, *Pioneer Days in Natal* (Pietermaritzburg: Shuter and Shooter, 1934), p. 59.
91 Haight concluded that it was tuberculosis of the spine, though he does not document his source.
92 Bodenheimer, *Real Life*, pp. 225–7.
93 *Times*, February 27, 1862.
94 George Kilgour, *Railway Extension in the Colony of the Cape of Good Hope, S. Africa* (Cape Town: Saul Solomon & Co., 1881).

## 3 INVESTING IN EMPIRE

1 GHL diary, October 6, 1860, MS Yale.
2 A. K. Cairncross, *Home and Foreign Investment, 1870–1913* (Cambridge University Press, 1975), p. 85; Daniel Thorner, *Investment in Empire: British Railway and Steam Shipping Enterprise in India, 1825–1849* (Philadelphia: University of Pennsylvania Press, 1950), p. viii; Ian J. Kerr, *Building the Railways of the Raj, 1850–1900* (Oxford University Press, 1995), p. 4.
3 Romesh Dutt, *Economic History of India* (New York: B. Franklin, 1970), p. 353.
4 P. L. Cottrell, *British Overseas Investment in the Nineteenth Century* (London: Macmillan, 1975), p. 23.
5 Helsinger, *Rural Scenes*, p. 227.
6 Gillian Beer, *Open Fields: Science in Cultural Encounter* (Oxford University Press, 1996), p. 42.
7 Margaret Homans, "Dinah's Blush, Maggie's Arm: Class, Gender, and Sexuality in George Eliot's Early Novels," *Victorian Studies* 36:2 (Winter 1993), 169.
8 Neil Hertz, "George Eliot's Life-in-Debt," *Diacritics* 25:4 (1995), 63.
9 Susan De Sola Rodstein has shown definitively the connections between David's trade, West Indian sugar production, and British consumption. She has also identified convincingly the allegory of authorship in the making of confections. See "Sweetness and Dark: George Eliot's 'Brother Jacob,'" *Modern Language Quarterly* 52:3 (1991), 295–317.
10 By the time Eliot began to invest her earnings, the West Indies were no longer the profitable British colonies they had once been. The only

shares Eliot owned in West Indian stocks were in the Colonial Bank. The Colonial Bank (later Barclays and then the Republic Bank) was established after the emancipation of slaves in the West Indian colonies of Jamaica, Barbados, British Guiana, Trinidad, and St. Thomas in 1837, to help the sugar industry by meeting the needs of planters. See Margaret P. Rouse-Jones, *The Colonial Bank Correspondence, 1837–1885* (Port of Newtown, Spain, and Trinidad: Paria Publishing Ltd., 1986). For an account of the decline in profitability of Jamaica after the abolition of slavery, including the diminution of sugar imports, see the review article published during Eliot's time as the editor of the *Westminster Review*, "British Philanthropy and Jamaican Distress," *WR* 59 (April 1853), 171–89.

11 Catherine Gallagher, "George Eliot and *Daniel Deronda*: The Prostitute and the Jewish Question" in *The New Historicism Reader*, ed. H. Aram Veeser (New York: Routledge, 1994), p. 126.

12 *Ibid.*, p. 127.

13 Charles Dickens, *Our Mutual Friend*, ed. Michael Cotsell (Oxford University Press, 1998), p. 114.

14 Mary Poovey, *Making a Social Body: British Cultural Formation, 1830–1864* (University of Chicago Press, 1995), p. 165.

15 Christina Crosby, "Finance" in *A Companion to Victorian Literature and Culture*, ed. Herbert F. Tucker (Oxford and Malden, MA: Blackwell, 1999), p. 233.

16 On money, speculation, and the novel, see Edward Copeland, *Women Writing about Money* (Cambridge University Press, 1995), Norman Russell, *The Novelist and Mammon: Literary Responses to the World of Commerce in the Nineteenth Century* (Oxford University Press, 1986), John Vernon, *Money and Fiction: Literary Realism in the Nineteenth and Early Twentieth Centuries* (Ithaca: Cornell University Press, 1984), and John R. Reed, "A Friend to Mammon: Speculation in Victorian Literature," *Victorian Studies* 27:2 (1984), 179–202.

17 Trollope, *The Way We Live Now*, vol. II, p. 100.

18 Crosby, "Finance," p. 230.

19 Haight prints:

| | | |
|---|---|---|
| 1872 on acct for Middlemarch | | 500 |
| "      do    do | | 1447 |
| "      Australian reprint | | 200 |

(*GEL*, 7:362)
But fails to print:
*New South Wales*
    Jan 24.7.6
    Jul 24.11.6
*Victoria*
    Oct 29.10
    April 29.2
(GHL journal, Memoranda, 1872, MS Yale)

20 *The Journals of George Eliot*, eds. Margaret Harris and Judith Johnston (Cambridge University Press, 1998).

21 Bertie's widow Eliza, who arrived in England with her children in April 1879, was to receive £200 a year. Agnes continued to receive £100 and Susanna (Lewes's sister-in-law) £75. GE diary, Memoranda, 1879, MS Berg Collection, New York Public Library.

22 Sambre and Meuse was a railway facilitating transportation for coal and iron mines in Belgium. See *Facts and Suggestions for the Holders of Ordinary Shares in the Sambre and Meuse Railway* (London: Effingham Wilson, Royal Exchange E. C., 1873).

23 For a copy of the will, see Blanche Colton Williams, *George Eliot* (New York: Macmillan, 1936).

24 Eliot's will is at the Public Record Office, Somerset House, London. Individual trust legacies were established for Bertie's children, Marian Elizabeth and George Henry Herbert Lewes. The investments fed into another generation of colonization when George Henry emigrated to Australia.

25 Russell, *The Novelist and Mammon*, p. 8.

26 *The Letters of Charlotte Brontë*, ed. Margaret Smith, 2 vols. (Oxford: Clarendon Press, 1995), vol. 1, p. 390.

27 Juliet Barker, *The Brontës* (New York: St. Martin's Press, 1994), p. 617.

28 *Ibid.*

29 Barbara Leigh Smith Bodichon, *A Brief Summary, in Plain Language of the Most Important Laws Concerning Women; Together with a Few Observations Thereon* (London: John Chapman, 1854), pp. 3–4.

30 Pam Hirsch, *Barbara Leigh Smith Bodichon: Feminist, Artist, and Rebel* (London: Chatto and Windus, 1998), p. 40.

31 James Mill, *A History of British India*, ed. William Thomas (University of Chicago Press, 1995), p. 332.

32 Alborn, *Conceiving Companies*, p. 38.

33 For an analysis of the relationship of nineteenth-century British feminism to the Indian empire, see Antoinette Burton, *Burdens of History: British Feminists, Indian Women, and Imperial Culture, 1865–1915* (Chapel Hill: University of North Carolina Press, 1994).

34 This information is taken from GE's diaries for 1879 (MS Berg Collection, New York Public Library) and 1880 (MS Yale) and also from Lewes's diaries of the 1870s (MS Yale).

35 Dickens, *Dombey and Son*, p. 82.

36 Sophia Andres, "Fortune's Wheel in *Daniel Deronda*: Sociopolitical Turns on the British Empire," *Victorian Institute Journal* 24 (1996), 94–5.

37 Thorner, *Investment in Empire*, p. 108.

38 John Chapman, *Principles of Indian Reform Being Brief Hints together with a Plan for the Improvement of the Constituency of the East India Co. and for the Promotion of Indian Public Works* (London: John Chapman, 1853), p. 34.

39 *The Cotton and Commerce of India, Considered in Relation to the Interests of Great Britain; with Remarks on Railway Communication in the Bombay Presidency* was announced by Lewes in the literature section of the *Leader* on February 8, 1851.

40 Thorner, *Investment in Empire*, p. 178.

41 *Ibid.*, p. 179.
42 John Chapman, introduction to the reprint of "Our Colonial Empire," *WR* 93 (1870), 1.
43 *Household Words* 2:51 (March 15, 1851), 593.
44 John Robinson, "The Future of the British Empire," *WR* 94 (July 1870), 30.
45 Kerr, *Building the Railways*, p. 35.
46 What she had not anticipated was that Thornie would return from South Africa and occupy her time and energy in the months between May 8, 1869, and his death on October 19. Work on *Middlemarch* continued during his illness.
47 See James L. Sturgis, *John Bright and the Empire* (London: The Athlone Press, University of London, 1969).
48 John Bright, *Speeches on Questions of Public Policy*, eds. John Bright and James E. Thorold Rogers (London: Macmillan, 1880), p. 57.
49 *Ibid.*, p. 58.
50 For example, TIAA/CREF began offering the "Social Choice" option in 1990. With the end of Apartheid, considerations about what it means to be socially responsible became vexed and inconclusive. TIAA has attempted to address concerns about tobacco and alcohol, military weapons and nuclear energy, animal testing, and the environment. This account aspires to keep its investors from losing money, acknowledging that often investing principles and social concerns don't mix. See John H. Biggs, "How to Make Choices for a Social Choice Account," *Participant*, August 1998, 2–3. Interest in the topic is demonstrated in John Hancock, *The Ethical Investor: Making Gains with Values* (London: Pearson Education Limited, 1999).
51 John Chapman, "India and Its Finances," *WR* 60 (July 1853), 95.
52 Robinson, "The Future," 22.
53 *Ibid.*, 23.
54 *Ibid.*, 34.
55 John Walter Cross, *Impressions of Dante and of the New World* (London and Edinburgh: Blackwood and Sons, 1893), p. 149.

4  *DANIEL DERONDA, IMPRESSIONS OF THEOPHRASTUS SUCH,*
AND THE EMERGENCE OF IMPERIALISM

1 Criticism focusing on connections between the empire and fiction other than *Deronda* include: De Sola Rodstein, "Sweetness and Dark," Susan Meyer's chapter on *The Mill on the Floss* in *Imperialism at Home*, Watson, "Jamaica, Genealogy, George Eliot," and Carroll, "The Giaour's Campaign."
2 Meyer, *Imperialism at Home*, p. 160.
3 *Ibid.*, p. 9.
4 Perera, *Reaches of Empire*, p. 2.

5 Terry Eagleton, *Criticism and Ideology* (London: Verso, 1978), p. 123.

6 Said, *The Question of Palestine*, p. 65. Said also made this point in his article "Zionism from the Standpoint of Its Victims," *Social Text* 1 (1979), 7–58. Significantly, this article was reprinted in 1997 as the first piece in a post-colonial reader, without revisions or qualifications, thereby reinforcing the authority of this interpretation of *Deronda*. See *Dangerous Liaisons: Gender, Nation, and Postcolonial Perspectives*, eds. Anne McClintock, Aamir Mufti, and Ella Shohat (Minneapolis: University of Minnesota Press, 1997), pp. 15–38.

7 Meyer, *Imperialism at Home*, p. 166.

8 Said, *Culture and Imperialism*, p. 66.

9 On gambling in *Deronda*, see Wilfred Stone, "The Play of Chance and Ego in *Daniel Deronda*," *Nineteenth-Century Literature* 53:1 (June 1998), 25–55.

10 On inheritance in Eliot's fiction, see Bernard Semmel, *George Eliot and the Politics of National Inheritance* (New York: Oxford University Press, 1994).

11 Bruce Robbins in "Forum," *PMLA* 108:3 (1993), 541.

12 *Ibid.*, 542.

13 Meyer, *Imperialism at Home*, p. 189.

14 This was done most explicitly in the contemporary sequel to *Deronda*, *Gwendolen: A Sequel to George Eliot's "Daniel Deronda,"* published anonymously in the US in 1878.

15 Said, *Culture and Imperialism*, pp. 95–6.

16 Claire Tomalin, *Jane Austen: A Life* (New York: Viking, 1997), p. 285.

17 Gayatri Chakravorty Spivak, "Three Women's Texts and a Critique of Imperialism," *Critical Inquiry* 12 (Autumn 1985), 244.

18 Susan Fraiman, "Jane Austen and Edward Said: Gender, Culture, and Imperialism," *Critical Inquiry* 21:4 (Summer 1995), 807.

19 *Ibid.*, 808.

20 *Ibid.*, 809.

21 *Ibid.*, 821.

22 Lewes and Eliot were reading *Mansfield Park* while Eliot was writing the early chapters of *Deronda*. GHL journal, June 29, 1874, MS Yale.

23 Said, *Culture and Imperialism*, p. 93.

24 See Michael Polowetzky, *Jerusalem Recovered: Victorian Intellectuals and the Birth of Modern Zionism* (Westport, CT: Praeger, 1995).

25 Said, "Zionism" in *Dangerous Liaisons*, eds. McClintock, Mufti, and Shohat, p. 19.

26 *Ibid.*, p. 21.

27 *Ibid.*, p. 22.

28 *Ibid.*

29 *Ibid.*, p. 23.

30 C. W. M. van de Velde, *Narrative of a Journey through Syria and Palestine in 1851 and 1852*, 2 vols. (Edinburgh: William Blackwood and Sons, 1854), vol. 1, p. 199. See also the review of this book by Margaret Oliphant, "The Holy Land," *Blackwood's Edinburgh Magazine* 76 (September 1854), 223–39.

31 Deirdre David, *Fictions of Resolution in Three Victorian Novels* (New York: Columbia University Press, 1981), p. 177.

32 Reina Lewis, *Gendering Orientalism: Race, Femininity and Representation* (New York: Routledge, 1996), p. 216.

33 Katherine Bailey Linehan, "Mixed Politics: The Critique of Imperialism in *Daniel Deronda*," *Texas Studies in Literature and Language* 34:3 (1992), 325.

34 Carolyn Lesjak, "Labours of a Modern Storyteller: George Eliot and the Cultural Project of 'Nationhood'" in *Victorian Identities: Social and Cultural Formations in Nineteenth-Century Literature*, eds. Ruth Robbins and Julian Wolfreys (New York: St. Martin's, 1996), p. 40.

35 Mary N. Layoun, *Travels of a Genre: The Modern Novel and Ideology* (Princeton University Press, 1990), p. xii.

36 *Ibid.*, p. 250.

37 Ian Watt, *The Rise of the Novel: Studies in Defoe, Richardson and Fielding* (Berkeley: University of California Press, 1957), p. 32.

38 *Ibid.*, p. 67.

39 Some have found imperialist ideology in poetry. See Laura Brown, *Ends of Empire: Women and Ideology in Early Eighteenth-Century English Literature* (Ithaca: Cornell University Press, 1993).

40 Lennard J. Davis, *Factual Fictions: The Origins of the English Novel* (Philadelphia: University of Pennsylvania Press, 1996), p. 213.

41 *Ibid.*, p. 221.

42 *Ibid.*, p. 222.

43 Lennard J. Davis, "Novel Worship," *Novel* 30:3 (Spring 1997), 407. See also Davis, "Reconsidering Origins: How Novel Are Theories of the Novel?" *Eighteenth-Century Fiction* 12:2–3 (2000), 479–99.

44 Eagleton, *Criticism and Ideology*, p. 110.

45 *Ibid.*, p. 126.

46 Brantlinger, *Rule of Darkness*, p. 8.

47 Patrick Brantlinger, *Fictions of State: Culture and Credit in Britain, 1694–1994* (Ithaca: Cornell University Press, 1996), p. 9.

48 *Ibid.*, p. 183.

49 George Levine, *Darwin and the Novelists: Patterns of Science in Victorian Fiction* (Cambridge, MA: Harvard University Press, 1988), p. 255. For other interpretations of Eliot's realism in relation to sociopolitical change, see Daniel Cottom, *Social Figures: George Eliot, Social History, and Literary Representation* (Minneapolis: University of Minnesota Press, 1987), and Catherine Gallagher, *The Industrial Reformation of English Fiction: Social Discourse and Narrative Form, 1832–1867* (University of Chicago Press, 1985).

50 Eagleton, *Criticism and Ideology*, p. 123.

51 Poovey, *Uneven Developments*.

52 See Ian Hacking, "The Making and Molding of Child Abuse," *Critical Inquiry* 17 (Winter 1991), 253–88, and Nancy Henry, "Ante-Anti-Semitism: George

Eliot's *Impressions of Theophrastus Such*" in *Victorian Identities: Social and Cultural Formations in Nineteenth-Century Literature*, eds. Ruth Robbins and Julian Wolfreys (New York: St. Martin's Press, 1996), pp. 65–80.

53 Eagleton, *Criticism and Ideology*, p. 124. See also Alison Byerly's argument that Eliot's representation of the arts suggests that her realism "acknowledges its own status as a fiction." *Realism, Representation, and the Arts in Nineteenth-Century Literature* (Cambridge University Press, 1997), p. 107.

54 For a fuller argument about the modernism of Eliot's last book, see my introduction to *Impressions of Theophrastus Such*, ed. Nancy Henry (Iowa City: University of Iowa Press, 1994).

55 Fredric Jameson, "Modernism and Imperialism" in Terry Eagleton, Fredric Jameson, and Edward Said, *Nationalism, Colonialism, and Literature* (Minneapolis: University of Minnesota Press, 1990), p. 44.

56 *Ibid.*, pp. 50–51.

57 *Ibid.*, p. 51.

58 On the implications of Jameson's work in relation to Said's, see Benita Parry, "Narrating Imperialism" in *Cultural Readings of Imperialism: Edward Said and the Gravity of History*, eds. Keith Ansell-Pearson, Benita Parry, and Judith Squires (New York: St. Martin's Press, 1997), pp. 227–46.

59 New critical attention has recently been paid to the "racially hybrid figure of Harry Transome" in *Felix Holt*, who, Tim Watson writes, "inherits the country estate in the novel but cannot be allowed to inherit that larger and more precious estate, England." Watson, "Jamaica, Genealogy, George Eliot," 15. Alicia Carroll writes of Harold Transome that "Eliot's Oriental is also an Englishman and an imperialist" and that both Harold and his son Harry are "posited as savage or of a lower order." See "The Giaour's Campaign," 238.

60 Benjamin Disraeli, Earl of Beaconsfield, "Speech Delivered at the Crystal Palace, June 24, 1872," *Selected Speeches of the Late Right Honourable the Earl of Beaconsfield*, ed. T. E. Kebbel, 2 vols. (London: Longmans, 1882), vol. II, p. 530.

61 See Winfried Baumgart, *Imperialism: The Idea and Reality of British and French Colonial Expansion, 1880–1914* (Oxford University Press, 1982).

62 Quoted in Byron Farwell, *Queen Victoria's Little Wars* (New York: Harper & Row, 1972), p. 219.

63 *A Monument to the Memory of George Eliot: Edith J. Simcox's "Autobiography of a Shirtmaker,"* eds. Constance M. Fulmer and Margaret E. Barfield (New York: Garland, 1998), p. 109.

64 Anthony Nutting, *Scramble for Africa: The Great Trek to the Boer War* (Newton Abbot, Devon: Readers Union, 1972), p. 80.

65 Anthony Trollope, *South Africa* (1878 edition), ed. J. H. Davidson, 2 vols. (Cape Town: A. A. Balkema, 1973), vol. I, p. 1.

66 Alexander Allardyce, "The Zulu War," *Blackwood's Edinburgh Magazine* 125 (March 1879), 378.

67 John Morley, "The Plain Story of the Zulu War," *Fortnightly Review* 31 (March 1, 1879), 348.
68 John Morley, "Further Remarks on Zulu Affairs," *Fortnightly Review* 31 (April 1, 1879), 562.
69 Allardyce, "The Zulu War," 376.
70 James Anthony Froude, "South Africa Once More," *Fortnightly Review* 32 (October 1, 1879), 455.
71 James Anthony Froude, *Oceana; or, England and Her Colonies* (London: Longmans, Green & Co., 1886), p. 9.
72 Froude, "South Africa," 452.
73 Trollope, *South Africa*, ed. Davidson, vol. 1, p. 194.

## CONCLUSION

1 Cross, *Impressions of Dante*, p. 296.
2 John Walter Cross to William Blackwood, January 17, 1893, MS Blackwood Family Papers, National Library of Scotland.
3 Gillian Beer, "Circulatory Systems: Money and Gossip in *Middlemarch*," *Cahiers Victoriens et Edouardiens* 26 (1987), 48.
4 John Walter Cross, *George Eliot's Life as Related in Her Letters and Journals*, 3 vols. (London and Edinburgh: Blackwood and Sons, 1885), vol. III, p. 259.
5 Gallagher, "George Eliot and *Daniel Deronda*," 138.
6 Bodenheimer, *Real Life*, p. 115.
7 *Ibid.*, p. 116.
8 Haight, *George Eliot*, p. 528.
9 Beer, "Circulatory Systems," 60.
10 Bodenheimer, *Real Life*, p. 118.
11 Fictionalizations of this episode include Terence de Vere White's *Johnnie Cross* (New York: St. Martin's Press, 1983) and Cynthia Ozick, "Puttermesser Paired," in *The Puttermesser Papers* (New York: Alfred A. Knopf, 1997), pp. 105–65.
12 John Walter Cross to his mother, April 13, 1872, MS Blackwood Family Papers, National Library of Scotland.
13 Dilke, *Greater Britain*, vol. II, p. 143.
14 Cross, *Impressions of Dante*, p. 222.
15 *Ibid.*, p. 223.
16 GHL journal, January 19, 1873, MS Yale.
17 Haight writes that her income in 1872 was "over £3000 and in 1873 nearly £5000 – more than half of it from investments." Haight, *George Eliot*, p. 458. Frederick Karl notes that "Cross had interceded in the couple's life and was investing moneys for Eliot and Lewes, at this time, £2000–3000, well over $150,000 in current spending power." Karl, *George Eliot*, p. 518.
18 Gillian Beer, "Passion, Politics, Philosophy: The Work of Edith Simcox," *Women: A Cultural Review* 6:2 (1995), 167.

19 John Walter Cross to William Blackwood, October 30, 1891, MS Blackwood Family Papers, National Library of Scotland.

20 Haight notes that: "In 1879 Eliza and her two children came to England, where GE arranged for their support, setting up in her will a trust fund of £12,500 to be divided equally between the children after Eliza's death or remarriage" (*GEL*, 1:lxxi).

21 Cross, *Impressions of Dante*, p. 173.

22 *Ibid.*, p. 176.

23 Haight, *George Eliot*, p. 477.

24 Dilke, *Greater Britain*, vol. II, p. 405.

25 Cross, *Impressions of Dante*, p. 296.

# Bibliography

## MANUSCRIPTS

The manuscript letters and journals cited are from the following collections:
Berg Collection, New York Public Library.
Blackwood Family Papers, National Library of Scotland.
George Eliot–G. H. Lewes Collection, Beinecke Rare Book and Manuscript Library, Yale University.

## PRIMARY SOURCES

Aimard, Gustave, *The Tiger-Slayer: A Tale of the Indian Desert* (London: Ward and Lock, 1863).

Allardyce, Alexander, "The Zulu War," *Blackwood's Edinburgh Magazine* 125 (March 1879), 376–94.

Ballantyne, R. M., *The World of Ice; or, Adventures in the Polar Regions* (London: T. Nelson & Sons, 1860).

  *The Coral Island* (London: Andrew Dakers Limited, n.d.).

Barter, Charles, *The Dorp and the Veld; or, Six Months in Natal* (London: William S. Orr & Co., 1852).

Bodichon, Barbara Leigh Smith, *A Brief Summary, in Plain Language of the Most Important Laws Concerning Women; Together with a Few Observations Thereon* (London: John Chapman, 1854).

Bright, John, *Speeches on Questions of Public Policy*, eds. John Bright and James E. Thorold Rogers (London: Macmillan, 1880).

Brontë, Charlotte, *The Letters of Charlotte Brontë*, ed. Margaret Smith, 2 vols. (Oxford: Clarendon Press, 1995).

Buchanan, Barbara, *Pioneer Days in Natal* (Pietermaritzburg: Shuter and Shooter, 1934).

Burton, Richard, *The Lake Regions of Central Africa* (1860; reprint, New York: Dover, 1995).

Chapman, John, *The Cotton and Commerce of India, Considered in Relation to the Interests of Great Britain; with Remarks on Railway Communication in the Bombay Presidency* (London: John Chapman, 1851).

  "Our Colonial Empire," *Westminster Review* 58 (October 1852), 214–34. Reprinted in *Westminster Review* 93 (January 1870), 1–18.

"India and Its Finances," *Westminster Review* 60 (July 1853), 93–104.

*Principles of Indian Reform Being Brief Hints together with a Plan for the Improvement of the Constituency of the East India Co. and for the Promotion of Indian Public Works* (London: John Chapman, 1853).

*The Colony of Natal. Compiled for the Use of Emigrants, from the Most Authentic Sources, by the Natal Land and Colonization Society Co.* (London: Jones and Causton, 1861).

Cross, John Walter, *George Eliot's Life as Related in Her Letters and Journals*, 3 vols. (London and Edinburgh: Blackwood and Sons, 1885).

*Impressions of Dante and of the New World* (London and Edinburgh: Blackwood and Sons, 1893).

*The Rake's Progress in Finance. Articles Reprinted from the Nineteenth Century Review* (London and Edinburgh: Blackwood and Sons, 1905).

Dickens, Charles, "The Noble Savage," *Household Words* 7:168 (June 11, 1853), 337–9.

*The Letters of Charles Dickens, Edited by His Sister-in-Law and His Eldest Daughter*, 2 vols. (London: Chapman and Hall, 1880–82).

*The Letters of Charles Dickens*, eds. Madeline House, Graham Storey, and Kathleen Tillotson, 11 vols. (Oxford: Clarendon Press, 1965–99).

*Dombey and Son*, ed. Alan Horsman (Oxford University Press, 1982).

*Nicholas Nickleby*, ed. Paul Schlicke (Oxford University Press, 1990).

*Great Expectations*, ed. Margaret Cardwell (Oxford University Press, 1993).

*David Copperfield*, ed. Nina Burgis (Oxford University Press, 1997).

*Our Mutual Friend*, ed. Michael Cotsell (Oxford University Press, 1998).

Dilke, Charles Wentworth, *Greater Britain: A Record of Travel in English-Speaking Countries during 1866 and 1867*, 2 vols. (London: Macmillan, 1869).

Disraeli, Benjamin, Earl of Beaconsfield, *Selected Speeches of the Late Right Honourable the Earl of Beaconsfield*, ed. T. E. Kebbel, 2 vols. (London: Longmans, 1882).

Eliot, George, "*Evenings in My Tent; or, Wanderings in Balad Ejjareed, Illustrating the Moral, Religious, Social, and Political Conditions of Various Arab Tribes of the African Sahara* by Rev. N. Davis," *Leader*, April 8, 1854, 330.

"*First Footsteps in East Africa* by Richard Burton and C. J. Andersen's *Lake Ngami*," *Westminster Review* 66 (October 1856), 309–10.

*The George Eliot Letters*, ed. Gordon S. Haight, 9 vols. (New Haven: Yale University Press, 1954–5 and 1978).

*Essays of George Eliot*, ed. Thomas Pinney (New York: Columbia University Press, 1963).

*The Mill on the Floss*, ed. Gordon Haight (Oxford University Press, 1981).

*Daniel Deronda*, ed. Graham Handley (New York: Oxford University Press, 1988).

*Felix Holt*, ed. Fred C. Thomson (Oxford University Press, 1988).

*Middlemarch*, ed. David Carroll (New York: Oxford University Press, 1988).

*Scenes of Clerical Life*, ed. Thomas A. Noble (Oxford University Press, 1988).

*Selected Essays, Poems and Other Writings*, eds. A. S. Byatt and Nicholas Warren (Harmondsworth: Penguin, 1990).

*Impressions of Theophrastus Such*, ed. Nancy Henry (Iowa City: University of Iowa Press, 1994).

*Romola*, ed. Andrew Brown (Oxford University Press, 1994).

*Adam Bede*, ed. Valentine Cunningham (Oxford University Press, 1996).

*Silas Marner, The Lifted Veil and Brother Jacob*, ed. Peter Mudford (London: Everyman, 1996).

*Felix Holt*, ed. A. G. Van den Broek (London: Everyman, 1997).

*The Journals of George Eliot*, eds. Margaret Harris and Judith Johnston (Cambridge University Press, 1998).

*Facts and Suggestions for the Holders of Ordinary Shares in the Sambre and Meuse Railway* (London: Effingham Wilson, Royal Exchange E. C., 1873).

Forster, W. E., "British Philanthropy and Jamaican Distress," *Westminster Review* 59 (April 1853), 171–89.

Froude, James Anthony, "South Africa Once More," *Fortnightly Review* 32 (October 1, 1879), 449–73.

*Oceana; or, England and Her Colonies* (London: Longmans, Green & Co., 1886).

Kaye, John William, "The Indian Civil Service: Its Rise and Fall," parts I–II, *Blackwood's Edinburgh Magazine* 89 (January 1861), 115–30; (March 1861), 261–76.

Kilgour, George, *Railway Extension in the Colony of the Cape of Good Hope, S. Africa* (Cape Town: Saul Solomon & Co., 1881).

Kipling, Rudyard, *"The Man Who Would Be King" and Other Stories*, ed. Louis L. Cornell (Oxford University Press, 1987).

Lewes, G. H., "Social Despotism in Austria," *Monthly Chronicle* 5 (June 1840), 500–508.

*"Five Years of a Hunter's Life in the Far Interior of South Africa* by R. Gordon Cumming," *Leader*, July 27, 1850, 423.

*"Narrative of a Mission to Central Africa* by James Richardson," *Leader*, April 2, 1853, 330.

"The Zulu Kaffirs," *Leader*, May 28, 1853, 502.

*"The Caucasus* by Ivan Golovin," *Leader*, January 14, 1854, 41–2.

"Lions and Lion Hunting," *Westminster Review* 65 (January 1856), 116–22.

"Hereditary Influence, Animal and Human," *Westminster Review* 66 (July 1856), 75–90.

"African Life," *Westminster Review* 69 (January 1858), 1–16.

"Uncivilized Man," *Blackwood's Edinburgh Magazine* 89 (January 1861), 27–41.

"Life in Central Africa," *Blackwood's Edinburgh Magazine* 89 (April 1861), 440–53.

"Mr. Buckle's Scientific Errors," *Blackwood's Edinburgh Magazine* 90 (November 1861), 582–96.

*On Actors and the Art of Acting* (New York: Grove Press, 1957).

*Versatile Victorian: Selected Writings of George Henry Lewes*, ed. Rosemary Ashton (Bristol: Bristol Classics Press, 1992).

*The Letters of George Henry Lewes*, ed. William Baker, 3 vols. (Victoria, BC: University of Victoria Press, 1995 and 1999).

Maidstone, Viscount [Earl of Winchilsea], *Abd-el-Kader. A Poem in Six Cantos* (London: Chapman and Hall, 1851).

Mann, Robert James, *The Colony of Natal. An Account of the Characteristics and Capabilities of This British Dependency* (London: 1859).

Mill, James, *A History of British India*, ed. William Thomas (University of Chicago Press, 1995).

Morley, John, "The Plain Story of the Zulu War," *Fortnightly Review* 31 (March 1, 1879), 329–52.

"Further Remarks on Zulu Affairs," *Fortnightly Review* 31 (April 1, 1879), 546–62.

Oliphant, Margaret, "The Holy Land," *Blackwood's Edinburgh Magazine* 76 (September 1854), 223–39.

*William Blackwood and His Sons. Their Magazine and Friends*, 2 vols. (Edinburgh and London: William Blackwood and Sons, 1897).

Ozick, Cynthia, "Puttermesser Paired" in *The Puttermesser Papers* (New York: Alfred A. Knopf, 1997), pp. 105–65.

Rees, Wyn, ed., *Colenso Letters from Natal* (Pietermaritzburg: Shuter and Shooter, 1958).

Reid, Mayne, *The Young Voyageurs; or, The Boy Hunters in the North* (London: David Bogue, 1853).

Robinson, John, "The Future of the British Empire," *Westminster Review* 94 (July 1870), 22–34.

Rouse-Jones, Margaret P., *The Colonial Bank Correspondence, 1837–1885* (Port of Newtown, Spain, and Trinidad: Paria Publishing Ltd., 1986).

Sidney, Samuel, "Indian Railroads and British Commerce," *Household Words* 2:51 (March 15, 1851), 590–95.

*The Three Colonies of Australia; New South Wales, Victoria, South Australia; Their Pastures, Copper Mines, and Gold Fields* (London: Ingram, Cooke, & Co., 1852).

Simcox, Edith J., *A Monument to the Memory of George Eliot: Edith J. Simcox's "Autobiography of a Shirtmaker,"* eds. Constance M. Fulmer and Margaret E. Barfield (New York: Garland, 1998).

Trollope, Anthony, *The West Indies and the Spanish Main* (London: Chapman and Hall, 1859).

*The Tireless Traveller: Twenty Letters to the Liverpool Mercury, 1875*, ed. with an introduction by Bradford Allen Booth (Berkeley: University of California Press, 1941).

*South Africa* (1878 edition), ed. J. H. Davidson, 2 vols. (Cape Town: A. A. Balkema, 1973).

*The Three Clerks*, ed. Graham Handley (Oxford University Press, 1989).

*The Way We Live Now*, ed. John Sutherland (Oxford University Press, 1992).

van de Velde, C. W. M., *Narrative of a Journey through Syria and Palestine in 1851 and 1852*, 2 vols. (Edinburgh: William Blackwood and Sons, 1854).

White, Terence de Vere, *Johnnie Cross* (New York: St. Martin's Press, 1983).

## CRITICAL AND HISTORICAL WORKS

Ackroyd, Peter, *Dickens* (London: Sinclair-Stevenson, 1990).

Adams, James Eli, *Dandies and Desert Saints: Styles of Victorian Manhood* (Ithaca: Cornell University Press, 1995).

Alborn, Timothy, "The Moral of the Failed Bank: Professional Plots in the Victorian Money Market," *Victorian Studies* 38:2 (1995), 199–226.

*Conceiving Companies: Joint Stock Politics in Victorian England* (New York: Routledge, 1998).

Andres, Sophia, "Fortune's Wheel in *Daniel Deronda*: Sociopolitical Turns on the British Empire," *Victorian Institute Journal* 24 (1996), 87–111.

Ashton, Rosemary, *G. H. Lewes: A Life* (Oxford: Clarendon Press, 1991).

*George Eliot: A Life* (London: Hamish Hamilton, 1996).

Azim, Firdous, *The Colonial Rise of the Novel* (New York: Routledge, 1993).

Barker, Juliet, *The Brontës* (New York: St. Martin's Press, 1994).

Baumgart, Winfried, *Imperialism: The Idea and Reality of British and French Colonial Expansion, 1880–1914* (Oxford University Press, 1982).

Beer, Gillian, *George Eliot* (Brighton: Harvester Press, 1986).

"Circulatory Systems: Money and Gossip in *Middlemarch*," *Cahiers Victoriens et Edouardiens* 26 (1987), 47–62.

"Passion, Politics, Philosophy: The Work of Edith Simcox," *Women: A Cultural Review* 6:2 (1995), 166–79

*Open Fields: Science in Cultural Encounter* (Oxford University Press, 1996).

Biggs, John H., "How to Make Choices for a Social Choice Account," *Participant*, August 1998, 2–3.

Bivona, Daniel, *Desire and Contradiction: Imperial Visions and Domestic Debates in Victorian Literature* (New York: St. Martin's, 1990).

*British Imperial Literature 1870–1940: Writing and the Administration of the Empire* (Cambridge University Press, 1998).

Bodenheimer, Rosemarie, *The Real Life of Marian Evans: George Eliot, Her Letters, and Her Fiction* (Ithaca: Cornell University Press, 1994).

Brantlinger, Patrick, *Rule of Darkness: British Literature and Imperialism* (Ithaca: Cornell University Press, 1988).

"Nations and Novels: Disraeli, George Eliot, and Orientalism," *Victorian Studies* 35:3 (Spring 1992), 255–75.

*Fictions of State: Culture and Credit in Britain, 1694–1994* (Ithaca: Cornell University Press, 1996).

Bristow, Joseph, *Empire Boys: Adventures in a Man's World* (New York: Harper-Collins, 1991).

Brown, Laura, *Ends of Empire: Women and Ideology in Early Eighteenth-Century English Literature* (Ithaca: Cornell University Press, 1993).

Burton, Antoinette, *Burdens of History: British Feminists, Indian Women, and Imperial Culture, 1865–1915* (Chapel Hill: University of North Carolina Press, 1994).

Byerly, Alison, *Realism, Representation, and the Arts in Nineteenth-Century Literature* (Cambridge University Press, 1997).

Cairncross, A. K., *Home and Foreign Investment, 1870–1913* (Cambridge University Press, 1975).

Carroll, Alicia, "The Giaour's Campaign: Desire and the Other in *Felix Holt, the Radical,*" *Novel* 30:2 (1997), 237–58.

" 'Arabian Nights': 'Make-Believe,' Exoticism, and Desire in *Daniel Deronda,*" *JEGP* 98:2 (April 1999), 219–38

Cheyette, Bryan, *Constructions of "the Jew" in English Literature and Society* (Cambridge University Press, 1993).

Copeland, Edward, *Women Writing about Money* (Cambridge University Press, 1995).

Cotsell, Michael, "Trollope: The International Theme" in *Creditable Warriors, 1830–1876*, ed. Michael Cotsell (London and Atlantic Highlands, NJ: Ashfield Press, 1990), pp. 234–56.

Cottom, Daniel, *Social Figures: George Eliot, Social History, and Literary Representation* (Minneapolis: University of Minnesota Press, 1987).

Cottrell, P. L., *British Overseas Investment in the Nineteenth Century* (London: Macmillan, 1975).

Crosby, Christina, "Finance" in *A Companion to Victorian Literature and Culture*, ed. Herbert F. Tucker (Oxford and Malden, MA: Blackwell, 1999), pp. 25–43.

" 'A Taste for More': Trollope's Addictive Realism" in *The New Economic Criticism: Studies at the Intersection of Literature and Economics*, eds. Martha Woodmansee and Mark Osteen (New York: Routledge, 1999), pp. 293–306.

David, Deirdre, *Fictions of Resolution in Three Victorian Novels* (New York: Columbia University Press, 1981).

"Children of Empire: Victorian Imperialism and Sexual Politics in Dickens and Kipling" in *Gender and Discourse in Victorian Literature and Art*, eds. Antony H. Harrison and Beverly Taylor (Dekalb: Northern Illinois University Press, 1992), pp. 124–42.

Davidson, J. H., "Anthony Trollope and the Colonies," *Victorian Studies* 12 (March 1969), 395–430.

Davis, Lennard J., *Factual Fictions: The Origins of the English Novel* (Philadelphia: University of Pennsylvania Press, 1996).

"Novel Worship," *Novel* 30:3 (Spring 1997), 405–8.

"Reconsidering Origins: How Novel Are Theories of the Novel?" *Eighteenth-Century Fiction* 12:2–3 (2000), 479–99.

Dawson, Graham, *British Adventure, Empire and the Imagining of Masculinities* (New York: Routledge, 1994).

De Sola Rodstein, Susan, "Sweetness and Dark: George Eliot's 'Brother Jacob,' " *Modern Language Quarterly* 52:3 (1991), 295–317.

Dryden, Linda, *Joseph Conrad and the Imperial Romance* (London: Macmillan, 2000).

Dunae, Patrick A., *Gentlemen Emigrants: From the British Public Schools to the Canadian Frontier* (Manchester University Press, 1981).

"Education, Emigration and the Empire: The Colonial College, 1887–1905" in *"Benefits Bestowed"?: Education and British Imperialism*, ed. J. A. Mangan (Manchester University Press, 1988), pp. 193–210.

Dutt, Romesh, *Economic History of India* (New York: B. Franklin, 1970).

Eagleton, Terry, *Criticism and Ideology* (London: Verso, 1978).

Edelstein, Michael, *Overseas Investment in the Age of High Imperialism in the UK, 1850–1914* (New York: Columbia University Press, 1982).

Edwards, P. D., *Anthony Trollope's Son in Australia* (University of Queensland Press, 1982).

Farwell, Byron, *Queen Victoria's Little Wars* (New York: Harper & Row, 1972).

Finkelstein, David, "Breaking the Thread: The Authorial Reinvention of John Hanning Speke in His *Journal of Discovery of the Source of the Nile*," *Text: An Interdisciplinary Annual of Textual Studies* 9 (1997), 280–96.

Fraiman, Susan, "Jane Austen and Edward Said: Gender, Culture, and Imperialism," *Critical Inquiry* 21:4 (Summer 1995), 805–21.

Gallagher, Catherine, *The Industrial Reformation of English Fiction: Social Discourse and Narrative Form, 1832–1867* (University of Chicago Press, 1985).

"George Eliot and *Daniel Deronda*: The Prostitute and the Jewish Question" in *The New Historicism Reader*, ed. H. Aram Veeser (New York: Routledge, 1994), pp. 124–40.

Gray, Beryl, " 'Animated Nature': *The Mill on the Floss*" in *George Eliot and Europe*, ed. John Rignall (Aldershot: Scolar Press, 1997), pp. 138–55.

Green, Martin, *Dreams of Adventure, Deeds of Empire* (New York: Basic Books, 1979).

Guest, Bill, and John M. Sellers, eds., *Enterprise and Exploitation in a Victorian Colony: Aspects of the Economic and Social History of Colonial Natal* (Pietermaritzburg: University of Natal Press, 1985).

Hacking, Ian, "Making up People" in *Reconstructing Individualism*, eds. Thomas C. Heller, Morton Sosna, and David E. Wellbery (Stanford University Press, 1986), pp. 222–36.

"The Making and Molding of Child Abuse," *Critical Inquiry* 17 (Winter 1991), 253–88.

Haight, Gordon S., *George Eliot: A Biography* (New York: Oxford University Press, 1968).

Hall, Catherine, "Going A-Trolloping: Imperial Man Travels the Empire" in *Gender and Imperialism*, ed. Clare Midgley (Manchester University Press, 1998), pp. 180–99.

Hancock, John, *The Ethical Investor: Making Gains with Values* (London: Pearson Education Limited, 1999).

Handley, Graham, *Trollope the Traveller* (London: Pickering and Chatto, 1993).

Helsinger, Elizabeth, *Rural Scenes and National Representations: Britain, 1815–1850* (Princeton University Press, 1997).

Henry, Nancy, "Ante-Anti-Semitism: George Eliot's *Impressions of Theophrastus Such*" in *Victorian Identities: Social and Cultural Formations in Nineteenth-Century Literature*, eds. Ruth Robbins and Julian Wolfreys (New York: St. Martin's Press, 1996), pp. 65–80.

"George Eliot and Politics" in *The Cambridge Companion to George Eliot*, ed. George Levine (Cambridge University Press, 2001), pp. 138–58.

Hertz, Neil, "George Eliot's Life-in-Debt," *Diacritics* 25:4 (1995), 59–70.

Hirsch, Pam, *Barbara Leigh Smith Bodichon: Feminist, Artist, and Rebel* (London: Chatto and Windus, 1998).

Homans, Margaret, "Dinah's Blush, Maggie's Arm: Class, Gender, and Sexuality in George Eliot's Early Novels," *Victorian Studies* 36:2 (Winter 1993), 155–78.

*Royal Representations: Queen Victoria and British Culture, 1837–1876* (University of Chicago Press, 1998).

Hughes, Kathryn, *George Eliot: The Last Victorian* (London: Fourth Estate, 1998).

Jacobson, Wendy S., ed., *Dickens and the Children of Empire* (Basingstoke: Palgrave, 2000).

Jameson, Fredric, "Modernism and Imperialism" in Terry Eagleton, Fredric Jameson, and Edward Said, *Nationalism, Colonialism, and Literature* (Minneapolis: University of Minnesota Press, 1990), pp. 43–66.

Johnson, Edgar, *Charles Dickens: His Tragedy and Triumph*, 2 vols. (New York: Simon & Schuster, 1952).

Jones, Robert W., " 'The Sight of Creatures Strange to our Clime': London Zoo and the Consumption of the Exotic," *Journal of Victorian Culture* 2:1 (Spring 1997), 1–26.

Kaminsky, Alice R., *G. H. Lewes as Literary Critic* (Syracuse University Press, 1968).

Karl, Frederick, *George Eliot: Voice of a Century* (New York: Norton, 1995).

Kayfetz, Sharon Leah, "Counterfeit Coins and Traffic Jams: Rewriting Masculinity in *Adam Bede*," *New Orleans Review* 24:2 (1998), 62–72.

Kerr, Ian J., *Building the Railways of the Raj, 1850–1900* (Oxford University Press, 1995).

Kestner, Joseph A., *Masculinities in Victorian Painting* (Aldershot: Scolar Press, 1995).

Koebner, Richard, and Helmut Dan Schmidt, *Imperialism: The Story and Significance of a Political Word, 1840–1960* (Cambridge University Press, 1964).

Layoun, Mary N., *Travels of a Genre: The Modern Novel and Ideology* (Princeton University Press, 1990).

Lazarus, Mary, *A Tale of Two Brothers* (Sydney: Angus and Robertson, 1973).

Leavis, F. R., *The Great Tradition: George Eliot, Henry James, Joseph Conrad* (New York: G. W. Stewart, 1949).

Lesjak, Carolyn, "Labours of a Modern Storyteller: George Eliot and the Cultural Project of 'Nationhood'" in *Victorian Identities: Social and Cultural Formations in Nineteenth-Century Literature*, eds. Ruth Robbins and Julian Wolfreys (New York: St. Martin's, 1996), pp. 25–42.

Levine, George, *Darwin and the Novelists: Patterns of Science in Victorian Fiction* (Cambridge, MA: Harvard University Press, 1988).

Levine, George, ed., *The Cambridge Companion to George Eliot* (Cambridge University Press, 2001).

Lewis, Reina, *Gendering Orientalism: Race, Femininity and Representation* (New York: Routledge, 1996).

Linehan, Katherine Bailey, "Mixed Politics: The Critique of Imperialism in *Daniel Deronda*," *Texas Studies in Literature and Language* 34:3 (1992), 323–46.

Low, Gail Ching-Liang, *White Skins/Black Masks: Representation and Colonialism* (New York: Routledge, 1996).

MacKenzie, John M., *The Empire of Nature: Hunting, Conservation and British Imperialism* (Manchester University Press, 1988).

MacKenzie, John M., ed., *Imperialism and the Natural World* (Manchester University Press, 1990).

Mangan, J. A., and James Walvin, eds., *Manliness and Morality: Middle-Class Masculinity in Britain and America, 1800–1940* (Manchester University Press, 1987).

McCaw, Neil, *George Eliot and Victorian Historiography* (Basingstoke: Macmillan, 2000).

Meyer, Susan, *Imperialism at Home* (Ithaca: Cornell University Press, 1996).

Miller, J. Hillis, "The Two Rhetorics: George Eliot's Bestiary" in *Writing and Reading Differently: Deconstruction and the Teaching of Composition and Literature*, eds. G. Douglas Atkins and Michael L. Johnson (Lawrence: University Press of Kansas, 1985), pp. 101–14.

Moyles, R. G., and Doug Owram, *Imperial Dreams and Colonial Realities: British Views of Canada, 1880–1914* (University of Toronto Press, 1988).

Nunokawa, Jeff, *The Afterlife of Property: Domestic Security and the Victorian Novel* (Princeton University Press, 1994).

Nutting, Anthony, *Scramble for Africa: The Great Trek to the Boer War* (Newton Abbot, Devon: Readers Union, 1972).

Parry, Benita, "Narrating Imperialism" in *Cultural Readings of Imperialism: Edward Said and the Gravity of History*, eds. Keith Ansell-Pearson, Benita Parry, and Judith Squires (New York: St. Martin's Press, 1997), pp. 227–46.

Paxton, Nancy L., *George Eliot and Herbert Spencer: Feminism, Evolutionism, and the Reconstruction of Gender* (Princeton University Press, 1991).

  *Writing under the Raj: Gender, Race, and Rape in the British Colonial Imagination, 1830–1947* (New Brunswick: Rutgers University Press, 1999).

Perera, Suvendrini, *Reaches of Empire: The English Novel from Edgeworth to Dickens* (New York: Columbia University Press, 1991).

Phillips, Richard, *Mapping Men and Empire: A Geography of Adventure* (New York: Routledge, 1997).

Polowetzky, Michael, *Jerusalem Recovered: Victorian Intellectuals and the Birth of Modern Zionism* (Westport, CT: Praeger, 1995).

Poovey, Mary, *Uneven Developments: The Ideological Work of Gender in Mid-Victorian England* (University of Chicago Press, 1988).

  *Making a Social Body: British Cultural Formation, 1830–1864* (University of Chicago Press, 1995).

Pratt, Mary Louise, *Under Western Eyes: Studies in Travel Writing and Transculturation* (New York: Routledge, 1992).

Press, Jacob, "Same-Sex Unions in Modern Europe: *Daniel Deronda*, Altneuland, and the Homoerotics of Jewish Nationalism" in *Novel Gazing*, ed. Eve Sedgwick (Durham, NC: Duke University Press, 1997), pp. 299–329.

Ragussis, Michael, *Figures of Conversion: The Jewish Question and English National Identity* (Durham, NC: Duke University Press, 1995).

Reed, John R., "A Friend to Mammon: Speculation in Victorian Literature," *Victorian Studies* 27:2 (1984), 179–202.

Ritvo, Harriet, *The Animal Estate: The English and Other Creatures in the Victorian Age* (Cambridge, MA: Harvard University Press, 1987).

Robbins, Bruce, "Forum," *PMLA* 108:3 (1993), 541–2.

Russell, Norman, *The Novelist and Mammon: Literary Responses to the World of Commerce in the Nineteenth Century* (Oxford University Press, 1986).

Said, Edward, *Orientalism* (New York: Pantheon, 1978).

*The Question of Palestine* (New York: Vintage, 1979).

"Zionism from the Standpoint of Its Victims," *Social Text* 1 (1979), 7–58. Reprinted in *Dangerous Liaisons: Gender, Nation, and Postcolonial Perspectives*, eds. Anne McClintock, Aamir Mufti, and Ella Shohat (Minneapolis: University of Minnesota Press, 1997), pp. 15–38.

*Culture and Imperialism* (New York: Alfred A. Knopf, 1993).

Sedgwick, Eve, *Between Men: English Literature and Male Homosocial Desire* (New York: Columbia University Press, 1985).

Semmel, Bernard, *The Liberal Ideal and the Demons of Empire* (Baltimore: Johns Hopkins University Press, 1993).

*George Eliot and the Politics of National Inheritance* (New York: Oxford University Press, 1994).

Shuttleworth, Sally, *George Eliot and Nineteenth-Century Science* (Cambridge University Press, 1984).

Smith, Grahame, "Suppressing Narratives: Childhood and Empire in *The Uncommercial Traveller* and *Great Expectations*" in *Dickens and the Children of Empire*, ed. Wendy S. Jacobson (Basingstoke: Palgrave, 2000), pp. 43–53.

Spivak, Gayatri Chakravorty, "Three Women's Texts and a Critique of Imperialism," *Critical Inquiry* 12 (Autumn 1985), 243–61.

Stone, Wilfred, "The Play of Chance and Ego in *Daniel Deronda*," *Nineteenth-Century Literature* 53:1 (June 1998), 25–55.

Sturgis, James L., *John Bright and the Empire* (London: The Athlone Press, University of London, 1969).

Thomas, Nicholas, and Richard Eves, *Bad Colonists: The South Seas Letters of Vernon Lee Walker and Louis Becke* (Durham, NC: Duke University Press, 1999).

Thorner, Daniel, *Investment in Empire: British Railway and Steam Shipping Enterprise in India, 1825–1849* (Philadelphia: University of Pennsylvania Press, 1950).

Tomalin, Claire, *Jane Austen: A Life* (New York: Viking, 1997).

Vernon, John, *Money and Fiction: Literary Realism in the Nineteenth and Early Twentieth Centuries* (Ithaca: Cornell University Press, 1984).

Wagner, Gillian, *Children of the Empire* (London: Weidenfeld and Nicolson, 1982).

Watson, Tim, "Jamaica, Genealogy, George Eliot: Inheriting the Empire after Morant Bay," *Jouvert* 1:1 (1997), 1–31.

Watt, Ian, *The Rise of the Novel: Studies in Defoe, Richardson and Fielding* (Berkeley: University of California Press, 1957).

Welsh, Alexander, *George Eliot and Blackmail* (Cambridge, MA: Harvard University Press, 1985).

White, Andrea, *Joseph Conrad and the Adventure Tradition: Constructing and Deconstructing the Imperial Subject* (Cambridge University Press, 1993).

Williams, Blanche Colton, *George Eliot* (New York: Macmillan, 1936).

Wohlfarth, Marc E., "*Daniel Deronda* and the Politics of Nationalism," *Nineteenth-Century Literature* 53:2 (September 1998), 188–210.

# Index

# CAMBRIDGE STUDIES IN NINETEENTH-CENTURY LITERATURE AND CULTURE

General editor
Gillian Beer, *University of Cambridge*

Titles published